Well-being for
Women

FAMILY
MEDICAL

Well-being for
Women

Helen Lawrence

**GEDDES &
GROSSET**

Published 2004 by Geddes & Grosset, David Dale House, New Lanark,
ML11 9DJ, Scotland

First published in Australia in 1991 by Thomas C. Lothian Pty Ltd

ISBN 1 84205 352 3

Printed and bound in the UK

FOREWORD

Well-being for Women is a book for women written by a woman. Helen Lawrence has had many years of experience as a physiotherapist as well as being a wife and mother. In 1984, she was the first physiotherapist in Australia to obtain a Fellowship in Physiotherapy in Women's Health. The information for this book has been gleaned from personal experience, literature survey and wide consultation with obstetricians and gynaecologists and other specialists involved in sexually transmissible diseases and the ageing process.

The book is about possible self-help, in conjunction with obtaining professional advice, and it will particularly appeal to those women who believe, rightly or wrongly, that they do not get an in-depth discussion from their doctors. Certain chapters may also be of benefit to partners who are at a loss to understand the special problems that confront women.

Such an effort in producing a very wide coverage of problem areas, from adolescence to the post-menopause, and in what circumstances physiotherapy may be of benefit, is to be commended.

J. F. Correy
AM MB BS (Syd.) FRCOG FRACS FRACOG
Professor of Obstetrics and Gynaecology
University of Tasmania

CONTENTS

INTRODUCTION

In my final year as a physiotherapy student I saw a baby born in its caul. This old term describes the membranes which cover the fetus and which usually rupture before birth, so it was unusual. The midwife peeled the membranes off like a rubber glove. It was an easy birth, the sixth I believe, but the mother was flat on her back and totally unconscious under chloroform. The following year found me feeling very young and inadequate, treating poliomyelitis victims, demonstrating breathing techniques in wards full of lung tuberculosis patients, and supervising the first walk for three years of ex-prisoners-of-war who had been immobilised in plaster beds with bone TB. Then, in Canada, I worked with children who had contracted cerebral palsy, many of them as a result of a traumatic birth.

The modern scene is dramatically different, particularly where birth is concerned. Technology has changed and is changing our lives: diagnosis is more precise, treatment is more specific, and if it fails we can sometimes be fitted with spare parts. But broad physiotherapy tenets remain the same as when I qualified. They are:

- to relieve pain
- to facilitate normal action of body systems, especially muscles and nerve pathways
- to maximise patient potential
- to teach people about their own bodies.

There has been a remarkable change in the last forty years. People are much more interested in their own health and much more knowledgeable, though of course there are still pockets of ignorance and wilful neglect. This awareness of what the human body needs appears to have come hand in hand with the realisation that the planet is very fragile and that we should take some responsibility for our own environment. The position of women is changing too. We make up a significant proportion of the work force, we expect reasonable equality with men and we want to make educated decisions about our own bodies. When I was about forty, a doctor used the words 'when you have your hysterectomy'. Hysterectomy is no longer mandatory except when there is a disease process present. I am glad to say that all my organs are still intact!

This book is mainly about the reproductive span of women and how physiotherapy fits in as a guided form of self-help for its varying stages, bringing a sense of physical well-being into our lives. Physiotherapy means 'body healing'; it is a tool of medical science. As well as being practical healers, physiotherapists carry out research and publish statistics. They work very closely with doctors, and in some countries they are allowed to treat the person 'off the street' as first contact practitioners. They use natural methods, often their own hands, and they do not prescribe drugs. In the popular mind there is a perception of hi-tech medicine as being opposed to natural medicine. Physiotherapy falls between these two extremes, often working as an adjunct to other medical treatments. The skills of the physiotherapist include a detailed knowledge of muscles, ligaments, bones and joints. She (or he) also has a practical understanding of the use of various forms of energy (electrical, sonic, magnetic, thermal) in treating the human body.

Fitness is receiving more and more emphasis in the pursuit of health. Sports physiotherapists are usually on hand at important matches both at home and abroad. When they think of fitness, some women imagine a glowing goddess of sport, but there are many activities that help us to maintain good health that do not involve actual sport and that can be adapted to our chosen lifestyle.

A working knowledge of our bodies helps us in everything we do and takes the mystery and folklore out of such vexed questions as safe sexual relationships and avoiding haphazard pregnancies. Once a pregnancy is established, physiotherapists as part of the obstetric team can show you how to breathe your way through short bursts of pain, for the remarkable fact is that women *ask* to be allowed to bear their labour pain if it is at all bearable, as an immemorial right of childbirth, rather than have it totally eliminated.

Physiotherapy plays an important part in the success of breast-feeding, particularly for the mother of a first baby. Successful breast-feeding seems to enhance every aspect of motherhood, and it needs to succeed from the very beginning. It is a confidence booster, a time and money saver, a health promoter and nature's bonding device. If physiotherapists can join in the assistance and encouragement of breast-feeding, more babies will obtain the start in life nature intended.

But women are not just child nurturers. With so many wishing to be active in the wider world, it becomes vital for young women to retain as much fitness as they can in pregnancy and to recover quickly if problems, such as a caesarean section, do arise. We no longer think of pregnancy as the ruination of the female figure. However, a woman may need a little prodding to spend time on herself in this extraordinarily self-giving stage of her life. Women on their own by choice or by circumstance have special needs and physiotherapy can offer not only physical assistance but also counselling and womanly understanding.

There are exciting new ways in which physiotherapists are helping women to overcome incontinence—the leaky bladder—which about a third of women find troublesome in middle to old age (and some at much younger ages), often instigated by giving birth. Genital prolapse is another legacy from birthing where physiotherapy has much to offer in rehabilitating the pelvic floor muscles and containing the prolapsing tissue. There are many aggravating symptoms associated with these two problems which are worth discussing with a physiotherapist who has a special interest in gynaecological conditions.

Too often stress and pain subtly erode our ability for coping and before we are fully aware we have the makings of a life-long problem. Understanding muscular and mental relaxation, honing our reflexes to work for us and re-examining an unrealistic self-image are not such difficult goals as they sound. Middle life leading up to menopause is a time to take stock. With a little foresight the scene can be set for tranquil ageing. It is a chance to review consolidating habits and attitudes. It may well be the last chance.

Physiotherapy is only one of the options open to women. It is not in any way exclusive. But it is a conservative, non-invasive way of conditioning the body which in most cases shows its true colours early in the course of treatment. It is useful to know a little about how it works. Every part of the seven ages of man, or woman, has its ups and downs. Often a fresh viewpoint is all that is needed to brighten a gloomy prospect or convert a negative to a positive, and physiotherapy is a very pragmatic and positive science.

1

FITNESS AND HEALTH

To understand how women's bodies work, it is useful to consider the differing strengths and weaknesses of the skeletal system and how the female anatomy influences fitness and health during day-to-day activities. It is also useful to see how women differ physiologically from men.

Females are generally smaller, lighter and fatter than males and, although they have only half to two-thirds the strength of men, they have certain physiological advantages in sport. They show greater endurance in some sports, and benefit in water sports from greater buoyancy and insulation due to extra fat. Top-class female athletes practising hard daily tend to reduce this fat proportion, though for swimmers the fat layer may be worth preserving.

Men can usually run faster than women for a good anatomical reason: they have a streamlined pelvis. Women's thighs are angled inwards to allow for the development of an obstetrically adequate pelvis, giving them a swinging gait. All women have this angling of the thighs, but some more than others. Men are generally stronger in the shoulders and trunk, but not necessarily the legs. Women have smaller hearts and lungs. They cannot store as much iron as men and have fewer red blood cells, giving them a lower oxygen-carrying capacity than males. Women may need iron supplements in pregnancy and sportswomen may benefit by additional iron. Some women competing in Olympic standard sport cease to have menstrual periods which causes them to worry about their fertility. Amenorrhoea may be related more to stress than to loss of body fat. When hard training finishes, the body will adapt and normal ovulation and periods will usually return.

As a female, you take longer than a male to produce a sweat. You can bring more blood to the vessels just under the skin (become pinker), and therefore sweat more efficiently and cool down more quickly than a man.

Back strain is common in women. It may occur after hormonal changes that soften ligaments in pregnancy and can have lasting results. But young women who have not been pregnant also complain of backache and some authorities believe that small, repeated traumatic episodes gradually weaken the outer casing of one or more discs. This sort of wear and tear can be reduced by taking care in lifting heavy weights. Lifting and twisting at the same time can be particularly damaging. Professionals such as nurses need to learn correct lifting techniques, shoulder lifts, lifting in unison, and so on. Women playing traditionally male sports like soccer may be prone to knee strain and contact injuries which are no longer a predominantly male phenomenon.

Overuse injury or repetitive strain injury (RSI) is often a female complaint, perhaps because more women use keyboards more consistently than men. Women seem a little more likely to develop calcification, a deposit of calcium material which is like thick toothpaste and which can collect around tendons and joint capsules. Older women are subject to bone and joint problems due to oestrogen withdrawal at the menopause. Women whose work involves sitting at desks or standing behind counters for long periods are especially at risk because the bones receive very little muscle stimulation.

All women are anatomically weaker than men in the floor of the pelvis; they are more likely to lose drops of urine during hard exercise.

Men are thought to be more logical than women but less intuitive; better at abstract thinking but weaker in language skills; good at long-term planning but poorer at day-to-day management. Although social and cultural conditioning has probably contributed to these differences, recent research suggests that men's brains may operate differently from women's. Desmond Morris, author of *The Naked Ape*, points out that men have better hand-eye co-ordination; they are traditionally better at sports such as shooting, fly fishing, archery, fencing, darts, golf and team sports, though there will always be many women who will beat them at their own game.

If the woman is the chief homemaker in her household, she will set the pace in the home. If the person in charge likes a hermetically sealed house, provides meals high on fat content and low on nutritional value, wears too many clothes and overclothes the children when small, sits about smoking, watching television or videos, popping pills for headaches and drinking coffee addictively, is it any wonder that the children may follow suit? Luckily fewer and fewer people adhere to this stereotype today.

Young plants at a nursery usually come with the recommendation that they have been 'hardened-off', which means they don't have to be kept behind glass. People should be hardened off too! In modern society this doesn't always happen: we sleep with closed windows; we dress in clothes like slacks and sweaters and track-suits (unless it's a heat wave); we eat more than we need and often the wrong type of food; and we sit about too much. We tolerate only a small range of temperature. In cold weather we tend to heat the whole house or workplace; if it is hot we demand air-conditioning. Humans have lived and survived in temperate zones for thousands of years without such adjustments to changing temperatures.

Outer over-clothing is common. Track-suits were first worn as after-sport wear when there was every reason to keep warm; now they are leisure wear. Jeans are sometimes so tight that they chafe a woman's genital area. Children's legs which used to be bare in all seasons are now encased in grow-suits, long trousers, even padded trousers (which may interfere with walking and encourage bow legs).

Women taking part in regular exercise are probably a motivated minority. Indoor sports, such as indoor cricket, tenpin bowling, aerobic classes, squash and badminton are very popular and an indoor exercise class is a quick way to have a weekly workout. But, while any sport is better than no sport, outdoor activities may be more beneficial from a general health point of view—and they are often free. For instance, cycling is an excellent knee muscle exercise but cycling in the fresh air is better for you than pedalling a stationary bike indoors. Swimming and surfing in the sea can be more invigorating than swimming several lengths of an indoor pool.

Figure trimming

At various stages in a woman's life the body tends to get a bit exuberant and out of hand. Puberty is the first danger point, then pregnancy, followed by the period after the birth or between births.

Middle life has its hazards and so do the menopausal years. These times are usually marked by feelings of tiredness, lack of drive, or a tendency to run to fat. The cause may be hormonal fluctuation.

It might sound as if a woman is constantly faced with problems caused by the vagaries of her body. That is not so. There are many years when we sail along, our weight not varying, our energy levels normal. And then, seemingly out of the blue, there will be a lapse.

Unexplained tiredness

Most women lose a varying quantity of blood at regular intervals throughout their reproductive life. Theoretically, this loss is quickly made up by the bone marrow, which continually produces new blood cells and haemoglobin (their oxygen carrying property) as the need arises. However, many women require extra iron, particularly in pregnancy (though there is some controversy about this), and women become anaemic more easily than men do. An interesting new theory is that women live longer than men because they accumulate less surplus iron. Vitamin B_{12} has been linked with a possible iron deficit in the reproductive years. Supplements of this vitamin may be worth investigation.

A blood test might not show any iron deficiency or other abnormality and yet the tiredness persists. This only means that the tests are not sensitive enough to pick up what is out of kilter. The problem is sub-clinical. As a young woman, I was told that my tiredness was 'in the mind' but eventually a course of iron pills was prescribed which effected a dramatic cure. Some types of iron are not well tolerated, but these days there are many to choose from.

Skeletal overview

Feet   A clue to good feet is the strength of the two arches: the long one which is easily identified and the transverse one under the bony metatarsal heads. It doesn't much matter if the long arch is flat (the condition commonly known as flat feet) provided the foot is mobile and the muscles are working correctly. However, a person with flat feet is unlikely to be a top sprinter. In flat feet the mid-foot doesn't lock properly and tends to be sloppy which prevents a good push-off in running. If the transverse arch is flat, pain (metatarsalgia) and corns develop and walking will be painful. Hammer toes and bunions are signs of overactive leg muscles and small arch muscles which have given up the ghost.

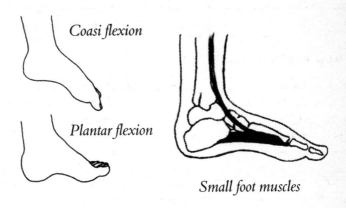

Coasi flexion

Plantar flexion

Small foot muscles

To exercise these small, crucial muscles, rest the foot on a flat surface and try to make a cave under the forefoot with the toes straight (not curled under). After a while it will be possible to exercise inside shoes. A satisfactory bulk of responsive muscle will develop, taking the place of claw-like long tendons with wasted muscles between them. Bunions may also be caused by pointy shoes and a faulty walk—striking the bone under the great toe hard at each step instead of transferring the weight along the outer edge of the foot. Surgery may be necessary to remove the bunion. Don't neglect exercising to improve the small foot muscles once the bunion has been corrected surgically.

Shoes should be chosen with care. It is only by being fussy that we can improve the available quality of the shoes we buy. Some manufacturers tend to make rather stiff shoes, quite unlike, say, the beautifully soft Italian leather equivalent. As students we were taught that it should be possible to fold a shoe in half, toe to heel. I wouldn't recommend this with anything but the most expensive European calfskin: you might be landed with the bill for a cracked shoe! But flexibility is a vital consideration for foot comfort and health.

Another difficulty is to find shoes of the right width. If you have problem feet, it may be prudent to spend more on everyday shoes that are low-heeled and comfortable to walk in rather than on dressy shoes and take the dressy ones to change into. Sometimes even standing in unsuitable shoes can cause intense pain, 'My feet are killing me!'

Shoes can certainly be the cause of much pain and misery and many shoe shops seem to run a sort of lottery where you pick up your size and get little help with fitting. Podiatrists and physiotherapists are left to pick up the bits. Perhaps they should also run the shoe shops!

Ankles   Many women say they have 'weak' ankles which 'give' or 'go over'. This is actually caused by imbalance of the six muscles which move the ankle joint. Often the muscles which turn the foot in or out are slow to respond when you stumble. All the ankle muscles can be strengthened by resistance exercises or by using a wobble board—an unstable board, like a seesaw, on which you stand and balance—which trains the ankle muscles to respond more quickly.

Women who take up jogging or squash without warming up can tear their Achilles tendon at the back of the heel. (Legend says that Achilles, a Greek hero, was dipped as a baby into a magic stream which was supposed to make him immortal. But his mother unfortunately held him by the heel, so he remained vulnerable in that one spot and he died when he succumbed to an arrow in the heel.) An Achilles tendon tear is a nasty injury which sometimes needs surgical stitching and then a long period of physiotherapy to stretch the tendon and bring swelling down. Shin strain is another sporting injury which must be treated if pain is to be relieved. This involves aching muscles in the front of the lower leg.

Knees   Some sports such as basketball, netball or skiing, involve sudden stopping and twisting on fixed feet. The knee can't tolerate this sort of action indefinitely unless the muscle at the front of the thigh, the quadriceps, is very strong. If it is weak, the kneecap can dislocate, or ligaments and cartilages can be damaged. The quadriceps actually encloses the kneecap and slots into the shinbone (the tibia). Some people develop a 'roughened kneecap', a type of arthritis which causes pain and swelling. Others have a kneecap which tracks sideways and has to be taped into place. Invariably the quadriceps is the key muscle which has to be strengthened to overcome the problem.

Hips The hip is a very strong joint which gives little trouble unless the pelvis is fractured or unstable or the hip joint becomes dislocated. A shallow hip socket predisposes to a possible disloca- tion before or at birth. This is more common in girl babies because females have more angulation of the thighs than males. Late in life, elderly women are somewhat prone to the same process because the hip socket has become worn on its upper side. Hip replacement is usually the answer in these cases.

Hands and wrists Hands are very susceptible to minor injuries such as cuts and burns. Some hand injuries are of the insidious, work-related kind. Musicians sometimes need treatment for repeti- tive injuries. One of these is a condition where the sheath or cover- ing of the finger tendons becomes tight or thickened. Another condition is called trigger finger. The finger is held flexed and is dif- ficult to pull back. When it is pulled passively, it gives a snap like the action of a trigger on a gun. Mallet finger is a sports injury where the extending tendon is pulled off its attachments and the end fin- ger joint can't be straightened.

Carpal tunnel syndrome is a painful hand condition where nerves, blood vessels and tendons become tightly confined behind a band of tissue covering the front of the wrist. Another condition is ganglion; a lump like a small pebble, usually on the back of the wrist, which is sore and may interfere with movement. Surgery is often the answer to these soft tissue problems, with physiotherapy as after-care. Movement in the hand is vital: if the grip is lost or weak, the hand becomes limited in all its actions. The so-called pre- hensile ability of grasping and holding and bringing the thumb to the fingers or to each individual finger has been refined to perfec- tion and used in every manipulation human genius can devise. Physiotherapists will go to endless trouble to try to maintain that prehensile ability, perhaps by splinting, but also by exercise. Some- times the action needs to be completely retrained because there is actual paralysis from nerve injury.

When an arm or wrist has to be splinted, it is most important to retain finger and hand movement. Some splints are called lively splints. They have rubber bands that stretch round the fingers to make sure the fingers get some movement against a slight resistance, a good way to ensure that muscles don't deteriorate.

Elbows   The forearm muscles originate in the elbow region and if these muscles are overused the elbow often becomes sore on its bony points. The ulnar nerve is very near the surface as it passes over the back of the elbow so it is easily bumped—the 'funny bone', and it may become trapped or bound down. Any interference with this nerve causes numbness or weakness in the outside part of the hand.

Shoulders and neck   There are conditions which involve the shoulder alone, but the neck is so often the instigator of shoulder problems that both are usually examined. The nerves for the shoulder and arm spread out from the spine in a large bundle called the brachial plexus. Parts of this network may become nipped or inflamed, causing referred pain down the arm. Stretching and mobilisation of the neck region can relieve symptoms like numbness and pain and weakness in one arm and hand.

However, some problems which occur in the shoulder have nothing to do with the neck. The joint covering or capsule can become bound down. The tendons running over it can become inflamed, or a pocket of fluid which prevents friction (a bursa) can adhere to bone and prevent full elevation of the arm. All these disabilities tend to be called 'frozen shoulder' because of the limitation of movement. A more modern term is 'rotator cuff injury', which is a name covering all aspects of movement. The term 'painful arc' specifically describes the restriction and pain when the arm is raised and moved away from the body.

Exercises for shoulder joint injuries should avoid lifting any weight. Arm swinging exercises are suitable or crawling up the wall with the arm supported by the wall or using a sling and pulley arrangement so that the good arm does most of the work.

Spine   People often imagine that their sore back or neck means there is a bone out of place. While it is true that spinal bones are altered in shape by the way children grow, by disease, by injury, and by wear and tear, it is *not* true that individual vertebrae migrate out of their habitual alignment. If they did, they would impinge on the spinal cord and probably cause extensive paralysis—which can happen if great force such as in a car accident is applied.

The discs between the vertebrae wear thin with age so that we all lose height eventually, and sometimes the soft structures tighten around the nerve roots where they leave the spinal cord causing pain along the course of a nerve. The pain of sciatica comes from the lower back, the lumbar spine; arm and hand pain come from the neck. Physiotherapists can do what is called a slump test to find out if the spinal cord is bound down or free to move within its canal during movements of the trunk. Disc pain is caused by a rent in the outer casing of the disc which allows fluid from within the nucleus of the disc to seep out backwards where it is very irritating to the nerves. Each disc looks a bit like a fried egg: in the centre is the nucleus and around it is a casing material. The nucleus should be dead centre. Lying on the stomach and propping up on the elbows helps to relieve disc pain as it bends the spine into a position that allows the fluid to be reabsorbed and the nucleus to float back into place.

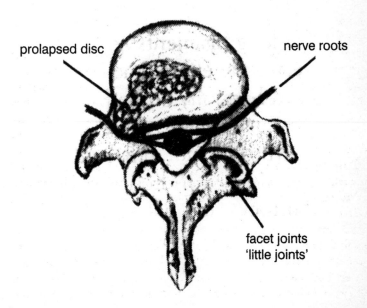

prolapsed disc

nerve roots

facet joints
'little joints'

Some people are born with slightly misshapen vertebrae, an extra rib or very tight spinal ligaments which make them more likely to get pain from these sources. Women have smaller vertebrae than men. They should probably not try to perform the same feats of heavy lifting unless they are specially trained. The lower part of the spine, the sacrum and the coccyx, seldom cause trouble unless they are badly injured: the coccyx, for instance, can be jarred in a horse-riding accident.

Antigravity muscles

Muscles that hold the body in an upright position are 'antigravity' muscles. They include the quadriceps, the buttock muscles, the stomach muscles and the shoulder blade muscles (rhomboids). They don't have to work very hard in a standing position, because the long ligaments attached to the spine hold it like straps with very little effort, and the body is balanced by muscles which work in harmony on both sides of the spine. But when any activity is performed, these muscles become very important. Women who are not physically active often have weak antigravity muscles, with droopy round shoulders, saggy abdomen, wobbly buttocks and flabby thighs. If these muscles are allowed to deteriorate, muscles on the other side of the joint (hip flexors, hamstrings, long back muscles and chest muscles) can become too tight. To test yourself, sit, legs straight, and stretch out to touch your toes with the ankles flexed back so that the toes are pointing up. If it hurts behind the knees your hamstrings and probably your heel tendon have become tight. Asian and African peoples are in the habit of squatting on their haunches, a good way of ensuring a long, flexible heel tendon. Westerners may be totally unable to squat with heels down by the age of 20!

Antigravity Exercises

These movements help maintain the correct spinal curves and strengthen the muscles that hold the body upright.

1. Cormorant
Stand with your feet apart and stretch your arms out and back, like a cormorant drying its wings.

2. Back flip
Stand with your legs apart, squat, then bend back until you are nearly horizontal. (Lean against something, if you have to, to steady yourself.)

3. Catapult
Stand with your hands clasped behind your back, and pull your shoulders down and back.

4. Kicker
Stand in front of a table or ledge and support yourself with both hands resting on the top. Raise one leg backwards as high as possible while keeping the trunk upright, then alternate.

5. Stork
Stand on one leg with the other knee clasped to your chest. Rise onto the ball of the foot of the supporting leg several times.

Exercise

In the past, exercise was often associated with a disciplined routine; the daily walk never to be missed, riding if you were rich, work for the poor. Children were taken out for an airing to bowl their hoops in the park, the babies in prams. Poverty kept many overworked and underfed, though not subject to the diseases of affluence.

Although jogging and other forms of exercise are beginning to alter lifestyles, there are still many modern children and adults whose habit is to sit glued to a television screen, perhaps having snacks in front of their favourite programme so that watching becomes associated with eating. As the body is also inert and almost certainly under-exercised, no wonder we are overweight as a nation! It is a wise move to take stock of your habits from time to time. Regular exercise, instead of tiring us, actually makes us ask for more.

First of all, what do you want to achieve with an exercise routine? A flat stomach? Shapely legs? Slim hips? Joints that are mobile and don't creak and crack? Stamina? Sports people often want to work on specific areas for special purposes. For the ordinary person it is best to aim at:

- strength in the antigravity muscles
- flexibility of joints
- attention to weak areas
- reasonable staying power.

Strength

The muscles to strengthen are the calves and the thigh muscle (quadriceps). Strengthen also the stomach and buttocks. To exercise the stomach, lie down on your back, knees bent. Now raise your head, shoulders and trunk. Do not attempt to work the stomach by raising both legs together with straight knees. The buttocks are used with the quadriceps in walking and running activities and coming up from a squatting position.

The shoulder and high back muscles, notably the rhomboid muscles which run almost horizontally between the shoulder blades and the spine, also need strengthening exercises. Lying prone (on stomach), with your elbows bent and head on hands, raise your torso as much as you can.

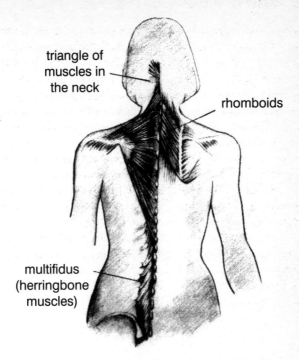

triangle of
muscles in
the neck

rhomboids

multifidus
(herringbone
muscles)

Muscles of the back

Stand tall often and make all the muscles mentioned taut as if a string is attached to the top of your head (see marionette, page 69). Don't forget to pull your chin in!

Flexibility

Yoga is excellent for increasing joint flexibility. At first you may think you will never make your rigid muscles flexible again, but with practice you will gradually achieve more range. Children are usually very supple. They sit cross-legged with their knees touching the floor. Easterners are in the habit of sitting like this and they keep their flexibility into old age. It is my belief that our loss of outward rotation of the hip, achieved when cross-legged sitting, is partly responsible for the modern frequency of hip arthritis and hip replacements.

Another area to assess now and then is shoulder rotation. Can you clasp your hands behind your shoulder blades, one arm coming up your back, one down?

Is your neck stiff? Perhaps it creaks when you move it? You can hear the crepitus close to your ears! Mobility exercises often help reduce this background noise. Cracking and creaking are not as sinister as they sound. A 'clunk' in the hip region only means that a big ligament is moving over a joint.

Weak areas

Ankles are liable to give way on uneven surfaces. To strengthen your ankles and make them more shapely, stand on one leg and rise up and down on the toe. If you tend to swell at the ankles (women do much more than men), sit on the floor and work the feet up and down and then walk across the floor on your bottom (progressive hip hitching).

Knees You can be weak-kneed or have weak knees! There may be a loose bit of cartilage in your knee joint which makes it lock in certain positions. Knees are also prone to ligament strain, and the kneecap to dislocation. Ask a physiotherapist!

Stomach A flabby, bulgy stomach that will not perform a sit-up is not only unattractive but it does not provide enough support for your internal organs or your back. At the end of the day you may feel so dragged down in that region that bed is the only place where you will find any relief. Some degree of stomach flabbiness is common for women in middle life. Women are more vulnerable than men (except those who consume large quantities of beer). We give birth which stretches our stomach muscles, our pelvis is more splayed and open, and we tend to collect fatty tissue in the abdomen and midriff. Remembering to pull in your stomach in odd moments will help. You may have a vertical gap between the two rectus muscles, the straight bands of muscle connecting the breast bone to the pubic bone. If so, you need to do resistance exercises. Don't be dependent on a panty girdle. Develop your own muscles!

Shoulder muscles It is difficult to keep shoulder muscles up to the mark. Even if you are a hillwalker who carries a heavy pack, you might still have a weakness in those crucial rhomboid muscles. To strengthen them, hold yourself up straight, and pull your shoulder blades down flush with the back chest wall. Weak muscles in the high back will give you the beginnings of a dowager's hump. Weak anterior neck muscles can cause neck, shoulder and arm pain and headaches. As well as tightening these slack muscles, it is best to consult a physiotherapist to mobilise your stiff neck if you have actual pain.

Back Pain in the waist area can be partly caused by weak stomach muscles. Bracing the stomach can enormously increase the strength of the back. For bracing see page 33.

Staying power

Try increasing your exercise tolerance. Do the same hard exercise, e.g., tennis or golf, once a week without fail. Take it seriously. If you prefer gardening, do it regularly, if possible, daily. You will find your stamina increasing automatically and you'll enjoy your mandatory routine exercise more and more.

Should I jog?

That depends on whether you enjoy it. If you want to jog, make sure you have suitable footwear, that is, padded, flexible gym shoes of good quality. Take them off when you come home. A change of footwear during the day is often neglected in this era of casual living. Foot health is important. If you think your feet smell, change your shoes and socks more often! Go barefooted! Let your feet breathe.

Jogging on a hard surface such as bitumen or gravel is not recommended. It causes jarring and shearing stresses on bones and joints. If possible, jog on grass.

Jogging may be dangerous if you have high blood pressure or heart disease and you should ask your doctor for a check-up before you begin a jogging programme. Develop a rhythm while you jog: breathe in as you take three strides, breathe out for two . . . But power walking might be a safer alternative.

Massage

Massage helps you relax and makes you feel good. But if you are hoping it will reduce your weight, you will be disappointed.

Sometimes massage can do what other things will not. Your physiotherapist may perhaps massage tight muscles in the neck and shoulder to enable him or her to mobilise or manipulate your joints. It is no good trying to perform a manipulation against the subconscious wishes of the patient!

Physiotherapists are often asked about vibrators. Are they any good? On the whole physiotherapists do not use them because they have no proven therapeutic value. Physiotherapists have better apparatus. Vibrators fall into much the same category as infra-red lamps which used to be a regular tool of the physiotherapist before the advent of ultrasound and interferential therapy. Now, they are considered a good home treatment if applicable. They help your muscles to relax.

Saunas, whirlpools, spa baths

The idea of humid heat is to make you sweat and lose fluid. The skin is a fairly good excretory organ so that you will also lose some waste products. You will tend to want to make up any fluid loss by being thirsty which is fine if you drink water. Drinking water will actually help you lose weight because it fills your stomach with a substance that has no kilojoules. But if you drink beer, spirits or even a soft drink after a sauna, you may put on as much weight as you lost by sweating.

Agitated water tends to be invigorating. It pummels you in much the same way as massage does. It is doubtful whether it does anything more than make you feel relaxed but the vibratory effect of turbulence has been found to reduce pain.

Injuries in sport and how to avoid them

Injuries in sport are, to some extent, inevitable. However, any known weak area should be protected. Sports equipment shops and medical supply shops sell ankle, wrist and knee supports made out of wetsuit material which moulds to the weakened area and reaches above and below a joint to reinforce ligaments. Physiotherapists can advise on this kind of splinting and also on strapping, using adhesive sports tape to protect joints and tendons. When any injury occurs it should be treated as soon as possible. Sometimes there is such heavy bruising that bleeding into muscles can form a build-up of blood called a haematoma. If a haematoma such as a 'cork leg' is not treated, the affected area may harden or calcify.

Ice is generally used first as a cold compress to staunch internal bleeding. Bandaging may be necessary and sometimes splinting. Later ultrasound or electrical treatment will possibly be used to disperse swelling and resolve bruising. Muscles or parts of muscles are sometimes torn, and these injuries are treated in the same way, although occasionally tissues have to be stitched up just like a skin injury is stitched if the wound is gaping.

Inflammation of a tendon can occur from long-distance running, golf, badminton or tennis. (Tennis elbow is well known but may not be caused by tennis.) Ligament injuries cause lack of stability and joint weakness and are often slow to heal as they have a relatively poor blood supply.

Muscles quickly weaken when immobilised. They must be retrained and the pull all around the joint normalised if the injury is not to repeat itself. Elbows suffer from being pulled, as in judo, or dislocated perhaps as the result of a fall in gymnastics. Ballet dancers are prone to ankle, foot and hip problems due to severe stretching of joints, while gymnasts can suffer wrist and arm problems and hyperextension of the trunk. Throwing can also cause wrist inflammation and a ganglion, a soft tissue swelling on the wrist. Netball, hockey and cricket may be hazardous for the fingers. Skiers often injure their ankles, tear a ligament, or more seriously fracture a bone. Fractures usually heal in a set period, depending on the kind of fracture and the amount of trauma to the bone. But if union is likely to be slow, electrical stimulation has been found to promote healing. Your physiotherapist can do this by making windows in the plaster and inserting moist pads with electrodes over them.

Other healing treatments include interferential therapy (IFT), pulsed electromagnetic energy (PEME) almost interchangeable with IFT, short wave, ultrasound, acupuncture, faradic and galvanic stimulation (these terms are explained in the glossary), specific pain relief, such as transcutaneous electrical nerve stimulation (TENS), and stretching, icing, mobilising, exercising or sometimes splinting, massaging and manipulating. Before any treatment is begun, the physiotherapist will need to investigate the problem thoroughly and often a body chart is filled in showing where pain or weakness or numbness is occurring.

At work

We have come a long way from the ill-lit factories and offices with heavy, back-breaking equipment that passed for acceptable work-places earlier this century. Most large employers have advisers who pronounce on suitable ergonomic office furniture, work breaks, user-friendly equipment and posture on the job but there are still, alas, too many employees who are rather neglected in this respect. It is amazing what a difference can be made by a headset for a tele-phone, a wrist rest for keying, or a tilted screen on a VDU.

Ergonomic chairs should be *bona fide* and therapeutic. These chairs are adjustable in height and the back rest can be placed at the right height and angle so that your spine is well supported. Desks should be at a height that saves you from leaning forward. Twisting to use a keyboard or screen can cause aches and pains, but a rotating chair will help. Ergonomics advisers can evaluate any job, for exam-ple, keying, writing, filing, stamping, sorting. If you feel you are badly done by in this respect, a physiotherapist or occupational therapist can approach the firm on your behalf, just as they may be asked at times to produce reports for workers' compensation cases, insurance bodies and the law courts.

Back care

Back strain is often caused by forcing the spine to move beyond its normal range. Maintaining good spinal mobility helps to prevent this. A minority of women are hypermobile and, when this is the case, joint stability is at risk if there is any muscle weakness in the area. If you have sustained a back injury, healing may tighten struc-tures round a joint so that it is prone to small repeated injuries.

Back-Strengthening Exercises

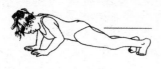

1. Push-ups
Lie on your stomach and push up on your hands, holding your body straight. Do not sag. Relax down after each push-up.

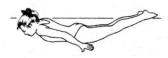

2. Press together
Lie on your stomach and lift both legs, keeping the heels pressed tightly together.

3. Knee hugs
Lie on your back and bend one knee to your chest (keep the other leg straight). Clasp your hands around the knee and raise your head towards it.

4. Crosswise
Lie on your back. Bend one knee to your chest and rotate the lower part of your body so that the raised knee touches the floor.

5. Straight leg raise
Lie on your back and raise one leg at a time. Keep your knees rigid.

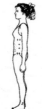

6. Bracing
Before lifting objects, stand, pull in your stomach and pelvic floor and then bear down slightly.

Sore backs should never be neglected. They seldom come right of their own accord. Physiotherapists can use passive movements of the legs, pelvis or upper torso to stretch scar tissue and restore mobility, making the back safer for possible future indiscretions that involve a heavy lift or a movement beyond your usual range.

Women are vulnerable to sacroiliac joint strain because these pelvic joints become mobile in pregnancy and may remain a bit looser than before. In fact, the female pelvis is structurally a less tight-knit unit than its male counterpart.

Young women are more prone to disc injury than middle-aged women because their discs are more elastic and thicker. As you get older, your discs wear thin. Back pain in later years is more likely to be due to strain in the little 'facet' joints at the back of the spine which can fairly easily slip out of alignment. Nerve pressure can occur in either case. Whatever your age it is vital to lift correctly, bending your knees and taking the strain close to your body.

The rope-like muscles that run parallel to the spine are often over strong, which can pull the vertebrae into a big curve in the waist region. It is important to strengthen the little herringbone-type muscles that hold the vertebrae at the correct degree of separation from each other and are responsible for postural control of the spine.

If you have to lift something heavy or awkward, do it by using the bracing method. Bracing involves contracting the stomach muscles in conjunction with the pelvic floor muscles, then doing a very slight bearing down movement (see page 33). Intra-abdominal pressure is thus increased, which helps to protect the spine while lifting. In bracing, the pelvis and abdomen combine to act like a box, with bone on three sides and a contracted stomach on the fourth. Underneath is a firm pelvic floor; the diaphragm creates the firm pressure from above. It is not easy to learn bracing, but once mastered it will serve you well and will become almost automatic whenever it is needed.

So, to minimise back problems:

- lift correctly
- brace when you lift
- keep reasonably mobile
- strengthen the right muscles.

Exercise evaluation

Adequate exercise creates a sense of well-being and should be a routine and essential part of life.

Exercise classes need to be undertaken with care. Aerobic exercise is meant to increase heart and breathing rates, but this must be done within the limits of your individual capabilities. There is a maximum heart rate which should not be exceeded. To calculate your maximum heart rate, subtract your age from 220 and then take 70 percent of the result. For instance, the maximum heart rate for a woman of 25 is 136 beats per minute. You can feel your heart beat in the wrist or in the carotid artery near your windpipe, just in front of the angle of the jaw. Count the number of beats for 15 seconds, then multiply by 4 to get the number of beats per minute; or count for 30 seconds and multiply by 2. Taking your pulse for a full minute is inaccurate as the beat slows considerably over that interval.

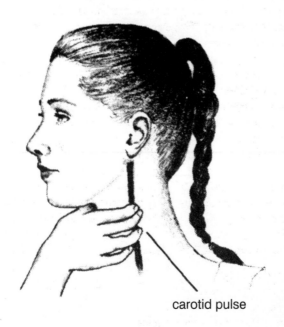

carotid pulse

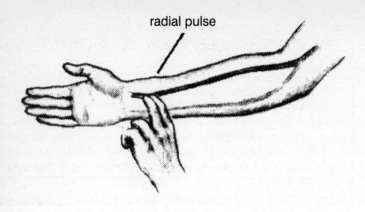

radial pulse

Any exercise routine should begin with a warm-up period before going into top gear, so that there is time for increased oxygen to reach the muscles. The basic metabolic rate increases after a session of exercise so that you burn up more kilojoules. The body also becomes more efficient at disposing of waste, through the skin, the lungs, the kidneys and the bowel.

Some exercises can put areas of your body at risk, so it is important to:

- avoid lifting *both* legs with knees straight
- bend your knees while doing sit-ups
- avoid star jumps if you have a weak pelvic floor, or if any part of your body reacts badly to shock (ankles, knees, hips, spine). Use Sorbothane® insoles and exercise on a soft surface.
- take care with back arching where you lie on your stomach and raise both legs and the upper torso. Over-use of extensor muscles may cause problems.

Some sports equipment may make an exercise too hard for your capabilities. For example, doing sit-ups on a ramp, head down, could strain your back or cause permanent separation of your abdominal rectus muscles if you have a tendency to separation (usually in pregnancy or postnatally).

Struts and Stays
Exercisefor Odd Moments

1. Lean your head against the car headrest. Pull in your chin and feel your head slide up the rest. (This contracts the anterior neck muscles which are often weak.)
2. Lean against the back of the car seat. Slide the shoulder blades down, flush with your chest.
3. Press your back into the seat back and pull in your stomach.
4. Sit right back into the seat and pull your pelvic floor muscles up off the seat.
5. With your feet directly under your knees, contract your calf muscles by pressing your feet against the floor.
6. Place your feet flat on the floor. Draw up the arches to make a cave under the feet (you can do this while wearing shoes).

   All of these movements can be done in the car, sitting at traffic lights or while standing in queues.

It is not wise to be tempted back to playing sport with an injury that is not completely healed. Strapping and moulded supports are acceptable after some injuries for a match where your presence is crucial, but it is prudent to seek advice on this point.

There is so much scope for the exercising twenty-first century woman that it is worth putting a little thought into what is best for *you*. So make sure you back the right horse in the race with your money, your time and your energy.

Smoking, alcohol and other drug abuse

So far we have talked about how to stay fit, or to fix up an injury and regain fitness. There are other factors which undermine fitness, namely smoking, drinking alcohol to excess, and use of other drugs.

Physiotherapists are more likely to see the end result of these addictions (particularly smoking) as they begin to affect a person in later life. Even if smoking does not lead to outright disease such as lung cancer or heart and blood vessel disease, it always affects lung function in time. Physiotherapists are often asked by a doctor to do a ventilatory function test (VFT) which is a standard test the doctor can use if he wants to know how seriously a patient is affected by lung or bronchial tube disease. If the candidate taking the test is a habitual smoker, her ventilatory function will be lower than the physiotherapist expects for her age. It is possible that the person taking the test has poor function because of some long-standing condition such as asthma and that she has never smoked. But poor results usually mean the person under investigation is a smoker.

Smoking, drug abuse or alcoholism in a pregnant woman can cause withdrawal symptoms and even death in the fetus. Often in these cases money is spent on the bad habit instead of on healthy food, and this further lowers the woman's resistance.

Occasionally people take stimulants, steroids or pain-killing drugs to improve their chances of winning in a sporting event. Not only is this illegal in competition but it is fraught with danger. The body will not function optimally for long if it is abused.

To exercise or not to exercise

People can always find excuses for not exercising. 'I'm too busy' is a common one and probably true. 'I do lots of housework. That's my exercise. I don't need any more!' is another. One study has found that housework, done at speed, uses more energy than a manual worker such as a navvy! But housework is a general term and some housewives are fussier than others, so what kind of housewife was this and did the navvy have a go-slow day? Neither housework, nor looking after babies or toddlers, uses all the muscles evenly. Formal exercise is needed as well, so that every muscle in the body, particularly the antigravity group, is worked. Rhythmical movement is desirable in any exercise programme because it is psychologically soothing and physically relaxing.

Poor weather stops us from doing all sorts of things. What a marvellous excuse! It's too cold, too wet, too windy, too hot, too humid . . . For those who live in regions of high temperature, either dry or humid heat, it is, of course, best to avoid the full heat of midday and the direct rays of the sun: early morning and evening are the ideal times. Two hints are: forego the main meal of the day until you have exercised; and wear cotton underwear. Clothes should breathe, allowing air to penetrate to the surface of the body, and cotton is more absorbent than synthetic materials.

Some people use a minor disability such as a bad back, either real or imagined, as an excuse not to exercise. If you have a bad back, you need advice and treatment: experts say that 95 percent of back-aches can be cured.

Treatment Schedule for Bruising, Muscle Tears and Joint Strains

Soon after injury:
- Use ice—ice cubes in a towel, pack of frozen vegetables, sprays, immerse in cold water
- Immobilise—bandage, strapping, rest
- Light massage (effleurage), stroking towards heart

If swelling is not going down within twenty-four hours:
- Seek physiotherapy treatment—IFT, PEME or electrical stimulation under pressure
- Gradually extend movement range (be guided by pain)

As condition improves:
- Deep massage (with liniment if you like)
- Ultrasound with liniment (to drive the liniment in)
- Stretch any tight tissue
- Mobilise joints in vicinity of injury
- Strengthen muscles

For return to sport:
- Wear support if necessary
- Warm up first
- Watch for weakness or fatigue

If you know some basic facts about how your body functions, you are in a position to protect it. For instance, neck manipulation may be dangerous. The vertebral artery runs close to the cervical (neck) spine. If it is kinked, part of the blood supply to the brain could be blocked. This shows up as dizziness, then slurring of the voice and it could obviously have serious consequences. It may be safer to have the individual bones 'mobilised', which is a gentle technique that nearly always results in a freer feeling in the neck.

This section on how to keep different parts of the body in good working order has covered only the common conditions that physiotherapists treat. Physiotherapists also work with all kinds of more serious disabilities such as nerve and brain disorders, fractures and dislocations, and rehabilitation after heart and lung surgery including treatment when the patient is incapacitated in hospital as well as after-care following orthopaedic surgery. Some physiotherapists work with disabled children and in hydrotherapy units, and there are physiotherapists in industry.

Responsibility for your own body and help with conservative, non-invasive, low-expense treatments will become more and more important in a technological world of already perplexing complexity.

Stress and relaxation

Being human means having perception, holding past, present and future in our minds all at once and having some insight into ourselves. In most ways this is a great boon. It has allowed the human race to soar above other animals. But there are disadvantages. Being conscious of self makes us particularly prone to stress.

We set goals for ourselves which may be unattainable or can only be realised at great cost. We worry about what impression we are making on other people. We compete, and agonise over failures. We want to influence others, and if we can't, we fret. Contemporary women are targets for all kinds of stress: as mothers organising a household and family in a complex world; as financial managers for the household; as part of the workforce; as carers for elderly relatives; as maintainers of standards in the home; as do-it-yourselfers who can mend a fuse, change a tyre, make a dress, build a rockery, start the mower . . . It is not always that we can't do whatever it is; rather that there are so *many* things waiting to be done. In addition there are stresses from financial worries, low self-esteem, demands and responsibilities, nervousness, and a wide range of fears about the future. Temperament is an important factor in how anyone will deal with stress. Certain temperaments appear to thrive on pressure while others are crushed.

Nervous and chemical reactions to stress

The body's nervous system works by sending impulses through its network, rather like an electrical current running along a wire. However, this is complicated by an ability to produce chemicals under certain conditions. These are called neurotransmitters. Stress factors are recognised by the cortex (the thinking part of the brain) and then passed on to the hypothalamus (the part of the brain that registers emotions and controls the organs' responses). The process can also occur at an unconscious level, bypassing the cortex. The hypothalamus processes sensations such as hunger and thirst, emotions and sexual feelings. It is also responsible for monitoring the female hormones that cause the cyclic changes which all women of reproductive age experience. The hypothalamus, together with glands such as the pituitary and the ovaries, regulates changes which include puberty, pregnancy and the menopause. Women's mood swings and emotions are thus inextricably linked to the reproductive functions.

Some important endocrine organs or glands which are very much concerned in the chemical transmission of stress are the adrenals which are situated one over each kidney. The adrenals can be directly stimulated via special emergency so-called 'fight-flight' nerves, or indirectly by hormones to produce adrenalin which can activate the production of at least eight other chemicals which cause increased heart rate and a speeding up of the metabolism. The effect on you may be just a feeling of excitement, a flood of fear (as happens when you narrowly escape a car accident), or pre-performance nerves (for instance, necessitating frequent visits to the toilet).

Stress can also affect the body's immune system. If you are in good health, and that means mental health as well as physical, you have a natural resistance to many diseases. But if you are living under constant threat of dire consequences, the stress may not only make you feel intellectually below par, but may also produce chemicals which could harm your immune system and make your body work against itself, in some respect.

Symptoms of stress range from feeling ill at ease to nervous tremor, from perspiring to having diarrhoea, from eating too much or too little to feeling faint or having a pounding heart. Stress can make you depressed or excitable, withdrawn with feelings of inferiority or loud and tactlessly outspoken.

Stress affects behaviour. It may make you smoke more, drink more, or take tranquillisers. These measures don't cure the stress although they may temporarily alleviate the symptoms and take your mind off your worries.

What you should be looking for is not just a palliative, but a new *modus vivendi*. The body is very clever at learning lessons from the messages it receives. There is also the possibility that it will unlearn one bad habit to take on another; let us say you succeed in controlling your palpitations which you used to get whenever you thought about talking in public only to find the body has taken on another bad habit. Just when you are about to greet some much loved member of the family you find you need to go to the toilet. The variations are endless.

Fortunately, there is a way to control your body, and to switch off the stress chemicals, or at least nip the process in the bud. You can learn to master relaxation. It may take a while, but it is guaranteed to succeed. If you persevere with relaxation, you bring on the opposing nerve transmission system which automatically switches off the chain reaction to stress.

Physical stress

Before the techniques of relaxation are explored, let us look at some of the conditions where physical stress, as distinct from mental stress, can cause havoc. In theory it is possible to divide the two kinds of stress but in real life they tend to overlap.

Over-use syndrome Over-use of the forearm muscles is currently a common problem among women, perhaps because a great many do keyboard work. The neck and shoulder muscles are often part of the picture, with some muscles overworking and others being lazy, creating an imbalance. Physiotherapy techniques aim at restoring the balance, either by massaging and relaxing movements, or by building up weak areas such as the shoulder girdle and teaching better co-ordination and flow in all movements in remedial fitness classes. Pause dynamics, which involve having little rests from work, and exercising muscles that are not part of the repetitive activity, have been introduced into some offices and factories.

If muscles are over-used, the tendons in the forearm, around the elbow, or near the shoulder may feel 'gritty' or 'creaky'. This indicates that the tendon is not moving freely within its covering sheath. All body organs are contained by a sheath or some sort of bag or capsule. Muscles and nerves also have sheaths. The sheath material around tendons can become inflamed with overuse—a condition called tendonitis. As there is very little room between a tendon and its sheath, any swelling or hardening will be painful in the extreme. Ultrasound treatment exacerbates tendonitis as the heat produced can increase the congestion. The physiotherapist might choose treatment with interferential current or pulsed electromagnetic energy (PEME). Both treatments promote healing by means of an electrical rhythm or 'beat' in the tissues.

Artists' stress   Performing artists such as dancers, musicians, acrobats, actors and media personalities are all subject to performance nerves. Physical stresses may occur from holding unnatural poses, using joints beyond their normal ranges and, in the case of musicians, using one small part of the body more than it would generally be used and to the exclusion of other parts.

Physiotherapy can usually alleviate such aches and pains and in fact there are some physiotherapists who have made esoteric studies of specific ailments such as clarinetists' thumbs!

Executive women   Head and neck problems must rate high on the list for women with special responsibilities. We talk about people having a heavy burden on their shoulders. No doubt this was originally meant as a real burden such as a sack or a yoke. Now it can be taken in its metaphorical sense. Travelling is probably a factor in increasing stress when it could, with training, be used as a time to relax.

Muscles in the scalp, around the jaw and in the neck tighten imperceptibly, pressing on nerves to the head and altering blood supply. The result is a tension headache.

It may be that you who have the headache are the only one who knows, while you try to carry on and function normally. But you probably give yourself away: your facial expressions will be less mobile than usual to those who know you well, and you may make little extraneous movements, twitchiness, fiddling with things, sighing or propping your head.

Indigestion is another sign of stress, possibly caused by missing meals, eating too fast because time is short, or eating when you are upset. Indigestion is a warning to slow down and eat sensibly before you get stomach ulcers.

Shop assistants, hairdressers, teachers   If you are one of these, your feet can suffer. Constant standing, particularly if there is little movement, allows blood to pool low in the body. The heart pumps blood through arteries to all parts of the body. The beat is lost by the time the blood reaches the veins which have tiny pockets in them to help prevent the blood from going backwards, but they have to be assisted by muscles to raise the blood to the heart, especially when the person is upright. The calf muscle is the most important pump for returning blood to the heart. Anyone who has to stand for long periods should work the calves, rising on the toes or standing on one leg and working the other ankle. Even with this sort of 'little and often' mechanism there is a tendency to get varicose veins—tortuous protrusions where a backlog of blood over the years has stretched the veins out of shape.

Fallen arches, ankle and knee weakness, and backache are further occupational hazards. Teachers constantly bending over desks may have pain between the shoulder blades, or neck or back pain. Added to the physical discomfort is tension. Pain causes tension of muscles; muscle tension causes more pain. It is a merry-go-round of stress.

Aerobics exercises are intended to make sure that the heart-blood vessel system is stimulated, as well as muscles strengthened and joints mobilised. If your job is sedentary or stationary, you need some form of workout at least once a week. Brisk walking is an aerobic exercise, so is swimming and most ball games (although croquet and bowls wouldn't rate very high on that score). Make sure you enjoy some antidote to the demands of your job.

Relaxation

To help channel the mind away from stress and pain, physiotherapists teach a triad of methods: **relaxation, breathing patterns** and **rhythmic movement,** which can be practised either singly or in conjunction, depending on the situation and on personal preference.

An understanding of the process of relaxation plays a vital part in learning to ignore disturbing bodily sensations. The technique is very old. It has been practised by Indian yogis for thousands of years. Exponents of relaxation therapy talk about an altered state of consciousness. This state can be measured by an electroencephalogram which shows alpha brain waves indicating reduced body metabolism. Relaxation is not sleep but a consciously controlled dormancy, an absence of reaction to stimuli.

Meditation is a common means of achieving this dormancy. It can be done by mental fixation on repeated words, focusing the eyes on a spot, or concentrating on the stream of one's own breath. Any of these devices tends to induce muscular relaxation. The English poet Tennyson, for instance, was able to fall into a state of meditation by silently repeating his own name. Meditation has been used by mystics to bring on altered consciousness where there is a loss of personality, a feeling of being beyond time yet deeply peaceful. Easterners are traditionally more accomplished meditators than Westerners and great feats of endurance are attributed to meditative techniques. Meditative relaxation could be called self-hypnosis, except that there is continual conscious awareness. It is a voluntary state which is comfortable and pleasurable. During meditation the multiplicity of sensations coming into the brain are reduced by focusing on one point of consciousness. The mind then seems to be able to discard the original device which cleared it of trivia and maintain the state of relaxation until the person returns to reactive consciousness by an act of will. However, it seems that not everyone is capable of reaching the same depth of relaxation. Relaxation can be divided into two streams, **still relaxation** and **rhythm relaxation**.

Still relaxation

Traditionally, still relaxation has been done in the lotus position or some sitting posture with a straight back. The upright position is used because lying down induces sleep and that is not the aim. However, physical comfort is important and a fully supported position is usually what is wanted, though not always.

Recumbent relaxation is familiar to most people. You are motionless, spread-eagled, fully supported and breathing easily in a state of deep comfort. (A contrasting mental picture of tension is of people in a dentist's waiting room sitting stiffly upright, knees crossed, hands clasped or leafing the pages of magazines, a prey to anticipatory stress.) A typical image of a relaxed person is one who is open, accepting; while that of a tense person is closed in, unaccepting. The internal feelings are diametrically opposed in the two states and in fact a different subconscious nervous system is operating. In the relaxed state the dominant system is the parasympathetic, the subconscious system of nerves that carry out the smooth inner workings of the body. The parasympathetic system maintains an even heart rate, breathing appropriate to the state of activity and normal intestinal, glandular and hormonal activity. It keeps us comfortable. On the other hand, in a state of tension, the sympathetic nervous system is dominant. This system comes into prominence in cases of sudden fright or sustained nervous tension and is known as the 'fight-fight' reflex. It is nature's way of alerting the body to react to a crisis. Heart rate and breathing rate increase, adrenalin is pumped into the bloodstream and the body becomes tense and ready for action.

The opposite number system An English physiotherapist, Laura Mitchell, worked out a system of relaxation whereby the muscles that are not usually part of the tension pattern are used to pull the body out of its tension habit. Mitchell relaxation is based on the fact that muscles oppose each other. If a joint is moved, one muscle performs the action while its opposite number lets go and allows the movement. Some muscles, such as the muscles that raise the shoulders, are often involved in a state of tension. Consequently, responding to the command 'Pull your shoulders down' will make the anti-tension muscles work and the tense muscles will then be given no option but to relax. At the next command, 'Stop pulling your shoulders down', you will have relaxed all around the shoulder joint. The technique can be used for every part of the body, easing it gradually out of its tension pattern. Mitchell relaxation is often used in antenatal classes to train women to relax in labour, but it can be useful for anyone.

Mental images for relaxation   Some people react better to mental images or words: 'heaviness', 'limpness', 'like a rag doll'. Relaxing the muscles in the face is often a good way to encourage general relaxation. Or imagine a simple face such as a child draws—three circles, two eyes and a mouth—then think of the circles widening out towards each other like the ripples on a pond. The eyes and the mouth are surrounded by circular muscles which, if relaxed, result in a lack of expression, a deadpan look to the face. A face in repose will quickly spread relaxation to neck, scalp, shoulders, arms and then trunk and legs.

Relaxation may lead to sleep; indeed relaxation with deep breathing can cure insomnia. But the object of relaxation training is to experience a form of consciousness where stress is eliminated.

Touch relaxation   can be very helpful if you find it difficult to relax. It should be done by someone you love and trust. Your partner runs his or her hands along your arms from the shoulders to the fingertips, while you imagine tension flowing out of your body under the moving hands. Sometimes, you will feel a pleasant tingling sensation. Your partner then runs his or her hands from your hips down to your feet in the same manner. The whole hand should be used in a soft but firm action, moulding the palm and fingers to the relaxed limb. Or you can lie on your stomach or on your side. Your partner then runs down your spine with both hands, starting at the seventh cervical vertebra (the bumpy one at the nape of the neck) and sliding the hands right down the spine and off the tailbone. This movement can be very comforting—it may even make you fall asleep.

Breathing patterns   Words can be introduced into a relaxation technique, to be said silently in time with breathing in a pattern of repetition. The mind is then wholly taken up with this exercise and has no opportunity to initiate irrelevant or inappropriate trains of thought. Words should be soothing and geared towards positive thinking. The words that evoke the right reactions can be left to the individual, whether it be the transcendental 'Om', or words from a poem, song or prayer. As long as the process doesn't become too wordy!

Relaxation Techniques

(anorexia, tension headache)

1. Grandma

Sit in an armchair high enough to support your head. Or use a rocking chair, if you have one, and rock occasionally—it helps relaxation. Become aware of your body all the way down from your head to your toes. Pay special attention to a feeling of sagging in the shoulders. Try to make your arms limp. Imagine your arms and legs are too heavy to lift. Let your face sag in and let the only movements (apart from rocking) be eye flutters and gentle breathing. Repeat to yourself a phrase such as 'feel good' every time your breathe in. Stay like this for about 15–20 minutes.

2. Stand still

Stand with your arms a little way out from the sides of your body. Shake your hands as if they were wet and you were shaking off drops of water. Feel loose in the shoulders and neck, but don't droop your head.

3. Spaced out

Lie on your back on the floor, in bed or on the lawn, looking up. Feel your body as you did in the chair. Notice the difference in this position. Gravity is acting differently on your spread-out body. Try making your body cover as much territory as possible. Spread your arms and your legs, stretch a little and then let go and let your body drift. Imagine you are weightless in space, floating.

Breathing generally becomes slow of its own accord. Try to use your diaphragm by taking air in slowly, making your abdomen rise slightly. On the breath out, sigh gently, letting the elastic recoil of your chest push the air out. Never try to force air out. Take as long as you can over each breath, without causing any degree of strain. Slowly, your own breathing will mesmerise you into a state of deep comfort, and a feeling of well-being will steal over you.

If you are in pain, use shorter breaths, opening the mouth and taking a little gasp and then sighing out. In this way you are pandering slightly to your pain while you mobilise the body's defences into conquering it. Pain becomes bearable if you let it wash over you, letting your subconscious anti-pain system subdue it. Try not to react to pain with stress and tension; this only makes it worse.

Concentrating on breathing can make an intolerable situation tolerable. It is helpful not only for labour, but for any type of pain, even mental suffering. Taking a deep slow breath 'in—out' before you speak can even control anger!

Rhythmic movement

While the first stream of relaxation is still relaxation, the second stream, rhythmic movement, is an instinctive way of inducing a calm state of mind. Babies love to be rocked. We all love music and dancing, though not always of the same kind. It has always been known that rhythm dulls jangling nerves and 'soothes the savage breast'—though the chemical process within the body is only beginning to be understood. A mental picture that can be used for rhythm relaxation is the old-fashioned one of an old woman sitting in a rocking chair by a fire, knitting: she is really quite active and yet she is relaxed. Another image of rhythmic relaxation comes from the southern states of the USA where summer is oppressively hot: the veranda swing. The swing creates a current of air which is cooling and the gentle rhythmic motion is relaxing.

Taking responsibility for your own relaxation

Many physiotherapists teach relaxation using only their voices and their hands, their rationale being that it is better not to make you too dependent on your therapist, but to teach you to control your own body. It is really a question of letting go of what we consider is a necessary control. It frightens us to give way absolutely and surrender ourselves to whatever is coming to us. We may let go in the safety of our own homes but it is another matter sitting in the dentist's chair or about to go under an anaesthetic!

Pain mechanisms

Pain is not only a physical sensation but also the conscious perception of that sensation; that is, how you see it and what it signifies. Pain is subject to psychological interpretation, depending on a person's ethnic background, environment, upbringing and personality. There are five ways in which pain may be felt:

1. Tissue damage: cutting, burning or bruising of skin and or underlying tissues.
2. Bone and joint pain.
3. Direct nerve pressure or compression of nerve endings.
4. Internal pressure and stretching.
5. Lack of oxygen.

It is interesting that surface damage such as cutting is felt as pain, whereas there are no nerves to record cutting and burning of internal organs. It is more important that the internal organs record pressure and stretch as, in some situations, severe pain is a sign of imminent rupture.

Bone is particularly sensitive to pain, especially in and under its covering membrane, the periosteum. If you have had a fracture, you know the fragile feeling caused by any untoward movement.

Nerves register all kinds of pain. They also react to any sort of interference in any sector of their pathway. Little nerve endings respond to the pressure of swelling in the tissues, and a direct assault on a nerve trunk causes pain like an electric shock!

If an internal organ is damaged, pain may be 'referred' somewhere else. For instance, angina pain is felt down the inside of the left arm.

Pain may also be due to oxygen starvation. This is very apparent in the excruciating pain of sudden cramp, caused by lactic acid build-up such as happens in a mild way when our muscles are stiff after exercise. A hot bath to relieve stiffness probably works by ensuring a good blood supply.

Pain tolerance

Painful labour and birth was traditionally thought to be the fate of women, so much so that when anaesthetics were invented many people considered it wrong to use them for any aspect of childbirth. In the mid-twentieth century this belief was challenged and some people came to consider labour pain as the result of years of biblical indoctrination or fear of pain as a race memory of traumatic childbirth in the past. Some people went so far as to say that, if fear of childbirth were removed, it should result in painless labour. This has not proved to be the case, although it is evident that a great deal can be done to reconcile women to the idea of constructive labour pain. Labour pain has been measured and found to be as intense as toothache, neuralgia or cancer pain, but fortunately each 'pain' is of short duration. Experiments have been done to find out how different races and cultures tolerate labour pain. Some cultures prohibit crying out but will allow a low moan; others encourage as much noise as a woman likes.

In many primitive communities not only labour pain but all pain demands stoic fortitude. Young boys and in some cases girls pass through what we would consider cruel and disfiguring initiation ceremonies. These obligatory rites serve, perhaps gratuitously, to teach the brain to ignore some types of pain.

In Western societies, psychological reaction seems to be bound up with pain expectation. We have apprehensions about pain and how severe it is likely to be. We also have fears about our behaviour during pain and whether we will stand the strain.

Pain chemicals and pathways

Pain sensations begin as a chemical called P substance in the tissue of origin, then change to electrical impulses as they zip up to the brain. The impulses carry messages of pain and other sensations such as heat, cold, touch or irritation. The nerves which carry these impulses do not connect directly with the brain. They transfer their messages to other nerves, or bundles of nerve fibres, and then to yet others, the process compounding itself in the brain. A nerve ends in a cluster of tentacles which meet the tentacles of the next nerve link across a 'gap' called a 'synapse'. The electrical nerve message becomes chemical where it jumps this gap, then changes back to an electrical impulse, then to a chemical in the spinal cord and back to an electrical impulse and so on. Think of it as a telephone message going to a central exchange.

When pain is in its chemical form, it can be influenced by another chemical called endorphine, which is produced by the body as an antidote to pain. For instance, endorphine can 'numb off' pain in situations of great danger, as when a soldier is fleeing from the enemy and doesn't realise how seriously wounded he is. Endorphine levels are raised during feats of endurance, such as jogging, running a marathon, or playing any hard game of sport, not to mention giving birth.

Pain intensifiers

Two factors make any pain worse, tiredness and expectation of outcome. If you know you only have to experience the pain for a short time, you will be more willing to put up with it than if you can see no real end to it. Pain that is inflicted during medical or dental treatment ought to be easier to withstand on this score as it is usually short-lived. However, it is often accompanied by fear, expectation of sudden severe pain, and sometimes also an element of distrust. What are they going to do to me?

Some pains indicate that disease is damaging the body, as is the case in AIDS. Awareness of deterioration can make the pain seem worse and harder to bear. By contrast, labour pain almost always has a desirable outcome and is usually seen in a context of optimism.

Pain is the body's device to alert the conscious mind to a situation that is potentially dangerous. Although quite curable nowadays, leprosy used to be renowned for its disfigurements. These are not actually caused by the disease itself: leprosy attacks the sensory nerves, making the area affected numb and unable to feel pain. This leaves hands and feet particularly liable to burns, cuts, abrasions and bruises. Pain is a warning, and it can be a very insistent warning.

So what is the best way to tackle pain?

Analgesia

An analgesic is a medicinal substance that relieves pain. Analgesics fall into four categories: painkillers taken by mouth; painkilling injections into muscle or bloodstream; painkilling injections to dull nerves and localised pain; and inhalation of gases.

Oral painkillers and injections   Aspirin is a very common oral painkiller, as are preparations which contain paracetamol. On the whole it is best to use these drugs for short term pain, although aspirin is sometimes prescribed on an ongoing basis for certain types of rheumatism.

Narcotics are stronger painkillers that are derived from the opium poppy. They have been around in some form or other for a long, long time. The Romans used a narcotic called laudanum. Various drugs which contain codeine are sold over the counter.

Stronger narcotics, morphine and pethidine, are prescribed by doctors in certain circumstances and are usually given by injection. All narcotic drugs are addictive and if used for long-term pain should always be taken under medical instruction. Since morphine-like substances have been found associated with nerve pathways in the human body, it has been realised that the introduced narcotic uses the same mechanism to suppress pain, the difference being that it is stronger. It acts to reinforce the body's own control of pain. Hence pethidine is used in labour to reinforce relaxation and breathing techniques (pages 138–147).

Muscle relaxants can also be used to control pain (as pain is often due to tension). Quinine is a muscle relaxant. Pain can also be suppressed by using non-steroid anti-inflammatory drugs (see page 193), cortico-steroids (hydrocortisone—usually by injection, for example for shoulder bursitis) and antihistamines.

Local painkillers Local analgesics can be given to dull pain that is confined to one region or to prevent pain in an area which has to undergo treatment that might cause pain. Sometimes nerves can be infiltrated with local anaesthetic—a nerve block. An example is a pudendal block, which numbs the pudendal nerves when forceps have to be used in labour. Nerve blocks are also used for other types of severe internal pain but unfortunately this seldom works as a long-term cure. Pain is very clever at finding new channels to zip up and worry the brain!

Epidural and spinal analgesia An epidural injection blocks pain messages from reaching the brain. It can be an enormous relief in labour, if pain has become intolerable. It is also used to block out back pain when there is severe nerve pressure from a spinal disc lesion. Epidurals have become quite popular as a method of analgesia for surgery and have a high safety record. Surgery below the epidural area can be carried out if the patient is agreeable. Caesarean section is often done with an epidural so that the mother can see her child born. For some surgery a light general anaesthetic might also be administered to save psychological strain. The brain is left largely unaffected and it appears that this inflicts less shock on the system than a total general anaesthetic. An epidural injection introduces local analgesic into the epidural space around the spinal cord where the nerves emerge. Your spinal cord is protected by a layer of tough material called dura, hence the name epidural (*epi*, outside; *dura*, hard). The needle stays outside this hard layer. Sometimes a 'spinal' injection is given with a very fine needle which penetrates the dura, and it acts more quickly than an epidural.

Epidurals and spinals are usually free from unwanted side-effects but occasionally fluid escapes from the spinal cord. This leakage can cause a nasty headache, and possibly a lowering of blood pressure (although this can be an advantage in labour when blood pressure may be too high).

Gas inhalation for pain　　Nitrous oxide and oxygen, often just known as 'gas', provides a quick and easy method of pain control. Dentists use a mild mixture of nitrous oxide and oxygen to allay nervousness in some patients. The same mixture is also used for women in labour. The mixture can be varied to suit the individual but the percentage of oxygen is always over 50 percent, ensuring good oxygenation of the fetus and preventing the mother from becoming too comatose. Many women feel comfortable with 30 percent nitrous oxide and 70 percent oxygen. The gas is inhaled through a mask with a valve which is self-activated by breathing.

There are several ways you can learn to control and sometimes banish pain without the use of drugs. Physiotherapists can help by teaching relaxation, or by using acupuncture, biofeedback or TENS.

Relaxation

Pain, like stress, nearly always causes muscle tension which makes the pain worse. Relaxation training can help you ignore your pain. Once the brain has learnt that you are not going to allow your body to relay pain messages to it, it may stop listening for them. Chronic pain may simply be repeated nerve impulses causing a habit. Constructive behaviour is capable of diverting the pain messages.

Acupuncture

Acupuncture is a traditional Chinese method of influencing healing and pain control by using points of lowered resistance in the skin. Mechanical stimulation (acupressure), electrical impulses or needle insertion can be used. Each process sets up a vibration in the tissues. You can think of acupuncture points as the places where the body allows systems to be accessible. Often there are bundles of nerves or clusters of blood vessels near these points. Acupuncture can also be used in diagnosis.

It has been found recently that acupuncture promotes endorphines in the fluid that bathes the brain and spinal cord. Results are sometimes immediate, but may take hours or days. After about six sessions you should know whether you respond to this kind of treatment. A side-effect of acupuncture can be feeling faint, and it is considered to be a good idea not to have a heavy meal before treatment. Women are said to respond more readily than men: perhaps women are less sceptical and any treatment is more likely to work if the patient's approach is positive.

Biofeedback

Pain usually results in muscle tension and changes in skin temperature. There is a machine which can measure muscle tension, skin temperature or resistance and relay it to the patient by a varying pitch sound. If you have a tension headache you will usually have a tight temporal muscle, the frontalis. This tension can be measured, signalled to your attention and you can learn to reduce the tension and monitor your own success.

TENS

TENS (transcutaneous electrical nerve stimulation) is becoming more and more accepted as a way to control pain. These stimulators, often called pain block machines, are transistor-powered and can be extremely small like a hearing aid. If the pain warrants it, they can be implanted in the body by surgery. However, pain can often be influenced by attaching the small leads from the TENS machine to any part of the body using a gel and attacking the pain from *outside*. A circuit is set up either around the local area of pain or at a site where the nerves would be expected to transmit the pain to the brain. In this way the pain pathway can be interrupted.

Your physiotherapist will design the right distribution, wave form, pulse rate and intensity to suit your particular condition. This electrical device works to produce endorphines in a similar way to acupuncture. TENS can even be used for labour pain because it can stimulate the inhibitory pain system and help switch off relays of pain signals to the brain, but it has not proved universally helpful as very strong contractions, where push-button pain control would be an advantage, appear to overwhelm the nervous system with rapid stimuli which may break through the electrical control rhythm.

A simple explanation of pain is the pain gate theory, although the actual mechanism is very complicated. When the 'gate' in the spinal cord is open, pain messages can flow up to the brain. When it is closed, pain messages are intercepted and might not reach the brain. TENS acts particularly well as an interceptor of pain messages. It helps to close the gate.

Some tension pain is the result of tightening of small areas of muscle or connective tissue about the size of a cent or a pebble. These are called trigger points and can easily be found by your physiotherapist. Sometimes they can be felt as a lump, sometimes as gritty areas. Treating these trouble spots will often cure your pain spontaneously.

Pain is such a personal experience that other people, even close family, can seem rather unsympathetic. Pain may not show and you may be accused of 'enjoying your poor health'. With so many avenues to explore, there is really no excuse for doing nothing about pain. Pain clinics and psychological treatment such as hypnotherapy can help, as can relaxation to reduce muscle spasm. Chronic pain leaves traces on your face and your body and drags you down. You should take every possible step to overcome it.

Reflexes

A reflex is an involuntary response to a stimulus. Some reflexes, such as the knee jerk, are innate. Others, such as retaining urine in the bladder until convenient to void, are learned. Many reflexes operate on a feedback mechanism. If one thing happens, another follows and feeds back to the original, modifying its effect. This happens with pain. A message signalling pain is sent to the brain which responds by evaluating the nature of the pain—whether it signals mild injury, destruction of tissue, or whatever—and deciding what the reaction will be. Sometimes two antagonistic reflexes go out at once. The brain attends to the most important reflex, suppressing the lesser one.

A conditioned reflex is the result of training. Learned reflexes begin to develop in infancy and we refine them throughout our lives as our skills increase. Many activities begin as a laboriously slow brain function of trial and error, experiment and correction. Take learning to drive a car, for instance, or even driving a strange car. You have to think out what you are doing. You feel a bit insecure and liable to make mistakes. Once you are accustomed to the complex actions you have to perform, it all becomes extremely easy. What has happened is that the movements have been incorporated into the reflex arc and are much less dependent on brain control.

When the body is moving, many reflexes occur, continually correcting potentially faulty movements. Obviously such reflexes are tremendously important in sports where fast-responding reflexes are needed for quick reactions.

Babies have righting reflexes which tell about the relationship of the body to the head, of being the right way up (which may be upside down in the uterus). Righting reflexes are innate in most animals, but many movement reflexes can be trained. Imagine the reflexes involved when a concert pianist, after years of intense practice, seemingly effortlessly tackles a complex concerto without a score.

Internal workings

Some people consider it a good idea to develop the bowel-emptying reflex by going to the toilet at the same time each day, usually around breakfast time. Some parents insist on their children having a bowel action at a regular time but undue parental pressure may be counterproductive. Nothing is worse than to induce straining to secure a result. However, there is value in self-training. The body can learn to effect the desired result at a convenient time and it *is* convenient to get that business over for the day.

For centuries people believed that missing a daily bowel action would poison the system. That belief was challenged in this century, leading to a very different attitude. Nursing staff no longer fuss if patients have no bowel action for a week after an operation. In fact, it is usually the patients who fuss! But true constipation is not a desirable state and straining at stool can lead to prolapse, particularly in women who have just had a baby, and whose tissues are stretched and vulnerable (see pages 172–175). Bowel content softeners can be taken to guard against this.

Constipation might also lead to diverticulitis, when a series of distended sacs protrude from the bowel wall and trap faeces. These pockets are easily inflamed. Symptoms are griping pain and passing mucus, followed by increasing constipation. The condition can be greatly improved by diet and training the reflex.

When you get a fish bone stuck in your throat, you usually end up by swallowing it because anything that goes far enough back into the throat cavity will initiate the swallow reflex. This doesn't matter as much as you might think. Once the bone gets past the windpipe which is protected by the cough reflex, the food mass engulfs it as it goes downwards through the intestines, and the intestinal muscles tend to align it with the tube. The intestines work by peristalsis, whereby the muscular walls behind the food mass contract simultaneously as the walls beyond the food mass relax. If the reflexes go wrong, build-up of wind and bowel contents may cause pain. This is possibly one reason behind obscure low abdominal or pelvic pain. It is known as dysmotility.

Hoodwinking the reflexes

Reflexes are often the cause of extreme distress. If you think you are going to vomit, you have a reflex on stand-by, ready to empty your stomach. Thinking about something entirely different might get you out of the situation and give the reflex time to cool off. The gag reflex can be very easily elicited by touching the soft palate at the back of the throat. Dentists always try to avoid firing off the gag reflex, but some people may be fairly susceptible to any manipulation in the region.

Sexual reflexes can be fired very easily if you know the mechanism. Brides in the prudish nineteenth century used to be told by their mothers to 'lie back and think of England!' which was supposed to switch off any feelings of revulsion or, horrors, sexual arousal! Many reflexes function during sexual intercourse but any one of them can be inadvertently dampened by a hostile attitude.

Reflexes are very elusive: we may want to switch one on or off but haven't the faintest idea how. On the other hand, a reflex may operate without our consent. Besides this, reflexes often give us false information. The bladder-emptying reflex may signal that the bladder is full when it is only half-full. The stomach reflex might tell us it is empty when it is not filled to the capacity to which it is accustomed. Eating bulkier food will trick the stomach into thinking it is full. Even drinking water can do this. Compulsive eating is often triggered by a clamorous stomach. Compulsive dieting is reflexly controlled by a non-compliant stomach. Both conditions can be overruled by reason and logic.

It is possible to prevent a sneeze by pressure on a branch of the facial nerve just under the upper lip, but mental control in time may also inhibit a sneeze. Pressure on the perineum (the bridge between the vagina and anus) will switch off bladder urgency. This is why little girls clutch themselves when they suddenly want to go to the toilet. The urge can be temporarily subdued.

After a stroke there is sometimes over-activity of reflexes. Usually when one muscle contracts, a reflex inhibitory message goes to its opponent. Spastic children and stroke victims may have lost some of this switching off mechanism. Physiotherapists treat these conditions by tricking the reflexes into submission and facilitating smooth movements. Repetition by the patient helps the brain to establish control over the erring reflexes.

A milder form of reflexes being out of balance is incoordination. Muscular reflexes are kept under the constant scrutiny of the main brain (cerebral cortex) and also the cerebellum which knows about the position of your body in space. The cerebellum tells the reflexes how to maintain balance and posture. If there is something wrong with the cerebellum, jerky movements called ataxia can be the result. You can use your eyes to help movements even if you have little movement sense.

Vasomotor reflexes

The vasomotor reflexes look after the constriction or dilatation of arteries. For instance, a reflex dilatation of the face and neck arteries may be caused by embarrassment—you blush. Stress can cause constriction of little branches of arteries and raise blood pressure. This is called a pressor reflex. Hot flushes in the menopause are instigated by vasomotor reflexes which have become unstable due to withdrawal of oestrogen from the system. Migraine is another condition where artery constriction and dilatation reflexes have overreacted.

Cold, whitish fingers in winter, and sometimes at other times, is an annoying case of the artery constriction reflex working overtime. This is called Raynaud's phenomenon. Doctors use various drugs to correct these over-zealous reflexes. The whole hand may become hot and pink or cold, bluish and moist, and light touching, heat, cold, air currents are all exquisitely painful. This is called causalgia or Sudeck's atrophy. Women seem to be a bit more susceptible than men to this type of painful burning. The hand may swell and become relatively useless. Treatment involves controlling the pain and exercises to stimulate circulation. Trigger areas can be infiltrated with a local anaesthetic using injections or sprays.

Swelling after a fracture, compression or some interference to blood supply can cause vasomotor reflexes to go astray. There are many physiotherapy treatments for reducing swelling.

Reasoned responses

Reflexes are a bit like children, full of quixotic requests. Reflexes can gain the upper hand and be very unreasonable. Reason comes from the brain. The brain can countermand a reflex because a reflex is a subordinate impulse. The brain may take matters out of mere reflex hands. But we do rely on our reflexes and our imperfections are sometimes found out by them. If you have to perform some intricate task in public, say, playing a piece of music, unless you have learnt it (reflexly), you may start making mistakes through sheer nervousness because your mind is on your critical audience. If you know your piece thoroughly (that is, reflexly), you will sail through it even if you are nervous because your automatic pilot will do it for you!

The best way to train a reflex is by repetition and it may take a long time and there may be occasions when it lets you down. Reflexes are mercurial. They are sometimes much easier to train than you think. (This goes for your children's reflexes too. Be kind but firm to reflexes and the results will be worth the effort.) Reflexes thrive on routine and repetition, and they work best in a climate of relaxation.

You can learn to control heart rate, blood pressure, skin temperature and muscle tension. It is possible to slow your heart rate by breathing more slowly and thinking relaxed thoughts. This in turn can lower your blood pressure. If necessary, a biofeedback machine can help you train reflexes by giving you information about your internal workings.

Even sleep is subject to modification by the conscious brain. We can decide when to go to bed, and programme ourselves to wake up. Research has shown that our patterns of sleep are important. If you have a lie-in after a sleepless night, you may sleep but you may also establish a pattern for sleeping in daylight hours. Shift workers often have trouble when they want to return to normal sleep hours because their reflexes are out of gear.

Subliminal reflexes

Advertisers know all about our reflex desires and they prey on our susceptibilities in a shameless way. If an advertisement brings out the right reflex response we will be kindly disposed to buying whatever it is although we may be unaware of what is going on because the whole transaction takes place below the water-line of our consciousness.

A physiotherapist faced with a patient with faulty reflexes will enquire into how they are upsetting that person's lifestyle. Perhaps faulty is too strong a word, as we vary in what we are prepared to put up with from our bodies. Treatment will depend on what kind of reflex has to be modified. Is it muscular, vasomotor, digestive, urinary or psycho-sexual? All are capable of modification. Knowing the means helps you to achieve the desirable end.

Lock and key mechanisms

Many body systems work on a 'lock and key' relationship; one special substance or molecule locking in where others would fail to fit. Reflexes belong to this system: a reflex can be switched on or off by the higher centres of the brain but one reflex can never become another. A reflex responds to its own unique stimulus and an unusual response can sometimes show that something is wrong. There is, for instance, a reflex action of the big toe called the Babinski reflex. By stroking the sole of the foot briskly, the big toe will point down. If there is something wrong with the central nervous system and inhibitory factors are missing in the reflex mechanism, the big toe will point up!

Women's reflexes

With one notable exception—motherhood—reflexes in men and women are basically the same. Female sexual reflexes have their counterparts in the male. For instance, the clitoris becomes swollen and erect, like the penis, and even emits drops of fluid.

It is possible that women are a little more successful than men at controlling unwanted reflexes. Men are notoriously bad dieters, and find it difficult to subdue hunger and thirst reflexes. Most women find it easier to control sexual impulses than men. Many women inhibit a sneeze to a minor event and modify a cough. On the other hand, we are inclined to neglect our postural reflexes. More women than men have poor posture.

Reflexes are constantly operating, telling the nervous system about tone in muscles. The reflex arc begins as a sensory message informing a centre in the spinal cord or brain what conditions are like in a part of the body—such as a muscle. The second section of the arc consists of a message which is sent to do something about it—a motor message. Muscles that hold us upright are made up of many 'slow twitch' fibres which are good at holding for long periods. We should heed the reflex messages that constantly adjust muscle response to keep the body erect. It actually takes less effort to remain erect than to sag.

Recognition of the role of action and reaction may prevent you from becoming a slave to one of your own reflexes!

Motherhood is governed by many innate responses which we call maternal instinct. As well, there are chemical reactions which maintain the pregnancy, terminate it, start labour contractions, bring in the lactating responses. The milk let-down reflex is a good example of nature's provision for a newborn child. The reflex is set off by the baby while the mother's physical response is enhanced by her emotional tenderness and the relative helplessness of her newborn.

Reflexes are inbuilt protectors of the species. Without them we would become extinct. We can guide them but never ignore them. A great deal of conscious time is spent in controlling this subconscious army of activity, restraining its exuberance and channelling its workings into reactions that profit the individual.

2

ADOLESCENCE

Adolescence for girls *and* boys is an inexact period between the onset of puberty and maturity. The word refers to growing up, and people do it at different paces. These few years, roughly between the ages of eleven and eighteen, are a transitional period of great importance.

To you who are in this age group, it may seem that you are viewed by younger and older people as a strange, rather unpredictable species. In primitive societies an initiation ceremony or 'rite of passage' was held to usher a child into adulthood. Everyone knew when childhood would end and adulthood begin. In this century we seem to have set the period of adolescence apart much more than appears to have happened in the past, perhaps because we spend longer at school; perhaps because of the increasing complexity of our lives. 'You are behaving like a child!' is an adult catch-cry. Unless we are in the midst of adolescence ourselves, we tend to expect immediate adult behaviour. The teenager is faced with a double standard: one moment you are supposed to grow up instantly and the next you are regarded as a misfit betwixt and between.

Humans are the only animal species to experience adolescence. In fact this period can be regarded as a prolonged learning experience, vital for the evolution of our species. Human adolescence has been called a 'psychocultural latency period'; in other words it is a time of life when responsibilities are limited and learning abilities are at their keenest so that the emerging adult can acquire the knowledge to help fit them for life. Concurrent with intellectual learning there is a coming to terms with newfound sexuality and with changes in body proportions.

Adolescence begins at puberty. For a girl this means budding breasts, widening hips and a more curvaceous body. Puberty is also heralded by the beginning of menstruation. Some girls develop and menstruate at 11, while others do so later—at 14 or even 16. Sometimes puberty brings on a great increase in appetite, and a tendency to put on 'puppy fat'. Or it may cause a rush of energy, perhaps to release tension and sidetrack disturbing bodily sensations, or because of a new delight in physical skills which are being refined and perfected. Sexual and aggressive urges are often channelled into sport, in a harmless letting off of steam.

Menstruation

The first period, known as the menarche, is a point which marks a girl's entry into adulthood, a sign that she is becoming sexually mature. Ovulation may not occur for some time and it is not at all abnormal for menstruation to be irregular at first. It is thought that the menarche takes place when the body accumulates a certain proportion of fat to body weight. There is some evidence that thin girls are late in menstruating. Better nutrition has lowered the average age of the onset of menstruating compared with the past.

The word *menarche* comes from *mensis*, month, and *arche*, beginning. Once the menstrual cycle settles down, it generally assumes a periodicity of 28 days or thereabouts, so that among primitive peoples it was thought to have some connection with the phases of the moon. Some people still believe in this theory but it is difficult to prove.

Joan of Arc was 19 when she died and it was widely believed that she had never menstruated, leading people to believe she was either a saint or a witch. This is not surprising as it is known that severe physical or mental stress may cause amenorrhoea (absence of periods). (For example, women in displaced persons camps after the Second World War are known to have stopped menstruating but to have begun again once they were rehabilitated.) Amenorrhoea was once considered a great benefit because, in the opinion of the time, menstruation was 'the curse of Eve', preventing women from entering public life, and from taking on a traditionally male role as Joan of Arc did.

Of all the signs of burgeoning femininity, the menarche is the most dramatic. Girls will notice the gradual laying down of breast tissue, the arrival of sparse pubic hair and some mucousy vaginal discharges. Some girls, eager to reach maturity, will be more aware than others of these early signs. It has been suggested that the conditions surrounding the first period affect the way a woman regards her menstrual cycle—whether she tolerates it cheerfully or thinks of it as woman's curse, but recent research discounts the emotional repercussions of the first period.

Repeated unpleasant side-effects of menstruation probably play a more decisive role in how the monthly cycle will be viewed.

Menstrual pain (dysmenorrhoea)

Menstruation may be painful, particularly in the first days of the period when the uterus contracts fairly strongly. The contractions may cause a temporary deficiency of blood to the muscular wall of the uterus which results in crampy sort of pain. A group of fatty acid substances called prostaglandins are responsible for these contractions, during periods and in pregnancy and labour. Some young women's systems are over-endowed with prostaglandins and hefty contractions of the uterus may cause them painful periods which can be very dispiriting and debilitating. The thought of being even partly incapacitated by menstruation is intolerable for a teenager wanting to swim or hike or rock climb or sail a tall ship. Backache is another complication, possibly because the nerve centres for the back in the spinal cord are very close to the nerve centres for the reproductive organs which allows a kind of overflow of pain from one to the other. The condition is often cured by pregnancy because of the improved blood supply to the uterus.

Menstruation pain may respond to two physiotherapy treatments which improve blood supply to the pelvic organs. One is to pass a form of gentle heat, called short wave, through the body, warming the internal organs, and producing a pleasant feeling of deep warmth. Short wave works in the same way as that tried and true remedy for period pain, a hot-water bottle clasped to the stomach. The other treatment, known as interferential therapy or IFT, is more recent and appears to be more effective. It is a 'cold' treatment, during which two electric currents are used which 'interfere' with each other, causing an increase in cell activity and accelerated movement of body fluids, including blood. Both treatments are given between periods.

Gentle Exercises to Relieve Period Pain

1. Donkey exercise

Kneel on all fours (hands and knees), with your back parallel to the floor. Hump your back up and then lower it to the horizontal position.

2. Salaam

Kneel, slope your back, lean on your arms and rest your head on the floor. Rest and relax in this position. (If the ache in the lower abdomen is very severe, spread the knees apart so that they don't press on the tender stomach.)

3. Hip hitching

Lie on your back. Make one leg longer than the other by sliding your hips. Alternate your legs and start slowly, gaining speed as the pain recedes.

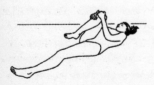

4. Half-roll

Lie on your back, hugging one knee. Roll your body to the opposite side and back. Repeat on the other side.

5. Rocking

Lie on one side, curled up with yours arms around your knees. Rock in a small movement, forward and back, developing a comforting rhythm.

Physiotherapy offers a very simple corrective, but you may also wish to consult your family doctor about period pain. She or he might prescribe a drug which inhibits excessive prostaglandin production, or a female hormone called oestrogen. In extreme cases a surgeon can cut the nerves that carry the pain into the body's communication system, but before considering such drastic action, it is worth exploring the physiotherapists' noninvasive techniques.

Premenstrual tension (PMT)

There has been much debate in recent years about premenstrual tension (PMT), in the lead-up to the period. The physical symptoms include extra fluid retention, a feeling of pelvic fullness, backache and stress-related headaches; emotional symptoms are signs of irritation, moodiness or vagueness. Studies have indicated that PMT stems more from cultural and environmental influences than from hormonal changes, that is, chemical changes in body fluids. It is likely that the more premenstrual tension is discussed, the more women will suffer from it. Many women do notice signs that herald the onset of their periods: a tenderness of the breasts, low abdominal discomfort and irritability or tiredness. However, a woman leading a largely sedentary lifestyle might overreact to signs that a healthy, active, well-integrated person may ignore.

If there are definite symptoms of PMT such as backache or low abdominal 'bloating', physiotherapists will be able to suggest a range of treatments. This might involve interferential (antipain) therapy (IFT) for bloating, neck mobilisation for headaches, relaxation techniques for stress or an exercise routine for backache. Nothing is too trivial to treat, even if its origin is more psychological than physical. Physiotherapists understand the interplay between physical and emotional factors.

Growth

Humans have a long childhood compared with other mammals. Growth is relatively slow between the toddler phase and the teenage. In puberty there is a growth spurt, bringing new physical and emotional needs. Hands and feet grow; legs and arms lengthen; the trunk grows sturdier. The lungs expand more and the breathing rate slows, as does the heart rate. Growing is complicated by sexual change: in females breasts grow, the areola around the nipple appears, the pelvic girdle broadens, and fat deposits cause bodily curves. At the same time unidentified aches may occur, often in the limbs, and usually at night or early morning. These so-called growing pains are usually not serious and can be relieved by heat or brisk massage.

Postural problems

The rapid growth changes going on in puberty can put considerable strain on body tissues such as joints, ligaments and muscles. A young woman in good health usually manages these changes well and grows up straight and shapely. But the undernourished or obese girl or one who has some bony abnormality, however slight, may compensate by adopting an undesirable posture. It has been said that poor posture only develops because some bodily defect makes it actually painful to hold the body erect. Once established, the blueprint for the posture can be very hard to eradicate.

Adolescent postural problems are common. Physical changes in weight distribution, such as development of the breasts and shaping of the adult pelvis may alter body mechanics and result in round shoulders, jutting chin or faulty pelvic tilt—how much you stick your bottom out or tuck it under so that you look like a banana! Psychological adjustment to changing body shape may contribute to the problem. Breasts seem to grow disconcertingly large or hardly at all. One seldom meets a female who is satisfied!

Some types of poor posture appear to be hereditary. Look at your older relatives to see how you might look at their age! Preventive therapy, an active lifestyle, corrective furniture and inculcation of good habits may all be needed to counteract the genetic effect.

No matter what the cause, poor posture should be treated as soon as it becomes evident, especially in the young before the pattern for the undesirable body carriage is laid down indelibly in the subconscious.

Physiotherapy has much to offer you if you have a postural problem. You can be relieved of pain, and your body alignment can be investigated with a view to re-aligning it in a way that is comfortable and will prevent other problems from developing. Gone are the rigid

Postural Exercises

1. Pintucks
Sit, stand or lie. Bring your shoulder blades together. Imagine the skin is like darts or pintucks on a dress. Don't raise your shoulders. Do this a little and often, every day. (This can cure round shoulders.)

2. Ironing
Lie on your back, with your knees bent and feet flat on the floor. Press your waist down onto the floor and feel your stomach tighten. (This helps a sway back.)

3. Fishtail
Hang from a bar or rings. Swing your legs, first to the right and then to the left. Keep your legs together. (This stretches the spine and helps mild curvature.)

4. Marionette
Stand on your toes, keeping your knees stiff. Walk with your head up, as if the top of it were attached to a string suspended from the ceiling. Walk stiffly like a puppet, without allowing your knees to bend.

5. Stork
Stand on one leg and hug the other knee firmly to your chest. Go up and down on the ball of your foot. Change legs. (This strengthens the antigravity muscles which help to hold us upright.)

6. Whoa!
Sir or stand. Pull in your chin and stretch the back of your neck. (Imagine you are a horse being reined in.)

backs and wasp waists of the Victorian era! Healthy posture is now individual, dynamic and natural.

Spinal curvature

If you are going through the growing period when bones are reaching their mature form, three main skeletal abnormalities can develop:

1. Exaggerated postural curves such as a sway back (lordosis) or a high forward curve in the spine (kyphosis), commonly called round shoulders or poking head.
2. A sideways curve which causes 'listing'. The medical name for this is *scoliosis*. Muscles are stronger on one side of the curve than on the other and they pull the bones out of alignment and may cause individual vertebrae to rotate. The curve starts as a simple C but progresses into an S curve.
3. Development of wedge-shaped vertebrae in the thoracic region, a condition called Scheuermann's disease.

Any of these aberrations of growth can cause backache, and early correction is important. Scoliosis is the most serious of the three. In mild cases, physiotherapy treatment may be enough. Moderate 'listing' can sometimes be corrected with a brace but severe cases may need surgery in which an operation using Harrington rods is performed to hold the errant vertebrae in place.

Scheuermann's disease is fairly common, but is usually arrested when growth stops. It involves a few vertebrae growing slightly wedge-shaped. If you do have one of these bony irregularities, good mobility and specialised exercises will save much pain and possibly deformity in the future.

Acne

Acne is the bane of adolescence, an ego-reducing disease. It is associated with hormonal changes during puberty, not caused by lack of washing. During puberty the apocrine sweat glands enlarge and you will notice more odour to perspiration. Some of the oily skin glands may not enlarge enough and they can become clogged and harbour infections particularly on the face and neck, so hygiene is important if you have acne, but lack of it is not the cause.

Peeling agents, taken internally or applied externally, have proved useful. Even rubbing the face hard with a washer under the shower will help because it stimulates blood circulation. In summer, sea water and outdoor pursuits are very beneficial. If acne is a year-round problem, the physiotherapist's ultraviolet (UV) lamp can help in colder weather or for those who have to work in an air-conditioned atmosphere. This treatment toughens up the skin and tends to annihilate harmful bacteria. Acne usually disappears with advancing age but, as it can leave nasty facial scars, it should be tackled early. (It is now known that strong sunlight over a protracted period can be harmful to the skin. Controlled UV treatment is given only for a few minutes to the affected area.)

Obesity

Some people are overweight because they were overfed in infancy causing extra fat cells to develop. If this was so, it can't be helped now. But further increase in size and number of cells during adolescence tends to be permanent and there is still an opportunity to double back on your tracks and avoid this permanent weight burden.

Immoderate fasting is foolish as it can cause deficiencies of iron, calcium and some vitamins. So can skipping meals and making up on hefty snacks. Fast foods are generally overloaded with fat, salt and sugar and usually lack fibre so they should be avoided. Wholegrain cereals should form a basic part of the diet. Refined carbohydrate and lack of fruit and vegetable fibre is implicated in colon cancer and other problems of the digestive system such as diverticulitis. Manufacturers are responding to the call for more fibre in food, but their claims should be viewed critically by consumers. A discerning shopper reads all the small print!

We often choose the food we eat by habit. Variety can be introduced to a diet by including new foods from other cultures. Be adventurous. Try making real wholemeal bread; buy free-range eggs; cultivate a liking for luscious home-grown fruits and vegetables. 'You are what you eat' is an old adage but a basically true one.

Slimming

Losing weight is really a matter of arithmetic. If you burn up all the kilojoules or calories you take in (4 kilojoules = 1 calorie), you stay the same weight. You can lose weight by substituting a food containing a high number of kilojoules with a lower kilojoule food. Morning and afternoon snacks, part of the psychological satisfaction given by the food habit, can be retained if, for example, a biscuit is replaced by an apple. Sugar intake can be cut if you teach yourself to drink unsweetened tea or coffee. Much can be achieved, even in the most unpromising cases by will power, weekly weighing and regular aerobic exercise. Beware of excessive dieting though: it can cause anorexia nervosa.

Anorexia nervosa

Anorexia is a condition of emotional origin where there is chronic loss of appetite. Teenagers are besieged by all sections of the media and clothing industry with images of an ideal female figure. This pressure and other subtle persuasion at home, school or work can drive some teenagers to a process of self-starvation. Its symptoms include radical weight loss, sallowness, menstruation disorders, apathy, agitation and tension. In the seventeenth century a person suffering this disorder was described as 'a skeleton clad only in skin'.

New research links anorexia with depression, in which a brain chemical activates the stress reflex. If this is so, meditative relaxation techniques can help switch off the stress reflex. An adolescent who is fat at puberty might try to lose weight due to a consequent horror of obesity. Anorexia is sometimes just overreaction: it takes off like a runaway horse. Gentle relaxation therapy can soothe the hyperactive element and induce restful sleep.

Sample Replacement Diet

This is a suggestion for losing weight slowly but surely. By changing your habits and eating low-calorie food you can maintain your new low weight. Learn to give up your old eating habits, represented by the current diet, and take on a new look by following the replacement diet. Note that the replacement diet gives a lot of variety and is much more nutritious.   *(Continued)*

Sample Replacement Diet (*Continued*)

Time	Current Diet	Replacement Diet
7.30 a.m.	2 cups of tea with full-fat milk and sugar	2 cups of tea with skimmed milk and no sugar
8.00 a.m.	2 slices of toast, 1 cup of coffee, black with sugar	Fresh fruit, or 1 bowl of wholegrain cereal with no added sugar (specified on packet), 1 slice of wholemeal toast, 1 cup of coffee, black or with skimmed milk, 1 boiled or poached egg
11.00 a.m.	1 cup of tea with full-fat milk and sugar, 1 biscuit	1 cup of tea with skimmed milk and no sugar, or fruit juice with no added sugar, or 1 piece of fruit
1.00 p.m.	1 salad roll, or 1 packet of sandwiches, 1 can of soft drink	Salad with cottage cheese or lean meat or hard-boiled egg, or salad, cheese or meat on a slice of Ryvita®, wholegrain, wheat or rye bread, fruit juice, or fruit, or unsweetened low-fat yoghurt
4.00 p.m.	1 cup of tea with full-fat milk and sugar, 1 piece of cake	1 cup of tea with skimmed milk, 1 low-fat, low-sugar wholegrain health bar or 1 wholemeal biscuit
7.00 p.m.	Meat, gravy and potatoes, or 1 pie or pasty, or 1 fried fish and chips, or steak and chips, or spaghetti, or pizza	Lean meat and 3 vegetables, or casserole and baked jacket potatoes, or steamed or baked fish with salad, or steak, vegetables and mashed potatoes with cottage cheese instead of butter, or omelette with brown rice and green salad
10.30 p.m.	Hot chocolate with full-fat milk and sugar	Hot chocolate with skimmed milk and no sugar, or a bowl of wholegrain cereal with no added sugar

In all questions of weight, either overweight or underweight, self-esteem is important. Once a person begins to feel in control of her own body, learning to know its vagaries and how it works, she will be in a position of power.

Combating tension

Asthma, migraine and tension headache occur at all ages and are not confined to women. However, they often appear for the first time in adolescence.

Teenage asthma

You may have had asthma of the allergic type as a child and then had stress in advanced school years bring it on again. Often the trigger is vigorous exercise. When this is the case a challenge test consisting of limited but hard exercise will produce wheezing. This characteristic wheezing is due to muscular spasm obstructing the airways. A bout of exercise may produce coughing, which is good because it helps expel mucus. Asthmatics can also be checked by a ventilatory function test (VFT) to measure the expiratory flow rate to determine how much impediment to air there is in the breathing tubes.

Not all forms of asthma are triggered by exercise. Psychological stress often brings on attacks of allergic or non-allergic asthma and you may be tempted to use the complaint as an excuse for not doing things that are irksome to you. Fear of an attack produces its own symptoms. During an attack or in anticipation of one, an asthma sufferer can expect to be tense, even panic-stricken.

It is not easy to overcome tension before and during an attack but the condition can be relieved by relaxation of the small breathing tubes. Inhalant sprays such as Ventolin® do this. Relaxation techniques will enhance the effect of the drugs and discourage total dependence on them.

Physiotherapy treatment for asthma aims at relaxation of the whole body and particularly of the breathing tubes during the expiratory phase; clearing obstructed airways of mucus; providing instruction in correct breathing habits; and increasing tolerance to exercise progressively.

Exercises for Asthmatics

1. Count down
Kneel, resting your elbows and forearms on a bean bag or chair. Breathe out very slowly, feeling your chest wall drop right down, and count in seconds. You may count aloud but you must do it all in one breath.

2. Squeeze box
Kneeling upright, place your hands on the side of your chest. Breathe out slowly, pressing inwards with your hands.

(In exercises 1 and 2 the breathe *in* should come in a relaxed way.)

3. Thistledown
Sit at a table with a ping-pong ball in front of you. Blow the ball across the table. Blow slowly and steadily.

4. Candid candle
Light a candle and put it on a table. Blow the flame horizontal, but don't blow it out! Do this as many times as you can in one breath.

5. Huff and puff
Obtain a bubble pipe and a bowl of soapsuds. Blow a large bubble. Take the pipe out of your mouth and gently blow the bubble off the pipe.

6. Exercise tolerance
Run round the house as many times as you can without wheezing. Stop if you wheeze. Try to increase your tolerance day by day. Progress gradually to a longer period, doing any exercise that increases your breathing rate, but always stop if you start to wheeze.

These exercises might make you cough but it doesn't matter—coughing helps to shift the mucus in your chest.

Migraine

The word 'migraine' comes from the German *hemikrania* or 'half skull'. The condition is usually felt on one side of the head with stabbing pain over one eye. It is thought to be due to excessive dilation of some arteries in the skull while others, possibly on the surface of the brain, are somewhat constricted. Or there may be a constrictive phase followed by a dilatory phase. The dilation can often be felt in the arteries of the neck and base of the skull as a more than normally strong pulsation. Sometimes there is temporary interference to sight, spots before the eyes, blurring or semi-blindness, sometimes nausea and vomiting. Migraine is sometimes associated with emotional disturbance and appears to be unusual in children but relatively common in adolescents. Some young women may find it has pre-menstrual associations. It can continue throughout the reproductive phase of a woman's life, so it is really important to treat it when it first appears. Often there is quite a long warning phase, when you will be aware that a migraine is coming on.

Biofeedback and relaxation can be used to prevent a migraine attack or to control its severity. Some people can ward off attacks by these simple methods (though not so simple to learn). Others need medication. Biofeedback helps you to learn a desired response by means of an electrical or mechanical recording device.

Another method, IFT, the electrical treatment mentioned before, may be quite dramatic in its relief of migraine because it works directly on the blood circulation. To have its full effect, this treatment must be applied when the attack is coming on. Interchangeable with IFT is TENS which can 'switch off' the painful throbbing. A doctor may prescribe drugs to stave off or minimise attacks but physical means of control can be used in conjunction with such a medication programme.

Tension headaches

If you are studying for long hours with your head bent forward over your books, this position puts strain on the neck muscles, particularly a little triangle of muscles which holds the skull onto the top few vertebrae. These muscles can go into a kind of spasm, squeezing nerves going to the scalp and brain and causing headaches.

Longer muscles connecting the area between the shoulder blades with the base of the skull can also become taut and painful. You might have chronic pain confined to the neck that comes after an hour or so of study. In another condition, an 'acute neck', you wake up with a stiff neck and find that your head won't turn, or you have to hold it slightly on one side and this is very painful.

Physiotherapists have an excellent record of curing such complaints quickly. In the case of an acute neck, one treatment of gentle mobilisation can leave you almost pain-free.

There are some other conditions that affect young people that appear under other headings or in other chapters. Above all, don't regard yourselves as different. Remember there is the enormous advantage of youth. Teenagers' problems are likely to be easier to treat because their bones, muscles and organs are young: if 'fully' adult women seem to have fewer problems, it may only be that they have become more expert at hiding them!

3

SELF-IMAGE, SEXUAL FULFILMENT AND SEXUAL SAFETY

For women sexual fulfilment is not confined to performance of the sexual act. There are women who have chosen a different path for their womanhood and remained virgin all their lives. Nuns devote their femininity to their order; some women pour their selfhood into their art or their work or into care of someone dear to them.

The ordinary woman has had to contend with a subordinate place in the scheme of things for most of recorded history. It is not surprising that the woman of today works towards being wholly liberated.

Power dressing

Whenever you meet someone, you take in not only their bodily image but their clothes. Even if you are walking at a distance behind someone in the street, you may recognise them by their clothes. Of course, you may also recognise them by some physical attribute, such as the way they walk, the colour and style of their hair or their actual size. Nevertheless, you will be unable to separate the person from the clothes they have chosen that day. Human beings seem to be unique in the animal kingdom in purposefully choosing bodily adornment. Without clothes most of us feel vulnerable. To feel comfortable, we like to be dressed for the occasion; a swimsuit is all right for the beach, but not for a night at the opera. We feel unpleasantly vulnerable when we don a hospital gown with no back to it, though we don't mind so much sitting in a nightie in a hospital bed.

In sexual encounters we may choose to meet on a vulnerable but privileged level. But I believe the human race has a fundamental psychological need for clothing. Perhaps this was triggered by the evolutionary discarding of the oestrus, of being on heat only at certain times of the year. The mature human female along with the primates is responsive all the time. Clothes are a protection not only from the weather but for the psyche. Sexual drive in animals is often ritualised. In human society, at all historical periods, we see the sexual ritual partially achieved by clothes. But we dress to emphasise our personalities as well as to attract the opposite sex. We shouldn't feel vain about dressing primarily to please ourselves. We dress to expose our standards and values, to maintain an authority suitable to our position in the workplace and to please others, both men and women. We also dress to compete and to conform.

Women are often prepared to go to extreme lengths to achieve an effect, sometimes even to the detriment of their health. Tight lacing into body corsets may have produced an hourglass figure; it also caused visceroptosis, the actual displacement of organs, squashing the bowel and other organs downwards. The empire line brought the waist up under the bust and the waist has been known to disappear altogether under the shift, the kaftan, the tent or the sack. Early in the twentieth century women's abdomens and breasts used to be bound down tightly immediately after the birth of a baby. The engorged tissue had to go somewhere, so breasts became pendulous and hung down to the waist. At this critical time they were squashed out of shape. The bra is a controversial garment, but large breasts look very ugly and feel very uncomfortable if they are allowed to droop or flap about. An underwire may be undesirable for a nursing mother but it does provide support at other times and comfort usually makes good sense in matters of health.

Women are not alone in creating bizarre unnatural effects. Men in ancient Crete wore increasingly tight belts from the age of seven to shrink their waists, according to some dictate of fashion. Buttocks also are sometimes stressed, sometimes not. There was that blatant Victorian sex lure, the bustle, and today we have tight jeans, whereas the 1920s flapper banished the buttocks.

Headgear and hair, make-up and beards are all part of dressing up for both sexes; the aim being either to emphasise sexuality or to cloak it in mystery. The impact tends to reflect some feeling prevalent in the era. The intent may be to shock the observer—witness the punk rocker!

There is usually a subtle reason for the decrees of fashion. Each generation wants to supersede the one before and right the mistakes of the immediate past. By dressing differently this wished-for change becomes symbolically realised. Paris fashions are only taken up universally if the skill of the designer is able to catch the spirit of the age.

Clothing and hairstyle may be used to accentuate an affiliation such as wearing a uniform and, because the person reveres the association, the uniform is also revered. We think of a uniform as comfort clothing but this wasn't always so. There was the hair shirt! The old-fashioned wimple was apparently responsible for headaches, and I once knew a case of actual indentation of the skull in a woman who coiled her hair tightly around her head; she belonged to a religious order where the hair must never be cut. Are sweat bands, a modern equivalent, too tight? How about bike helmets?

Hats have again become fashionable, not just to keep us warm in cold weather but also to shade out the direct rays of the sun and protect us from the hole in the ozone layer. Hair is probably cleaner and healthier than it has ever been. But beware of harmful chemicals. Dyes may eventually cause your hair to lose its lustre. Some hairsprays harbour carcinogens, and watch out for irritating genital sprays which may encourage cystitis.

Subtle use of cosmetics enhances our good features, but caked on make-up will spoil the resilience of the skin and it may fall into a mass of wrinkles by middle age. There is a sheet of muscle in the skin of the neck called the *platysma*. Use of this muscle helps to prevent saggy folds developing too early. Grimace, bringing your teeth together and drawing the corners of your mouth down. (Not to be done in public—it makes you look like a Frankenstein monster!)

Our sexuality is a mishmash of emphasis and concealment, of display and mystery to keep the other sex guessing. If we are wise, we will choose clothing that plays down a defect, such as a protruding stomach or thick thighs. We may use high hats and high heels to increase our stature. Desmond Morris in his book *The Naked Ape* makes a pertinent comment about the way women jeopardise foot health in the name of fashion. He says of high heels that they may show off the calf but they also 'severely limit the action of walking (as well as permanently damaging the feet)'. Men are not immune from using artifice to create an effect and have worn platform soles, tights, maquillage, the codpiece, the kilt, loincloths, togas, tunics, g-strings and thongs, all to emphasise or disguise their manhood. Women may hide their knees or expose them, swathe their arms, cover their heads, wear low-cut or see-through dresses (or even bosom-revealing bodices as did the Cretans—ancient Crete had a real eye for the body!). Both sexes cover the eyes on occasion with masks and dark glasses, and adorn face and body with tattoos, piercings, powder and paint. It's all part of the art of using body language and body power, and the power is sexually based; either it is an affirmation of our sex to ourselves and others of our sex, or it is a ritual for attraction of opposites. And have you ever noticed how very fussy our sexual partners are about what we wear? 'You can't wear that! It makes you look too young, too old, too casual, too flamboyant, too sexy . . . '

Good grooming may not always secure you a job (though it may help) or a partner, but it will inevitably raise your self-esteem.

We never really see ourselves as others see us. Fleeting glances in mirrors and shop windows often come as a bit of a surprise. This is because we keep a self-image tucked away in some corner of the brain and, although it is *like* the real thing, there is an element of idealism in it. Taking a long appraising look in a good mirror at figure and features can be rewarding, as it is the only way to blend the image and come to terms with reality.

Sexual intercourse

In this modern era when we are better informed than ever before about the workings of our bodies, we want to get the most out of our sexuality. Most women would like to be good sexual partners; partly for their partner's sake, but also for their own. We know that if sexual health is possible to achieve, it helps enormously with our overall sense of well-being.

It might appear that the male should be attracted to the female as a bee to a flower and that everything in the garden is lovely. Obviously, men are not always susceptible to coercion. In fact modern society condones a variety of relationships. There are men who expect their partners to accept that they have relationships with other women; and women who expect the same. You may be justifiably upset and humiliated over your partner's intimate relationship with another woman, whether it includes sexual intercourse or not. Of course, women offend against men in this way too.

In the whole area of sex, sexuality and initiation of pregnancy there is a great deal of scope for exploitation between the sexual partners. Childbearing is often unfortunately dragged into these complicated manoeuvres. (For instance a pregnancy might be started to try to save a relationship.) Planning families nowadays is usually a joint venture. Nevertheless, a woman is still at risk of being impregnated against her will, whereas it is unlikely that a man could be persuaded to procreate if he didn't want to. He might accidentally procreate or he might be duped into that act by his female partner who assures him it is 'safe' when she knows it is not!

It is imperative that a woman understands her own anatomy, and not only because it will help her have a full and rewarding sexual life. In the female the sexual organs are entirely within the bony pelvis. The movement of the pelvis during intercourse is called pelvic rocking, or pelvic tilting. For a woman, this is a forward thrust of the pelvis, rounding the lumbar curve of her spine and tucking her buttocks under and forward. The movement is the same whether you are on your back, on your side, on your front, kneeling or in any other position for sexual intercourse. Women who have difficulty in performing pelvic rocking in aerobic classes or antenatal fitness classes, where it is often taught, are not necessarily sexually inhibited: they may simply not be well-co-ordinated. That is, they lack proprioception, the ability of the brain to translate ideas into actions. When they are taught to do this basic pelvic movement, it improves their sexual function.

The vagina is the entrance to a woman's sexual and reproductive organs. Sliding two fingers into the vagina (or one if it is tight) will make you familiar with its structure, its relationship to the urethra and the rectum, and the exploring fingers can also feel the muscles of the pelvic floor. (Tighten your muscles around the two fingers.) There is no need to wear a rubber glove. The vagina is not sterile. It is advisable, however, to wash your hands first and not to introduce bowel matter into the vagina. This exploratory manoeuvre can be done comfortably in the bath.

Positions for intercourse

When you are well practised, in good health and free from pain or discomfort, positions for intercourse can be chosen as the mood takes you. But if you are a learner, for a woman, lying on your back with your partner on top will probably be the easiest position for you both. If you still have trouble connecting, a small pillow under your buttocks will angle your vagina a little more advantageously.

On your hands and knees, with your partner behind you, is helpful if your back is aching. This is also convenient in pregnancy. If your partner has backache or some other disability, he can lie down with you on top, or sit in a chair with you astride. Either way, his body is splinted and supported.

Sometimes the only impediment to satisfactory sexual intercourse is too much intellectual content. C. S. Lewis paints an amusing word picture of a couple, with reference books laid out on bedside tables, trying desperately to achieve sexual harmony. Intercourse is a matter of feeling. Too much thinking can block the necessary sensory system and wreck the whole endeavour.

A partnership between a man and a woman at its best can be one of a mutual appreciation society, each partner developing confidence in the other. Sensitivity and understanding can help cure the distressing problem of impotence; while a man's patience and tenderness can make sexual intercourse a revelation for a woman.

Sexual satisfaction

It is well known that men achieve sexual satisfaction more easily than women, which can cause frustration for their partners and sometimes estrangement, so men may often need instruction. For most women, to be enjoyable, sexual intercourse has to take place in an atmosphere of safety and freedom from distraction. Because the 'parasympathetic' nervous system is involved, a climate of sensual relaxation is most conducive. The parasympathetic nervous system (which is the opposite condition to the 'fight-flight' reflex) is responsible for suffusing blood to the vaginal area and clitoris, without which orgasm cannot happen. Sexual intercourse is largely a muscular activity: not only are the ordinary muscles under the control of the will working, but also involuntary muscles in the upper vagina which give the cataclysmic contractions of orgasm. Physical well-being, some understanding of the mechanism and security in the relationship are all necessary for sexual satisfaction.

Men are not always aware of the anatomical vagaries of the human female. Female human beings have evolved a vagina that is angled forwards, as is the bladder tube (all other similar mammals have a 'straight' vagina). It is possible that adoption of the upright posture with its tilting effect on the pelvis led to the acute anatomical angle of the vagina leaving the uterus, and the urethra leaving the bladder. Hence human intercourse face to face is usually easier, though many other positions are possible as expertise develops. However, an inexperienced male may try to penetrate straight in instead of angling his penis backwards along the vagina. This means that he is aiming for the bladder rather than the cervix, which can be disconcerting for him and painful for his partner. Fortunately, men are becoming increasingly aware of the anatomy and sexual needs of women.

Sexual difficulties

Difficulties with sexual intercourse have many causes, both physical and psychological. It is beyond the scope of this book to deal with them all. However, a few words of advice must be included on the importance of the pelvic floor.

The pelvic floor   Once correct penetration has been achieved, for more enjoyable sex a little muscle called pubo-coccygeus should be explored. This muscle is like the letter U with two arms swinging from the pubic bone and the loop incorporated into the fibrous bands surrounding the vagina and anus and finally reaching the coccyx. If the loop is drawn forwards by contracting the whole pelvic floor muscle, it becomes shorter, narrowing the vagina and gripping the penis. The pubo-coccygeus can be imagined like someone's arms as they chin a bar. The strength of the 'chinning' can be estimated by the male partner who acts as a kind of human perineometer (a perineometer is a biofeedback machine for recording pelvic floor strength). In some cultures girls are taught this exercise before marriage, a practice which might improve their chances of avoiding a prolapse. Women often report with delight that both they and their partners enjoy sex more as the pelvic floor exercising results in more firmness in the vagina.

The tissues in the genital area are delicate and easily bruised. If you have been given rough treatment by your male partner and find yourself sore and swollen, don't hesitate to go to a doctor. Women should certainly not be expected to put up with traumatic sexual encounters, rape being the extreme case of this. A thoughtful partner allows a woman time for arousal, so that the vaginal mucus glands can lubricate the channel to a slippery state for easy entry of the penis. If you find you are too dry, use a cream such as KY® gel to enhance your natural lubrication.

Frigidity   Vaginismus is a condition, sometimes called frigidity, when the woman switches off and her vagina becomes narrowed by surrounding muscle spasm. This may happen through some subconscious fear or preconditioning, even where there is every wish to participate in intercourse. Physiotherapists can teach women to overcome vaginismus by examining the action of their pelvic floor muscles and by training the muscle to relax when relaxation is called for.

Other embarrassments   There are some functions of the human female that cause embarrassment. One of them is losing urine on the point of orgasm. This is usually due to weakness of the urinary sphincter. If you read chapter 5 you will find out how to strengthen the sphincter and cure this condition, which may certainly be off-putting.

There is no embargo on having intercourse when you have a period, but if it is a day of heavy bleeding you may not fancy the mess.

If there is any unpleasant discharge from the vagina you should see your doctor. It is very likely that some form of medication can clear up the problem quickly, and hopefully you can be relieved by having a simple diagnosis.

Relaxation and sex   Anxiety that you have very little sexual drive or libido may actually be compounding your problem. Learning to relax can do two things:

- stop you worrying and thus increase your sexual ardour
- relieve you from caring so much that your libido is low.

The female wish for sexual intercourse varies with time of life, cyclical changes and moods, and state of health. It also varies from person to person. Sometimes there isn't very much we can do about it. Aphrodisiacs were the magical answer, but so far the perfect one from a scientific point of view has not been found.

Orgasm   In our time sex is such a talked-about pursuit that we tend to expect ecstasy and are disappointed when we get less. We also expect orgasms. Orgasm is an involuntary muscular action high in the vagina brought on by stimulation of the extremely sensitive nerves of the clitoris (above the urethral opening) and the vaginal wall, particularly a special area of the vagina located on the inner surface of the pubic bone (called the Grafenburg spot or G-spot). Touching the G-spot gives a woman an exquisite sense of delight. Although it is possible to enjoy sex without having an orgasm, of course orgasm gives release and satisfaction.

Patients consult me from time to time on the subject of their pelvic floor muscles and how they can make sex more enjoyable, both for themselves and for their partners. The pelvic floor muscles are quite an important part of sexual function but people with little or no musculature can still enjoy sex. Conversely, a woman might develop an admirably strong pelvic floor, and still get no satisfaction from sex. One woman described the sex act as 'Push-push and then it's all over!'

Balance in the sexual act between couples is a delicate matter that can only be resolved as a joint enterprise. Sadly, there is often imbalance. And when the life of a partnership is being sapped by selfishness, quarrels and lack of trust, the sex act suffers too. Another source of unhappiness is when couples badly want a child and can't achieve conception. Sexual intercourse then almost becomes a chore. Investigation of both partners can be a tedious business, but the results are worth the effort. In any sexual partnership there needs to be mutual support, and this covers all aspects of daily living.

In managing sexuality the sexes should complement, not compete against each other. A woman's subtle feminine component is a power for good in a relationship, smoothing rough edges and promoting harmony.

Sexual safety

To be entirely safe in your sex life is probably an impossibility as there is an element of luck in avoiding all contagious ills, but engaging in unprotected sex with unknown partners must be seen as high-risk behaviour.

According to the National Survey of Sexual Attitudes and Lifestyles' ten-year survey on sexual behaviour patterns, people are having more sexual partners in their lifetime, the average age for first intercourse has dropped to 16, and homosexuality has increased. In this climate of sexual freedom many relationships begin haphazardly, without due thought to lasting and often detrimental consequences. Your sexuality is a very important part of you. Used responsibly, it can be a source of delight to you and your partner. Throughout the animal world, patterns of sexual behaviour are very complicated and varied and protective of the species. Humans have evolved in such a way that sexual protection has become more intellectual than instinctive.

Face-to-face copulation is also a human characteristic: it heightens stimulation, refining and prolonging the sexual interlude. Some anthropologists think it may have developed along with speech. Young people are at the peak of desire in their late teens and early twenties (males a little earlier than females) so that, quite apart from the danger of sexual diseases, society has invented a great many checks and balances to prevent us from breeding like rabbits. Tribal communities instituted the incest taboo; although this, like any other human law, was broken when it suited people. In ancient Egypt brothers married sisters because the ruling family wanted to retain sole power within close family confines.

Tribal leaders used initiation ceremonies like the corroboree to instil sexual mores into their people. As human beings, our culture guides us as to how to behave sexually and this tends to be confusing because societal values change. There has been a great change from the constricting taboos faced by our grandparents' generationto the free-wheeling attitudes of the present one—so much so that responsibility for sexual behaviour is now largely on teenagers themselves rather than on parents laying down the law. However, most parents are very ready to be confided in and anxious to help.

Sexually transmitted diseases (STDs) are those which can be passed from one person to another by the act of sexual intercourse. They are caused by viruses, bacteria and parasites, and are also known as sexually transmitted infections (STIs). They are probably as old as mankind and are also referred to as venereal diseases, after Venus, the goddess of love. STDs have always flourished where humans live in close proximity, as in city slums, army camps or ghettos. Moses envisaged this kind of trouble when his people were encamped in the Sinai desert. In the biblical book of *Leviticus* (which just means 'law'), sufferers from STD (possibly gonor-rhoea) were instructed to wash themselves and their clothes carefully and to abstain from sexual intercourse for a week.

Today STDs are on the increase all around the world, particularly among younger people. The World Health Organisation (WHO) recently estimated that, excluding HIV and hepatitis, 1.5 million people catch an STI every day of the year. In July 2001 the British government, alarmed at the increase in the figures, launched the first national strategy for sexual health and HIV services. In 2003, Dr Kevin Fenton, consultant epidemiologist at the HIV and STI divi-sion at the Health Protection Agency (HPA) communicable disease surveillance centre, reported 'sustained increases in new diagnoses of STIs and increasing attendance to genito-urinary medicine (GUM) clinics'. He drew the conclusion that 'high-risk sexual behaviour undoubtedly remains a significant contributing factor'.

It seems that in spite of warnings about HIV and other STIs, people are not following the advice to use condoms, especially when having sex with a new partner. They believe that if they are unfortunate enough to catch something it can be easily treated, when in reality many STIs are becoming resistant to treatment, and are often spread without the infected person knowing because there are no obvious symptoms.

Syphilis

It was widely believed that Columbus brought syphilis to Europe from the Caribbean. Europe did have an epidemic of syphilis soon after Columbus returned to Spain. But Tannahill, author of Sex in *History*, thinks it unlikely that Columbus's men were responsible and notes laconically that, if they were, 'his 50 crew members must have had a very strenuous time'. It is much more probable that the disease is centuries older and was common in the days of the Romans.

Italians called syphilis 'the French disease'; other nations, no doubt including the French, called it the Flemish, Dutch, Castilian, Portuguese, Persian, Turkish, German, Russian, and Polish disease, or simply the Pox.

Although syphilis had until recently been almost eradicated in developed countries, it was still prevalent in the third world. In parts of Africa 20 percent of pregnant women have syphilis. If it is diagnosed early and treated, the disease can be quickly cured but this does not always happen and then the unborn child is in danger of contracting the disease from its mother. A famous example from history is of King Henry VIII who is thought to have passed syphilis on through the wife who bore his only son. The boy died as a teenager soon after succeeding to the throne. Terminal syphilis was as worrying for other generations as AIDS is for us now. Syphilitic ulcers developed on the mouth, breasts, fingers, eyelids or sex organs. Mushroom-shaped growths erupted over the genital area and eventually all systems of the body were invaded: heart, arteries, bones, nerves and the brain, causing what was called 'general paralysis of the insane'. Syphilitics were ostracised and often thought to have leprosy.

Today syphilis is again on the increase in many parts of the world. Between 2001 and 2002 syphilis infections in Britain rose by a staggering 63 percent.

Gonorrhoea

Another very old STI is gonorrhoea or clap; in fact it is probably the oldest. The clinical signs were recorded by a Chinese emperor in 2337 BC, and it is mentioned on an Assyrian clay tablet. Gonorrhoea means 'flow of seed', named thus by the Roman physician Galen who thought that the whitish discharge exuding from the penis was seminal fluid, when in fact it was pus. An inflamed urethra makes urinating painful or difficult, or even impossible. The French name for gonorrhoea was *chaud pisse* (hot urine!). Sometimes gonorrhoea has no symptoms so that the infected person acts as a carrier.

Treatments for gonorrhoea in the past were quite horrific, often making the sufferer worse. For instance, Rhazes, a ninth century

Persian physician, pushed silver catheters up the urethras of patients with urinary retention, succeeding only in spreading the infection further, both in the patient and in the population. Medical expertise of the time recommended live insects, fleas and lice to eat out the noxious emissions! Tissue damage was caused by mercury, arsenic or acid preparations, and wine, brandy or rose-water syringed into the affected areas caused more havoc.

For most of the last century gonorrhoea, a bacterial infection, was very speedily cured by antibiotics. Today, rising rates of infection are not the only problem. Recent research published in the *Lancet* reported that the antibiotic resistance of gonorrhoea increased from 3 percent to almost 10 percent between 2001 and 2002.

Crabs

Crabs (*pediculosis pubis*) is another STI which has been with us for a long time, although it is less prevalent since the era of good hygiene. Crabs are pubic hair lice and are usually sexually transmitted although they can be picked up by close physical contact or by sharing sheets, blankets or towels. They cause quite severe itching but nowadays can be easily eradicated by using a special shampoo or lotion. In the days of old wayside inns with dirty blankets, crabs abounded and must have caused much misery. They can be easily seen and their white eggs (nits) can also be seen clinging to the shaft of a hair.

Chlamydia

A few years ago a different form of gonorrhoea, non-gonoccocal urethritis, which has probably been around for a long period of time, was identified. The culprit causing the infection is *Chlamydia trachomitis*, a bacterium also implicated in the eye disease trachoma. The most common sequel of chlamydia is inflammation of the fallopian tubes (salpingitis) or pelvic inflammatory disease (PID). Chlamydia is a very common STI and one of the most serious as it can cause infertility in women.

Chlamydia is a small inflammatory agent that attaches itself to the lining membrane of the cervix and moves up the genital tract. The infection may show no symptoms but still damage the uterine tubes, which leads, in some cases, to sterility or tubal pregnancy. Partners are nearly always infected and, if you are a carrier, your partner must also be treated, otherwise you can be reinfected. Symptoms are vaginal discharge (often smelly), painful urination with itching and burning, abdominal pain and abnormal bleeding.

Chlamydial infection can cause cancer of the cervix so that regular Pap smears are essential for anyone who has ever had chlamydia. These involve taking a few cells from the cervix and vagina and examining them to detect cancer at an early stage. If you have chlamydia and are pregnant, your newborn baby is in danger of contracting conjunctivitis or pneumonia through contact with vaginal secretions.

Genital herpes

Another disease that has reached epidemic proportions is genital herpes. It is caused by a virus, and viruses are not easily subdued by antibiotics. Viruses in general have two ways of operating. They work on either the DNA or the RNA factor in cells. These are strands of material which form a pattern for cell life in all living creatures. The problem with drugs used to kill a virus is that they might kill the life-stuff DNA as well. Vaccines work better. They alert the immune system to develop antibodies to the particular virus or bacteria. This is a very effective way of ambushing the invader in its own stronghold.

Herpes viruses are a gang of five: two types of herpes (types 1 and 2), the chicken pox and shingles virus, cytomegalus virus and mononucleosis or 'kissing disease'. Herpes viruses are 'clever' enough to hide when attacked. The cytomegalus virus, a type of herpes which can kill newborn babies, is so successful at taking evasive action that no one quite knows where it hides. Many herpes viruses hide in nerve cells or ganglia (collections of nerve cells).

Genital herpes (type 2) is an on and off type of disease. When it is 'off', the virus has migrated to the nerve cells at the bottom of the spinal cord. When it is 'on' it is down in the genital area causing a rash, blisters on the penis or in the vagina, fever and swollen glands. A first attack of the herpes virus takes only four days to incubate, which means that the sexual contact can usually be traced. In the past, genital herpes was probably confused with syphilis, gonorrhea, leprosy and smallpox. Nowadays a pathology test can be done on the fluid taken from the herpes blisters to confirm the diagnosis. In women, genital herpes is associated with the risk of developing cancer of the cervix. Cervical cancer can be treated so long as it is detected early.

Genital herpes recurs with depressing regularity. Personal hygiene helps to confine the sores to one place. If you can strengthen the body's natural defence mechanisms by good diet and a judicious mixture of rest and exercise, the recurrences may grow less frequent. Saliva is infectious, so avoid using it as a lubricating agent in intercourse. Maintain good hygiene, particularly if you are touching children's eyes, mouths or genital area.

Cold sores are another herpes virus and a source of infection particularly if any form of oral sex is indulged in. They are very common and it is thought that some immunity to genital herpes can be acquired in this way. Both forms of herpes can be transferred between the mouth and the genital area, even on the fingers. Herpes viruses, once contracted, are in the system for life. They can be treated but as yet there is no complete cure. A drug called Acyclovir® is helpful in relieving symptoms of both primary and secondary herpes.

HPV

The human papilloma virus (HPV) can cause genital warts in both women and men but there are types which are asymptomatic. It is one of the most common sexually transmitted infections. (Another type of the virus causes the common warts that occur elsewhere on the body.) The warts may be visible, appearing as flat smooth small bumps, or larger 'cauliflower-like' lumps. They may itch, but are usually painless. The virus may be inactive for weeks, months or possibly even years after infection. The warts may be removed by freezing or laser treatment, or a liquid or cream such as Podophyllo-toxin® may be prescribed. Unfortunately, their removal does not necessarily prevent the spread of the virus, nor does it guarantee against the recurrence of the warts. Sexual intercourse should be avoided after treatment until the area has healed. HPV is more easily passed on to another person when there are visible warts present. For this reason, whilst warts are present and for at least three months after treatment, it is advisable to use condoms to avoid re-infection.

It is important to note that with the type of HPV that is asymptomatic, which means that those infected do not have any symptoms, many people are unaware that they have HPV. In women who are infected, this type of HPV can lead to abnormal changes in the cells of the cervix (the neck of the womb or uterus). This cervical intra-epithelial neoplasia (CIN) is not cancer but in some women it can develop into cancer if left untreated. It is therefore important that women have regular cervical smear tests. Treatment for CIN is very effective, and the risk of CIN recurring after treatment is low.

Hepatitis A

Hepatitis A (HAV) is a virus that resides in faeces and can be transferred by a contaminated hand passing the infection to the mouth. The disease can be picked up from infected food or water but also from oral-anal sex. Any form of hepatitis can do damage to liver cells, which could lead to cirrhosis or cancer. Some people exhibit no symptoms but can still pass on the virus. An immune serum made from hepatitis A antibodies (gamma globulin) is helpful in lessening the severity of the disease. If you know you have been in contact with hepatitis A, go straight to a doctor. Don't wait for symptoms to appear.

Hepatitis A is a common infection in many parts of the world so it is very important to be immunised if you are travelling to a country with a high rate of hepatitis A.

Hepatitis B

Hepatitis B (HBV) can cause chronic liver disease and cancer. It is very common worldwide and highly infectious. It can be passed on by having unprotected sex, by sharing contaminated needles or equipment used for tattooing, acupuncture or body-piercing. It can also be passed from an infected mother to her baby, or through a blood transfusion in a country where the blood has not been tested for the virus. Symptoms can be flu-like and also include tiredness, diarrhoea, nausea and vomiting, loss of appetite and weight loss. The skin may become jaundiced and itchy. Some people can exhibit none of these symptoms and still pass on the virus.

Diagnosis is by a simple blood test. If you are infected then you should use a condom during sex and your partner should be immunised. You should also limit the amount of alcohol you drink, and avoid sharing toothbrushes or shaving equipment.

People who are considered as being at high risk of acquiring the virus, such as midwives, can receive immunisation from sexual health (GUM) clinics or their GPs. Babies of HBV-positive mothers should be immunised at birth to prevent them becoming infected.

HIV/AIDS

HIV stands for human immunodeficiency virus. This virus can damage the body's immune system so that it cannot fight certain infections. A person infected with HIV does not have AIDS (acquired immune deficiency syndrome) until the virus seriously damages their immune system, making them succumb to a range of infections, some of which can lead to death.

In a healthy human being, special cells (T cells) roam about the body like a police force, killing off any 'wild' cells that are not bred true to type. HIV affects this immune system, rendering it powerless to deal with infective organisms. It weakens the body's defences so that diseases such as pneumonia and other infections can gain a foothold. These are called opportunistic diseases for obvious reasons.

AIDS was first recognised in 1981. Since then about 40 million people worldwide have been infected with HIV and about a third of them have died. There is still no cure for HIV although developments in treatment since the mid-nineties have improved the life expectancy for many of those diagnosed with HIV in the UK.

The HIV virus is present in the body fluids of an infected person and is transmitted by having unprotected intercourse with that person, or by using needles infected with the virus, or by receiving infected blood or donated organs as part of medical treatment. It can also be passed from a woman with HIV to her baby before or during birth, and also by breastfeeding.

There has been a good deal of overreaction to HIV/AIDS. Toilet seats are not a source of infection unless, as one writer put it, two people occupy the seat together! Nor does the virus appear to be spread by insects such as mosquitoes. Nowadays all blood in UK blood banks is tested for the virus to eliminate the risk of receiving contaminated blood in a transfusion.

HIV infection is diagnosed by taking a blood sample which is then checked for antibodies to the virus. Today all pregnant women in Britain are offered testing as part of their antenatal care. If the result is positive, then steps can be taken to reduce the likelihood of the infection being passed to their baby, through the use of anti-retroviral drugs, giving birth by caesarean section and avoiding breastfeeding.

Practising safe sex by using condoms is a preventative measure against HIV. But as the condom does not give total protection in every single case (it might have a minute hole in it and viruses are 500 times smaller than sperms), it is very important to know and trust your sexual partner.

Many vaginal discharges are caused by relatively minor infections, which, although contagious, are not necessarily contracted through sexual intercourse. These common infections cause vaginal inflammation.

Trichomoniasis

The infection trichomoniasis (sometimes called TV) is caused by a flagellate parasite (which means that it has a tail which it thrashes about to propel itself forward like a sperm). It is very sensitive to the amount of acidity in vaginal secretions and can cause no symptoms while living in the vagina until some change such as menstruation, sexual intercourse or an illness occurs. When the vaginal acidity increases, the parasites multiply and can invade other territory such as the urethra. There is copious vaginal discharge, which is slightly greenish and frothy, and there is itching at the entrance to the vagina. Sexual intercourse can transfer trichomoniasis to the sexual partner, hence it is usual for both partners to be treated for this disease.

Candida albicans (thrush)

Most people have heard of the fungus type organism, *Candida albicans*, or thrush, which grows in clusters in the vagina and develops long threads of discharge like cooked cheese. The organism feeds on glycogen and is common in pregnant women when the vagina contains a lot of glycogen, and in diabetics when urine can be high in glycogen. Thrush causes itching in women and irritation under the foreskin of their male partners. It can cause oral thrush in newborn babies. Normally *Candida* lives in mouths, intestines and vaginas without doing much harm, but it can run riot in the system. It often responds to treatment such as medication or control of diet.

Non-specific vaginitis

This is a female complaint although men can carry the bacteria but remain symptomless. There is itchiness and a greyish discharge with a fishy odour and the vaginal wall looks as if it is covered with flour paste. It can be cured by drug treatment.

Itchiness and redness at the entrance to the vagina do not necessarily mean you have an STD. This kind of itchiness, usually worse at night, may be psychological, even due to sexual frustration. Don't scratch. It is to be hoped that it will go away! An application of vitamin E cream or Savlon® might ease the itch. It is always wise to seek medical help.

There are two conditions, cystitis and mononucleosis, which you could contract without knowing where they came from. They are not STDs but they may be aggravated by sexual contact, particularly in the case of cystitis.

Cystitis

Cystitis can be caused by bacteria (*Escherichia coli*) that grow harmlessly in the gut. If these bacteria enter the urethra and bladder, they can set up inflammation. You can help prevent this by wiping yourself from front to back after urinating or defaecating, not from back to front. Pregnant women are more prone to cystitis than the ordinary population, as are diabetics and the elderly.

Although cystitis is not a sexually transmitted disease, it can be triggered by sexual contact. Sexual intercourse can cause bruising of the vagina and damage to the urethra and this can make infection of the bladder system more likely. Infection may even travel to the kidneys which causes acute pain. Bladder infection *per se* is uncomfortable and occasionally brings fever or nausea but mostly there is just a feeling of urgency, or wanting to go to the toilet often. The reason for this is that the mucous membrane of the bladder is swollen and the little nerve endings which remind you that your bladder is filling or full tend to be stimulated all the time. Sometimes there is blood in the urine, a rather alarming symptom but usually only temporary.

Cystitis can be diagnosed from a urine specimen and treated with antibiotics. You can help yourself a great deal by drinking copious amounts of water. Some women also find that cranberry juice or barley water can help clear up an attack, and there are alternative or complementary treatments like aromatherapy that may be worth investigating.

Mononucleosis (glandular fever)

Mononucleosis is caused by a virus belonging to the herpes family. It lives in the throat and its symptoms are fever, swollen glands and transient weakness. Mononucleosis is also known as glandular fever or kissing disease. It was not recognised until the 1880s and was often confused with leukaemia. Mononucleosis can be transmitted in blood, but it is mainly spread through saliva. The virus can't survive unless it has a warm, moist environment. Coughed out virus particles die. The disease is not too serious as it usually disappears in 2–6 weeks but it can recur and it is debilitating. It is particularly common among teenagers and it may ruin a student's chances of success in exams.

Pain after pelvic inflammatory disease (PID)

Infections involving the reproductive organs may cause adhesions, a sort of gumming up of one piece of tissue to another. When movement stretches these adhesions, they hurt. Because the urinary system and the bowel are so close to the reproductive organs, they can also be affected.

Physiotherapy can help women in the post-inflammatory phase of this condition. By the use of interferential therapy (IFT) the adhesions can often be broken down or dissolved. Young women who have had their infection treated by the doctor before it can do too much damage usually respond very quickly to the added help that the physiotherapist can give, because their tissues are young.

How to Avoid STI and Genital Problems

There are four golden rules to observe. They are:

- Know that you and your partner are not infected with any STI or use the protection of a condom. (Condoms are available at chemists, supermarkets and machines in public toilets.)
- Don't ever share needles. Needle sharing is very dangerous.
- If you work in the medical arena, avoid needle prick injuries.
- Understand that you are not at risk in ordinary social contact with people who have HIV/AIDS.

In addition:

- Maintain good hygiene. Wash the genital area at least once a day and more often if necessary. (Some women need to wash after a bowel action to prevent cystitis.)
- Don't wear nylon underwear. It encourages moisture in the genital region which makes it an ideal warm wet climate for organisms such as thrush. Wear cotton briefs and choose tights with a cotton gusset.
- If you think you have an STI, go to a doctor. In the UK, you can find details of your nearest NHS sexual health clinic in the phone book under genito-urinary medicine (GUM), sexually transmitted diseases (STD) or venereal diseases (VD). Or phone your local hospital and ask for the GUM clinic. Your partner will need to be identified and treated if an STI is confirmed.
- Peer pressure makes many girls have sexual intercourse before they want to. Think carefully before you say yes. It is *your* body and *you* have the right to reserve it.
- Try to avoid genital contact until you are in a stable relationship and you feel you can trust your sexual partner.
- Avoid any form of oral-genital sex when you have an infection. Mouth germs can be transferred to the vagina or urethra and vice versa.
- If you have any itching, burning or soreness in the vaginal opening or in the urethral opening, or any unusual feature such as a rash or blisters in the genital region, visit your doctor and have the problem professionally diagnosed.

There have been some studies which show that using intrauterine devices (IUDs) as a contraceptive will increase the chance of PID because the pull-string on the IUD can be the vehicle for the infective organism to gain access to the uterus and tubes. Menstrual blood actually feeds the bacteria. But good hygiene and safe sexual practices go a long way towards prevention.

A PID infection involving the fallopian tubes is called salpingitis. Pus is produced in the tubes and may spill over into the pelvic cavity.

Pelvic pain can be acute or just a chronic ache. It is often made worse by intercourse or any pelvic movement. Pain in the pelvis may be symptomatic of tubal (ectopic) pregnancy or appendicitis, so it is important to have it checked out by a doctor and accurately diagnosed.

Physiotherapy is an after-care treatment. Sometimes the after-effects of PID last for months, exhibiting persistent pain and abdominal tenderness. The physiotherapist's electrical machines give a range of anti-pain treatments. Electrical currents have a special ionic effect which promotes healing at a cellular level.

Infertility

If a woman's reproductive system is gummed up by repeated infections, her chances of delivering a fertilised egg into the womb may be remote. About 70 percent of women with blocked fallopian tubes have at one time had a chlamydia infection, even though many may have been unaware of it. In some cases surgical measures to remove the blockage may be successful but in others in-vitro fertilisation (IVF) may be suggested. IVF involves a cycle of drugs to stimulate the ovaries to produce eggs. The eggs are retrieved, usually by ultrasound guidance, and conception takes place in the laboratory. About 72–80 hours later the embryos are replaced into the uterus, through the cervix. The risk of multiple pregnancies depends upon the number of embryos replaced.

Ovulation problems are another reason for female infertility. Often drug treatment helps the ovaries to start ovulating again, although there can be an increased risk of multiple births. Polycystic ovary syndrome (PCOS) is the most common hormonal disturbance among premenopausal women and will affect one in five women during their lives. It is the leading cause of infertility due to lack of ovulation. Endometriosis, where parts of the endometrium (the tissue lining the uterus) are found on the ovaries and elsewhere inside the pelvis, is another condition that can cause infertility, depending on its severity. In severe cases surgery may be required to remove all the endometriosis by either cutting it out or burning it away with diathermy or laser, leaving as much normal ovary tissue as possible.

Infertility is of course not just a female problem. In about 30 percent of infertile couples, the problem is a male one to do with the production of sperm, in about 30 percent it is a female one, and for the rest it is a joint problem or the cause is unknown.

Infertility can be extremely frustrating and stressful, and the stress may in itself be a factor. In some 60 percent of cases where couples have experienced unexplained infertility for up to 3 years, the woman will fall pregnant in the next 3 years without any treatment. The subconscious mind is the unknown element in the equation. It keeps all medical researchers guessing how much can be attributed to science and how much to the elusive human psyche.

Birth control

Since the last century women have been freed from obligatory pregnancy. They can choose when to be pregnant and how many children to have. These choices allow for vigour in pregnancy and a greater chance of contentedness.

In the past women literally wore themselves out gynaecologically because contraception was not fully understood. Attempts were made to prevent conception, even by Stone Age communities. Primitive woman probably had an average of five children with a three or four year gap between each. This gave her a rest from menstruation for the best part of twenty years as she breast-fed for an extended period using nature's own contraceptive.

Birth rates fluctuate for political, economic and social reasons. During the 1930s the birth rate in the United States fell, in spite of the fact that there was still no reliable method of birth control. After the Second World War it rose, only to fall again in the 1960s when zero population growth (ZPG) was the credo.

The modern practice of men taking some of the responsibility for family limitation is now quite common in over-populated countries.

Surgical sterilisation of men is a relatively simple and painless process. Vasectomy involves cutting and tying the two *vas deferens* or spermatic ducts so that sperm cannot travel from the testes to the penis. Vasectomy does not affect a man's sexual performance. He continues to have normal erections and ejaculations, but he cannot impregnate a woman unless his ducts are joined again, and success in this reversal is not guaranteed.

In the past men used withdrawal as a means of preventing pregnancy. Withdrawal is considered to be about 50 percent effective. But modern women would not consider that good enough. The condom has a better record.

Abstaining

Doctors quite often say that if they ask a young woman if she enjoyed her first experience of intercourse, she says no. (Of course she will not tell her boyfriend that!) This is exactly what you would expect to find for three reasons: she is somewhat embarrassed; the man may have been a virtual stranger; she expected too much (advertising has built up sex to such a pitch that women expect an explosion of delight); or it hurt. If a woman is asked after she has formed a stable and satisfying relationship the answer would in many cases be yes.

So do female teenagers really want to go all the *way*? Girls give in to male coaxing for a variety of reasons, sometimes alcohol can have something to do with it, and they may even take the initiative themselves in our modern sexually liberated society. Young men, teenage and older, are unsure of themselves and sexual prowess is sometimes used to prove themselves to themselves and to their mates. But if a worthwhile relationship is developing the woman in question becomes more important than the mates.

There is a tendency to think that if you don't use your bodily attributes you may lose the ability. This is not true for sex. Your sexual ability will not wither on the vine. Sex is a shy customer. To get the most out of it, it needs to be wooed, slowly bringing it to full bloom. The old courtship period which began with walking out, talking, then touching more intimately had much to be said for it. It titillated the senses and made intercourse a prize at the end of a long and delightful apprenticeship.

To our cost we have taken the romance out of sex. We have made it a prosaic everyday affair. By reserving her favours a woman once had mastery and mystery. Some psychologists who deal with sexual problems where the male partner is impotent or the female partner frigid, have a routine which cures the affliction by a process which can only be called *tantalisation*. In the first week only light touching between the partners is permitted. Intercourse is forbidden. In the second week there is deeper touching, genital touching, until finally after a long prohibition period they are 'allowed' to have true sexual intercourse. It usually works! The human is a very contrary animal.

The first time

One myth (sometimes used as a confidence trick) is that a girl will not get pregnant if it is the *first* time she has had intercourse. This error probably stems from putting too much reliance on the hymen. If this membrane across the opening of the vagina, which can be torn or broken during the first sexual encounter, is even a little bit open, as it often is at puberty, sperms can make their way into the uterus. Remember sperms can swim! They don't like our cold, hostile world but prefer the dark, warm moistness of the uterus and teenagers need to protect themselves rather than leaving it to fate or good luck.

It is well known that many teenagers have sex without a condom. This could be because it feels nicer not to have an unnatural impediment between two people who want to be as close as possible; because sexual encounters often 'happen' without any planning; or because they believe some of the folklore circulated about sex that you can 'get away with it' in certain circumstances. Some of this folklore includes the following beliefs:

- If the man withdraws his penis before ejaculation no pregnancy will occur. FALSE and very risky. He can spill semen inadvertently into the entrance to the vagina.
- Having intercourse just as menstruation is drying up is safe. FALSE. Some women ovulate early, and sperms can live for a few days.
- Douching after intercourse protects you. FALSE. Sperm have been swimming upwards since ejaculation. Douching is much too slow to catch these freestyle experts!

- Urinating after intercourse is protective. FALSE. Urination in the female is via a separate channel. It can't wash sperms out.

Modern planning against pregnancy is assisted by a wide choice of contraceptive methods including the condom, the pill, the diaphragm and the intra-uterine device (IUD). Of these, the condom offers the best protection against STDs.

The condom

How safe are condoms as a contraceptive? About 98 percent safe if they are used properly, and they will protect you to a large extent from STDs as well. The male condom must be unrolled over the erect penis and the vagina must be lubricated before the penis is inserted (either by your own secretions or by a lubricant such as KY® gel). A small space must be left at the end of the condom for the semen, otherwise it will squeeze out backwards past the penis. During withdrawal, the condom must be held on by the man so that it doesn't spill its contents. No semen must be allowed to come in contact with the vagina.

Female condoms are made from thin, soft, lubricated plastic which lines the vagina when in place. The closed end of the condom is inserted high into the vagina. The open, outer ring lies just outside the vagina. To remove the condom after sex, the outer ring is twisted to keep the sperm inside and the condom is pulled out.

The pill

The contraceptive pill is probably the safest method known to prevent pregnancy—it has only a 0.25 percent failure rate. A few women experience side-effects which include depression, weight gain, loss of libido and a tendency towards thrombosis, but there are many types of pill (e.g., the progestogen-only pill (POP) or the combined pill which contains two hormones, oestrogen and progestogen) and one can be selected to suit the individual.

Most doctors will prescribe a contraceptive pill for women whether they are in a stable relationship or not. There are, however, some conditions which may make taking the pill unwise. These include liver disease, malignancies in the breast or genital organs, diabetes or heart disease.

One of the great advantages of the pill is that it does nothing to take the pleasure out of sex and, if used according to instructions, is more than 99 percent safe against pregnancy (but not against STDs).

The morning-after pill or PCP

The morning-after pill is the most common type of emergency contraception, and is particularly valuable in cases of rape. Since 2001 it has been available in Britain over-the-counter in pharmacies to women of 16 years and over. It can also be provided free on NHS prescription or from a local Family Planning or GUM clinic. Its use is not confined to the morning after but up to 72 hours after unprotected sex; for this reason it is now often referred to as the postcoital pill (PCP). If taken within 24 hours it prevents about 95 percent of pregnancies from developing; its effectiveness thereafter decreases to an estimated 58 percent if taken within 48–72 hours, so it is important to take the first dose as soon as possible.

The older type of morning-after pill, which is no longer available, contained large doses of oestrogen and progestogen which led to side effects such as nausea, headache, diarrhoea and dizzines. The new pill contains only progestogen with very few side effects. It works by either stopping an egg from being released or stopping a fertilised egg from implanting itself in the womb.

The contraceptive implant

The contraceptive implant is a small, flexible tube about the size of a hairgrip. It is inserted under the skin in the upper arm by a trained doctor or nurse and slowly releases the hormone progestogen. It is over 99 percent effective and works for 3 years.

Contraceptive injections

Contraceptive injections contain progestogen and are 99 percent effective. They are injected into a muscle and the hormone is released very slowly into the body, giving protection for two or three months at a time, depending on the type of injection.

Foams, creams, impregnated sponges

These spermicidal substances are meant to kill sperms but they may let some through the net. It is better to use a spermicidal agent with a condom or a diaphragm so that you have double protection.

The diaphragm

A diaphragm is a kind of cap which fits over the cervix and prevents sperm from entering the uterus. It is really more suited to women who have a widened vagina, as it has to be inserted by the woman (under the doctor's direction at first), and it must fit. Women who have had babies can use these devices very well, but insertion may be difficult for teenagers whose vaginas are likely to be narrow.

The intra-uterine device (IUD)

An intra-uterine device prevents the ovum from lodging onto the uterine wall. It is made of plastic and copper and is inserted into the uterus by a doctor or nurse. The IUD is 98 to over 99 percent effective and will usually last from three to ten years depending on the type. It is not, however, suitable for women who are at risk of getting an STI.

The intra-uterine system (IUS)

Like the IUD, this is a small T-shaped device that is inserted into the uterus by a doctor or nurse. The IUS is plastic and contains the hormone progestogen. It is 99 percent effective and gives protection for five years.

The 'safe period' or natural family planning (NFP)

There are several ways to work out what is the safest time in the month to have intercourse. Teenagers whose periods are often irregular may have difficulty determining the safe time. The aim is to avoid having intercourse at the time of ovulation, a few days before, and a few days after. Ovulation can be detected by observing the changes in the vaginal mucus. Mucus is wetter and more slippery if you are ovulating. Alternatively you can take your temperature first thing in the morning before getting up. It goes up a little at ovulation and stays slightly elevated until the next period. (If you are pregnant it doesn't go down.) Or you can examine the cervix. It usually feels like the tip of your nose, but if ovulation is occurring it feels softer. None of these methods are very easy, and all are a bit of a nuisance.

Commercially available kits make the job easier and have been found to be 94 percent effective in European trials. The Persona® system is available from leading chemists and consists of a small hand-held computerised monitor and disposable urine test sticks. The monitor uses built-in date from thousands of women plus chemical information you give it by inserting our own urine test sticks eight days a month. The test sticks collect hormones from your urine and converts them into a form which can be read by the monitor. The monitor reads, stores and uses the information to tell you which days you are fertile and most likely to fall pregnant . You can then avoid having intercourse during this time. The system is not suitable for women with irregular periods or who are breast-feeding or going through the menopause. (This system can obviously be useful when you are actually trying to fall pregnant as it enables you to pinpoint when you are most likely to conceive!)

The 'safe period' method is not as reliable as some of the other contraceptive methods. It is fine for stable relationships where pregnancy would not be a calamity, but full of hazards for casual or transient friendships.

Conception

Frequency of intercourse heightens the chance of conception and the most fertile period of a woman's life is when she is in her mid-20s. If you want to become pregnant at a certain time or you are having difficulty becoming pregnant, you can increase your chances by observing your vaginal mucus. As we discussed in the section on the 'safe period' (page 105), cervical mucus makes the longest 'thread' just before ovulation. It is thin, wet and transparent and the cervix is soft and a little open. Another way of increasing your chances of pregnancy is to record your basal body temperature each day before getting out of bed. A woman's temperature rises slightly at ovulation, and fertilisation is more likely just before this time. If you have conceived, the temperature stays at the higher level. You can of course also use a commericial kit such as the one described in the previous section to determine the days on which you are most likely to conceive.

After contraception

Contraception is susceptible to human failure. Even the pill, which is the safest method, can fail. You can forget to take it. Natural 'rhythm' methods are up to 30 percent unsafe due to all kinds of human error.

Once conception has occurred a woman is faced with three options: coming to terms with the pregnancy, abortion or adoption. To abort a fetus, however young, is to take life and there are many people who condemn such an action, but it may be the right decision medically or psychologically for you.

Abortion

In criminal situations, such as incest or rape, a woman is very vulnerable. A pregnancy resulting from either cause is a good reason for having an abortion and the law recognises this. Women can protect themselves by having their antennae out for being propositioned. Avoid lonely places, look business-like as you walk along the street, and be wary of suspicious behaviour. And if you are caught—scream, fight or run. If you have been sexually attacked and are worried that you might be pregnant, then the morning-after pill or PCP (see page 104) is effective in stopping a pregnancy if taken within 72 hours, the sooner the better.

A fetus is considered viable by the World Health Organisation if it is 22 weeks old or 500 grams in weight. This does not mean it will live if it is born then as the life of such a tiny baby is very uncertain. If an abortion has to be done at all, the earlier it is done the better. There is a technique called menstrual regulation or aspiration which is carried out in the fourth to sixth week following the last period before tests for pregnancy are reliable. It is a simple procedure which requires only local anaesthetic, but a disadvantage is that some patients will have it unnecessarily as they will not be pregnant. Prostaglandins and other substances can be used to initiate contractions of the uterus when more force than just suction is needed to dislodge the implanted ovum from the uterus. Side-effects such as vomiting, abdominal cramps, shivering and bleeding can occur so that the procedure must be performed by registered medical practitioners who can prevent distress where possible or treat it if it occurs.

Therapeutic abortion requires that the abortion is medically necessary as the woman's life or psyche is threatened (as in a case of rape) or when the child is likely to be grossly abnormal. Laws vary in their attitude towards abortion; countries may be liberal or the reverse in what they will allow. Legally in England, Wales and Scotland, a woman can have an abortion up to the twenty-fourth week of her pregnancy, with the agreement of two doctors, but it is best if the abortion happens within the first 14 weeks.

Septic abortion means that the uterus has become infected, usually from an abortion of the 'backyard' variety. Endotoxic shock can follow uterine infection and can lead to death.

Early abortion may be a way out for some, but if it is left until after movements are felt, the young potential mother may have developed quite a strong unconscious attachment to the child. It has been known for some teenagers to exhibit deep depression at the end of nine months. And a possible further result of the 'deprivation' is another pregnancy in quick succession.

Adoption

Some young women become pregnant unwittingly. If you learn late in the pregnancy that you are to have a child you may be totally unready for it. I once had to explain about labour and birth to a teenager who was seven months pregnant. She thought the baby's movements (very strong by then!) were indigestion. This is not as rare as one might think. Some women know they are pregnant but procrastinate until it is too late for an abortion.

Women can still opt out of bringing up a child and there is no need to have feelings of guilt about doing so. One of my clients at antenatal classes was going to have her baby adopted because she was in the midst of a glowing career in the army. She had thought it all through and was at peace with her decision. When she had given birth, she was encouraged by hospital staff to hold and breast-feed her baby. This strong-minded young woman did not waver from her initial decision but it didn't make things easy for her!

Many young women on their own these days have been to some extent conditioned into keeping their babies. The situation forty or so years ago was very different. Suitable childless couples could adopt a much wanted child with relative ease. The climate of opinion has changed, partly because it is now considered acceptable to have a baby out of wedlock and partly because it is believed that the natural mother is the best one to bring up the child. Not every young girl is suited to bringing up a child, even among older teenagers. Psychologists have noted that after a year, as the child becomes more and more demanding, the main responsibility is often handed over to mother or grandmother. To expect a girl to be an adequate mother at an immature age is asking her to be utterly unselfish. A teenage mother may have to give up a chance of a good job, a normal social life or further education. Her dreams and plans may have to wait. She is at the beck and call of another demanding immature human being. Sometimes this leads to anger and bitterness and both young mother and child suffer.

To give a child up for adoption is always a wrench. Relatives and advisers can only be supportive. The decision can really only be made by the mother unless there are medical grounds preventing her from keeping her baby. Maternal feelings do sometimes develop at a very early age and many teenagers make a success of bringing up a family. After all, in the past it was not uncommon to be married at 16 and to have two or three children by the age of 20. However, it is a different matter if you are a single mother, particularly if there is no extended family willing to share the responsibility. The married teenager or girl in a stable unmarried relationship has a better chance. Unfortunately, life is inclined to be a bit unstable and what looked like a good set-up at the beginning of pregnancy may look different or even fail as the pregnancy advances.

The medical facts are that the pregnant female who is under 20 has a greater risk of developing high blood pressure and toxaemia of pregnancy and a greater likelihood of having a small or premature baby. Her labour will probably not be more difficult because she is young. It has been found that most women are physically mature enough to bear children (vaginally) from the menarche (though they have to be ovulating). Pelvic dimensions keep pace with 'biologic' age and teenagers run no greater risk of obstructed labour than their older sisters. Nevertheless it has been suggested that some teenagers have disproportionately long labours. This could be because nervous anticipation inhibits the hormonal climate in which the uterus works best; or in some cases the labour is long because the obstetrician is trying to avoid the uterine scar involved in a caesarean section in one so young. Naturally, teenagers have their fair share of feto-pelvic disproportion—a baby too big for the particular pelvis or whose head is awkwardly positioned within the pelvis.

Determining sex

An ultrasound scan can determine the sex of a fetus and women will usually be asked at the time whether they wish to know the sex of their baby or not. The fact that the sex of the baby can be identified in this way has led to some fetuses being aborted purely because they were the wrong (usually female) sex. Some countries, such as China and India, which have a tradition of female infanticide have acted to prohibit antenatal sex-determination and the selective termination that can follow, except for sound medical reasons.

IVF techniques have now become so sophisticated that scientists can separate out sperm that will produce girls from those that will produce boys, giving parents the opportunity to increase the chances of having a child of a particular sex. Medically assisted sex selection for non-medical reasons is currently banned in the UK, but there are, of course, occasions when it is especially important to know the sex, for example where there is a risk of a severe genetic disorder being passed on to one sex, as in a male child inheriting haemophilia or muscular dystrophy.

There are natural ways of increasing the likelihood of conceiving a particular sex. For a girl, if a couple has intercourse timed to stop two days before ovulation, the sperm with the X chromosomes (the female determinant) will still be alive when the egg comes down, having outlived its Y comrades. For a boy, sex just after ovulation gives a chance for the fast-swimming Y-chromosome sperm (the male determinant) to beat the Xs to the ovum.

Research has suggested that sperm can transmit harmful substances which can affect the development of the baby. If the man drinks or smokes to excess or takes drugs at the time of conception, the baby might suffer as a result. So it is not only mother who has to give up her vices for pregnancy; potential fathers should also give them up in anticipation of paternity!

4

PREGNANCY AND BIRTH

Fitness for pregnancy

Fitness in youth is considered the norm; fitness in pregnancy can be jeopardised by laziness or physical disability. Rest is very important in pregnancy but there are few prohibitions on exercise these days and lazing about is not recommended unless the doctor has specifically ordered total rest. This only happens when there are problems such as high blood pressure, a placenta that is not nourishing the baby adequately, or an insecure pregnancy where it is feared that the baby may be born prematurely.

Physiotherapy fitness classes cater for the vast majority of women who are pregnant and who have no physical disabilities. You can do exercises with all parts of the body, often in a relaxing way to music, while the physiotherapist-instructor monitors the effect of gentle aerobics on your pulse rate, makes sure your stomach muscles are not overstrained and that the positions used do not interfere with the baby's blood supply.

Modification of exercise may be necessary if there is a legacy from your pre-pregnancy life, something you may have had since childhood like asthma or a back problem, which can be made better or worse by pregnancy. Do bring them to the attention of the physiotherapist instructing the class because exercises may need to be deleted or extra ones added.

Considering that pregnancy puts strains on both the skeletal system and the soft tissues, not only by additional weight but by some change in the composition of tissues, it is quite surprising that a large proportion of pregnant women look blooming and feel better than ever. If you are in this group your possibilities for maintaining your fitness are high. Physiotherapists often find that pregnant women can continue with fitness classes right up to their due date. Even with their additional weight, they can do low impact fast movement, and co-ordination and balance exercises are particularly valuable as the baby increases in size. Breathing exercises can be incorporated into movements of arms or legs and rhythms developed which might be useful in labour.

If you have a medical problem your doctor may restrict what you can do. You may even be asked to rest in hospital. But if you can't come to the physiotherapist, the physiotherapist can come to you. Often it is not clear until very late in the pregnancy whether a cae-sarean section will be necessary, so that when a medical problem confines you to bed it is advisable to prepare for both a vaginal and a caesarean birth. A physiotherapist can instruct you on relaxation and breathing techniques, taking into account your specific needs.

A few years ago it was discovered that lying flat on the back for any length of time could restrict the amount of blood that reaches the fetus. The weight of the uterus in this position slows the blood flow back to the woman's heart by putting pressure on a big vein which drains blood from the lower part of the body. Although there is no absolute prohibition on lying on your back—you might wake up in that position—it is not advisable to stay like that if you feel faint. Any lightheadedness is a sign that you should change position. Try lying on your side or kneeling on all fours.

It is now also known that hyperthermia (overheating) can cause damage to animal young, so that saunas, very hot baths and gross over-exercising are considered a bad idea, particularly in the first three months when the fetus is forming and developing. Of course, you may not know you are pregnant in the early weeks but, as soon as you do know, or if you are trying to become pregnant, avoid arti-ficially heating your body. You can sweat but the fetus is dependent on your blood supply for cooling down.

If you are smoking heavily and eating only junk food, you run a greater risk of placental insufficiency, an underdeveloped placenta (afterbirth) which does not supply enough oxygen to the baby. Some babies can compensate for this by sending the available blood to the more important organs. Eventually the deprivation becomes marked and the baby may die unless the condition is diagnosed and

In all varicose conditions, standing for long periods is bad. Standing still is worse. If standing is utterly necessary, moving from one foot to the other or up and down on the toes will, to some extent, mitigate the offence to the veins. The advice 'never stand when you can sit, never sit when you can (half) lie' is good advice in pregnancy. Half-lying in physio language means reclining with the feet up, in the *chaise longue* position. (The Romans used it for dinner parties. It would be interesting to know if Roman matrons avoided varicose veins.)

Cramp

Most people are familiar with the sudden incapacitating pain of cramp. Cramp occurs more often than usual in pregnancy, possibly because the slowed blood from the veins periodically gushes into lower limb muscles such as the calf. Cramp can be triggered by overworking a particular muscle or by bringing a muscle into action suddenly from a state of rest, for instance, during sleep. Cramp of the uterine ligament is one form of cramp peculiar to pregnancy. A sharp pain stabs into the groin area, either on the right or left side. This is caused by stretching of the round ligament of the uterus, which is quite short in the non-pregnant woman but must lengthen considerably as the uterus grows and rises from the pelvis into the abdomen. Application of heat, brisk rubbing or just resting for a few minutes will usually relieve this form of cramp.

As cramp is more likely to occur in the lower limb muscles, exercises involving foot, knee and hip movements are appropriate. All foot movements (up-and-down, in-and-out, and circling) should be done strongly and often throughout the day, followed by thigh tightening and hip-hitching. Hip-hitching consists of drawing alternate hips towards the shoulders while keeping the knees straight. This is a good all-purpose exercise in pregnancy, very easy to do, and it can be performed quite fast and energetically, even in bed. It appears to help prevent varicose veins and cramp by the massaging action on the deep pelvic blood vessels. Some women find it relieves backache as well (see page 66).

Carpal tunnel syndrome

This condition is not limited to pregnancy, and is one of the conditions associated with over-use. However, an increase in fluid retention in pregnancy may make some women susceptible. You are usually aware that you are retaining fluid: your rings become tight and perhaps your ankles are a bit thick. A band of tissue holds the tendons and nerves to the wrist, preventing them from springing out. Congestion behind this band causes pressure, resulting in pain and tingling in the hands.

Bad circulation may also be a factor, or a shortage of vitamin B_6, a deficiency of which causes thickening in tendons or their sheaths. During pregnancy all available stores might be used up. Vitamin B_6 can be found in wheatgerm, molasses and brewer's yeast and many fresh vegetables and fruits.

Hydrocortisone injections can be helpful in treating carpal tunnel syndrome, but they are not usually advised in pregnancy. The best treatment seems to be wearing light splints at night, and during the day if practicable. Physiotherapists custom-make these splints out of a plastic material which can be moulded to fit the individual. They can also be obtained at medical supply shops.

Intercostal pain

Pain in the rib area is an aggravating condition usually occurring in the last trimester. Short women who are carrying their babies high and have very little room between the uterus and the rib cage are sitting ducks for this problem. A persistent nagging ache develops around the lower ribs. There may be a painful band around the ribs originating in the dorsal spine, suggesting that there is pressure on the spinal nerve on that side. The condition is nearly always one-sided. It is not serious except that the woman gets very little relief and often can't sleep. It may be unclear as to whether the pain originates in the spine or simply from stretch and pressure of the intercostal muscles, the muscles that work the ribs. You may complain of a 'foot-in-the-ribs' or a bruised feeling. Many cases of intercostal pain are very stubborn and resist treatment which usually consists of stretching exercises with perhaps IFT or ultrasound. It is probably fair to say that treatment may not work, or may give only temporary relief. Knowing this, you can then make up your own mind whether to try it.

Indigestion

Indigestion or heartburn is an unpleasant side-effect of pregnancy. As the uterus rises it puts pressure on the stomach, forcing it up against the diaphragm. Some people have a rather loose opening in the diaphragm where the oesophagus (food tube) enters the stomach. Pregnancy can cause pressure against this area and further laxity, allowing some of the food in the stomach to reflux into the oesophagus. Food in the stomach is mixed with a very strong acid, whereas the climate in the oesophagus is alkaline. Acid reflux of even a small quantity of food causes a burning, lump-in-the-throat sensation which is worse when the body is horizontal. Because of the effect of pregnancy hormones on involuntary muscle tissue, food may remain in the stomach for up to 48 hours, which further exacerbates the condition.

Propping yourself up with pillows in bed and avoiding stooping positions is advisable. You might need to take some sort of antacid preparation or a little milk after meals. Eating small meals and chewing everything well helps, as do stretching exercises over the back of a chair (see page 126).

Constipation and flatulence

During pregnancy hormones reduce the motility of the whole intestinal tract. In some women this leads to constipation. On the other hand, because of the added support to internal organs from the uterus, there are women whose insides behave better when they are pregnant. Diet is probably the most important factor to keep bowel motions comfortable and normal. If you add unprocessed bran or rolled oats to your diet, more water will be taken up in the food mass and there will be better stimulation of peristalsis (intestinal movements). There should also be less of a tendency towards flatulence. If wind is a problem, there are exercises which can help, such as stomach tightening, hip-hitching, and humping the back on all fours, known as the donkey exercise (see pages 126, 128). All these exercises have a mechanical effect on the abdomen, acting as a stimulus to the passage of food residue and gas.

Breathlessness and palpitations

The modern pregnant woman often goes to some trouble to maintain her fitness. She attends antenatal, fitness or yoga classes. She may participate in sport. Nevertheless changes to the body mean that few will go through the whole pregnancy without becoming breathless. The body adjusts to the extra demands for oxygen by increasing the lung capacity. In ordinary circumstances a pregnant woman can keep up with the need for extra oxygen (but if you run upstairs or climb a long slow hill, you will puff a bit!). The same type of adjustment affects the action of the heart. More blood has to be pumped around the body. Most women are unaware of these changes but some develop a sensitivity to a heartbeat that has become stronger and more rapid and once it is noticed, it may concern them. Neither breathlessness nor rapid heartbeat should worry you in pregnancy unless there is some known malfunctioning of the heart or lungs, in which case a specialist will be brought in for consultation by your doctor.

Stress incontinence

Stress incontinence is a distressing condition that is dealt with in detail on page 181. A mild form is common in pregnancy. If a sneeze or cough erupts suddenly, it is quite likely that you will not be able to hold your loaded pelvic floor muscles against the onslaught and will leak a little urine. Pelvic floor exercises are a necessity during pregnancy, not only to help prevent this situation but to make the area flexible for the stretching it will have to undergo during the birth. No one need be unduly worried about mild stress incontinence in pregnancy. A more serious form of stress incontinence involving loss of a considerable quantity of urine several times a day is another matter. If this happens you should check with a physiotherapist. You may be exercising the wrong muscle. (It is quite easy to check that you are using the correct muscle by tightening your pelvic floor while passing urine at the toilet. If you can slow or stop the stream, there is no doubt that the right muscle is working.)

Insomnia

In the first trimester the extra hormones in the system may make for excessive drowsiness. In the third trimester wakefulness may be the bane of your existence. Discomfort from the large uterus, cramp and other aches and pains can interrupt sleep, as can pressure on the bladder and irritation of its muscular wall.

If you use relaxation techniques conscientiously you should be able to sleep or go back to sleep once awakened. A semi-prone position treatment begun. The treatment for the mother is rest, often in hospital, a better diet, and frequent checks on the baby by means of ultrasound scans and fetal heart monitoring. Fetal movements tell about fetal wellbeing. Any change in fetal movement pattern should be reported to the doctor.

Controlled Spinal Mobility Exercises

(For early pregnancy)

1. Serpentine
Lie on your stomach and press up on your hands, curving your back until your elbows are straight. Then sit back on heels into the 'salaam' without moving the position of your hands. Reverse the movements to lie on your stomach again.

2. Echidna
Lie on one side with your knees to your chest. Roll to the other side then straighten right out. Curl up again, roll to the other side and straighten right out. Then curl up again and roll to the other side.

3. Three-legged
Crouching on your hands and knees, bend one knee to your chest then stretch the same leg backwards. Alternate legs.

(Continued)

Controlled Spinal Mobility Exercises (*Continued*)

4. Counterweight
Sit in a frog position, grab your toes with both hands and rock on your bottom. If you can, rock onto your back and come up again, using the momentum you have generated. Don't let go of your toes!

5. Whirlbird
Sit with your legs out straight then bend and cross the right leg over the straight left leg. Swing both arms and the torso to the right and back. Change legs (left over right) and swing to the left.

6. Anglepoise
Lie on your back with your right knee bent and your hip rotated out so that your knee touches the ground. Repeat with your left leg.

Some women can distinguish all of their baby's actions, for example, limb movements, rolling, hiccups and often whether the baby has moved from breech position to head-down. If movements are becoming fewer and more feeble, the fetus may be suffering from lack of oxygen. An ultrasound scan can detect limb and trunk movements and tone of the fetus, whether it is lying limply in its sac or floating more actively.

You may be understandably embarrassed about your condition if you are unwillingly pregnant. If you lack support from a partner or parents, a member of the paramedical team might help by taking on the support role. You should never feel you have no one to turn to: there are all kinds of kindly disposed people and organisations waiting in the wings to help you, such as pregnancy support, social welfare counselling, church assistance groups, family planning and antenatal classes.

Antenatal classes

Antenatal classes or pregnancy fitness classes are a good idea. If they are taken by a physiotherapist, any discomfort of pregnancy that you may be complaining of can be examined and the physiotherapist can give you helpful hints and exercises specifically for these annoyances.

You can take a support person to these classes. This could be the baby's father, your mother, sister or a friend. The potential father is often engrossed with classes. Something that was not of interest because it is still months away becomes much more real and immediate. Classes bring out the protective instinct in the fathers-to-be.

Pregnancy side-effects

In the past women put up with a good many discomforts that are associated with pregnancy, believing they were inevitable. Some doctors may even have said, 'Oh well, you're pregnant. What else can you expect?' But many common discomforts can be dealt with which might save you weeks of low-level pain.

Backache in pregnancy

Fifty percent of women suffer from backache in greater or lesser degree. Pregnancy backache is a broad term. It is generally thought to be caused by the stretching of pelvic ligaments and alteration of posture. During pregnancy the hormone relaxin is released into the bloodstream along with many other hormones. Relaxin helps to soften the ligaments which will assist in the slight enlarging of the diameters of the pelvis for labour and birth.

The joint most commonly affected is one of the sacroiliac joints, to the left or right of the spine. Often the fetus is putting more weight on one side, and this is probably a factor in the one-sided nature of the condition. The subconscious brain is aware of the extra weight and the very slight slackening of ligaments, so a small, key, triangular muscle deep within the pelvis tends to tighten up or go into a spasm, and the woman complains of an ache in her buttock.

A physiotherapist can often put a finger on the sore spot and the pressure will cause pain. Treatment using mobilisation, ultrasound or IFT will usually relieve the muscle spasm and correct the problem.

Sometimes the pain is concentrated more in the joint itself. Treatment is similar and is often effective. Certain exercises can also help relieve the spasm and pain.

Weight gain

Back pain can also be caused by alteration of postural pressures on the joints of the spine. If there is a sharp angulation of the pelvis to the spine (a sway-back), there may be pain because the weight of the baby is dragging on the spine. Correcting your posture will help, along with tightening your stomach muscles and avoiding high-heeled shoes. Back pain can develop surprisingly early, often before the first three months of pregnancy are over. This may well be due to the high level of hormones operating, but it may also be the result of the beginnings of extra bulk in the pelvis. If you are in early pregnancy, you can usually do a wider range of exercises because you will still be able to lie on your stomach. Controlled spinal mobility exercises can be very effective in reducing painful muscle spasm and postural aches (see page 113).

Sciatic nerve pain

Nerve pressure is often a sequel to spinal joint or disc problems and this can be made worse by actual pressure of the fetus. The large nerve that supplies most of the leg muscles, the sciatic, is often the one affected because it is bulky (about as thick as a finger) and it travels right through the pelvis underneath the fetus. It is rather disconcerting when one leg suddenly 'gives way' or pain shoots down it like an electric shock! This is not usually as serious as it sounds; it is momentary and seldom persists after the baby is born. A maternity belt may be the answer. These belts are strong pieces of wide elastic with Velcro fastenings. They carry some of the baby's weight, support the back and may relieve nerve pressure. The physiotherapist will advise whether treatment or a belt would be more appropriate or perhaps both. The belts are much more supportive than the usual maternity corset sold in department stores, and can be bought at medical supply shops.

If the pressure on the sciatic nerve is mainly affecting motor fibres (the fibres that carry messages to the muscles), the leg muscles may be temporarily affected. The leg feels weak all the time and, as there may be a tendency to trip, some women need to use a stick. Don't worry; you have not become prematurely old! The weakness goes as soon as the pressure on the nerve (the baby!) is removed. Very occasionally a toespring splint is necessary.

Coccyx (tailbone) pain

The old schooldays trick of pulling a chair away just as somebody is about to sit down can injure the coccyx, as can falling off a horse or falling downstairs. When the coccyx is painful during pregnancy, the condition usually stems from a previous injury. During the birth the coccyx is bent back, hyperextending the joint, to make more room for the fetus's head. If the coccyx is mobile, this is no problem, but if it is stiff, as it can be after injury, a definite crack can be heard and the joint may temporarily subluxate (go out of joint). This leaves a very sore area which makes sitting painful or impossible, sometimes for weeks. If the coccyx fractures, it will heal slowly but this is a painful process as it can't be splinted. When a woman complains of a painful coccyx in pregnancy, a few ultrasound treatments will often relieve pain and, by bringing more blood into this rather bloodless area, the joint should be in a better condition for movement at birth. A physiotherapist should be able to tell if there is a lack of flexibility in the joint and may be able to mobilise it.

Separation at the pubic symphysis

The pubic symphysis is the joint in the pubis, centred under the pubic hair. Unlike an ordinary joint, it doesn't normally move. The joint moves during labour by taking up fluid and can produce an estimated temporary separation of from 1 to 12 millimetres. If, however, the separation occurs in pregnancy, it causes trouble. The whole pelvis is a strong, tightly-knit structure which has to carry the weight of the trunk and, in pregnancy, the weight of a heavy uterus. A pubic joint that has too much give in it makes the woman feel unsafe, as if her pelvis is going to fall apart, and it may reduce her walk to a waddle. A hip belt is the answer, making for a secure held-together feeling, a great comfort. The belt, called a trochanter belt, is made out of seat-belt material. Women having their first baby seldom suffer from this malady; it generally happens after the pelvis has been stretched by one or more vaginal births.

Separation of the rectus muscles

Nearly every woman has separated rectus muscles by eight months pregnant. The rectus muscles are the straight bands of muscle reaching from the breast bone to the pubic bone. Before a woman has children, her rectus muscles are joined together with a tough fibrous membrane or sheath. As pregnancy advances, the sheath tears and the two bands separate. The separation can be seen when you try to sit up from lying. Your abdomen rises in a V shape. Anyone teaching pregnancy exercises will recognise this tendency and any obvious separation should lead to a less vigorous exercise routine, deleting any exercises which over-strain the stomach muscles. Sit-ups are usually only appropriate during the first and second trimester of pregnancy. Your physiotherapist will judge your capabilities.

After the baby has been born, it will be necessary to exercise to fill the gap, done by working up the rectus muscles against resistance. If these muscles have been overstrained during pregnancy, the mother starts with a post-natal handicap. There is no need for despair, however, as muscle has marvellous powers of regeneration if the will to work is there. Badly separated rectus muscles will need an abdominal binder for a few weeks. In all these cases where belts or binders are necessary, a physiotherapist should be consulted about type and fitting.

Varicose veins

Although the tendency towards varicose veins is hereditary, you can do a lot to prevent them from occurring in pregnancy if you start early enough. In the later part of pregnancy veins may stand out prominently, but a simple exercise routine can prevent them from becoming unsightly and painful. An aching leg from distended veins means that varicose veins are developing. This may be partly due to hormonal changes on the walls of the veins but is aggravated by standing for long periods (hairdressers beware!). Aching legs in pregnancy should be rested *and* exercised. Supportive stockings may also be worn.

Clots in veins

Some varicose conditions may be less obtrusive but can blow up suddenly into venous thrombosis where there is a partial blockage caused by blood moving so sluggishly in the distended veins that it forms a clot. The condition is potentially dangerous because the clot could travel in the bloodstream to the heart, lungs or brain. The symptoms of venous thrombosis are local redness, hardness or soreness. Any such symptoms in pregnancy or in the post-natal period should be immediately reported to a doctor. However, most varicose veins do not lead to clotting. Although the bloodstream is slowed and the little valves in the veins are somewhat incompetent, allowing blood to pool in the lower limbs, there is no blockage or clotting.

Haemorrhoids

Two more conditions must be included among varicose problems. Haemorrhoids (piles) and vulval veins, which can form a cluster like a bunch of grapes on the entrance to the vagina, are both common conditions. If necessary, haemorrhoids can be treated postnatally with ultrasound which will shrink them quite rapidly.

Treatment of circulatory problems

Varicose veins of all types need movement to accelerate the circulation and help drive the blood in the veins in the lower part of the body back to the heart. Resting with the feet slightly elevated is an essential routine, and general exercise such as walking is beneficial although a brisk walk is much better than the window shopping variety. Exercises using the calf and thigh muscles are important and can be done incidentally, many times a day. These routines can prevent varicose veins from developing or stop them from getting worse. For haemorrhoids and vulval veins exercises contracting the pelvic floor muscles will help. When the pelvic floor muscles are used effectively, blood in the veins around the vulva and the anus is pushed on, the circular massaging action working to clear the overloaded veins.

Exercises for Specific Problems

1. To prevent extreme separation of the rectus muscles while still working the stomach muscles:

a) tighten your stomach many times a day (pulling in under the baby); and

b) hold your stomach 'together' (with hands) in a half-lying position, with your knees bent, and raise your head.

2. To prevent or control varicose veins:

a) do a lot of foot pedalling—feet up—feet down; and

b) do some energetic hip hitching, either stationary or progressing across the floor.

3. To prevent leg cramps:

a) do some loose hip hitching before going to sleep;

b) follow this by taking your legs apart and back.

(Both of these movements can be done in a half-lying position.)

4. To relieve intercostal pain:

Stand and stretch your arms parallel over your head and move them first to the left, then to the right. Stretch *away* from the side that hurts, with more pull.

5. To relieve indigestion:

Hang your shoulder blades over a chair and stretch your midriff. Alternatively, kneel and prop your elbows on a chair.

6. For wind pains:

Position yourself in the 'donkey' position (on all fours) and hump your back.

7. For swelling in the hands:

Raise your arms above your head and alternately make a fist and then stretch your fingers. Follow this by circling from the wrists, arms still in the air.

In all varicose conditions, standing for long periods is bad. Standing still is worse. If standing is utterly necessary, moving from one foot to the other or up and down on the toes will, to some extent, mitigate the offence to the veins. The advice 'never stand when you can sit, never sit when you can (half) lie' is good advice in pregnancy. Half-lying in physio language means reclining with the feet up, in the *chaise longue* position. (The Romans used it for dinner parties. It would be interesting to know if Roman matrons avoided varicose veins.)

Cramp

Most people are familiar with the sudden incapacitating pain of cramp. Cramp occurs more often than usual in pregnancy, possibly because the slowed blood from the veins periodically gushes into lower limb muscles such as the calf. Cramp can be triggered by overworking a particular muscle or by bringing a muscle into action suddenly from a state of rest, for instance, during sleep. Cramp of the uterine ligament is one form of cramp peculiar to pregnancy. A sharp pain stabs into the groin area, either on the right or left side. This is caused by stretching of the round ligament of the uterus, which is quite short in the non-pregnant woman but must lengthen considerably as the uterus grows and rises from the pelvis into the abdomen. Application of heat, brisk rubbing or just resting for a few minutes will usually relieve this form of cramp.

As cramp is more likely to occur in the lower limb muscles, exercises involving foot, knee and hip movements are appropriate. All foot movements (up-and-down, in-and-out, and circling) should be done strongly and often throughout the day, followed by thigh tightening and hip-hitching. Hip-hitching consists of drawing alternate hips towards the shoulders while keeping the knees straight. This is a good all-purpose exercise in pregnancy, very easy to do, and it can be performed quite fast and energetically, even in bed. It appears to help prevent varicose veins and cramp by the massaging action on the deep pelvic blood vessels. Some women find it relieves backache as well (see page 66).

Carpal tunnel syndrome

This condition is not limited to pregnancy, and is one of the conditions associated with over-use. However, an increase in fluid retention in pregnancy may make some women susceptible. You are usually aware that you are retaining fluid: your rings become tight and perhaps your ankles are a bit thick. A band of tissue holds the tendons and nerves to the wrist, preventing them from springing out. Congestion behind this band causes pressure, resulting in pain and tingling in the hands.

Bad circulation may also be a factor, or a shortage of vitamin B_6, a deficiency of which causes thickening in tendons or their sheaths. During pregnancy all available stores might be used up. Vitamin B_6 can be found in wheatgerm, molasses and brewer's yeast and many fresh vegetables and fruits.

Hydrocortisone injections can be helpful in treating carpal tunnel syndrome, but they are not usually advised in pregnancy. The best treatment seems to be wearing light splints at night, and during the day if practicable. Physiotherapists custom-make these splints out of a plastic material which can be moulded to fit the individual. They can also be obtained at medical supply shops.

Intercostal pain

Pain in the rib area is an aggravating condition usually occurring in the last trimester. Short women who are carrying their babies high and have very little room between the uterus and the rib cage are sitting ducks for this problem. A persistent nagging ache develops around the lower ribs. There may be a painful band around the ribs originating in the dorsal spine, suggesting that there is pressure on the spinal nerve on that side. The condition is nearly always one-sided. It is not serious except that the woman gets very little relief and often can't sleep. It may be unclear as to whether the pain originates in the spine or simply from stretch and pressure of the intercostal muscles, the muscles that work the ribs. You may complain of a 'foot-in-the-ribs' or a bruised feeling. Many cases of intercostal pain are very stubborn and resist treatment which usually consists of stretching exercises with perhaps IFT or ultrasound. It is probably fair to say that treatment may not work, or may give only temporary relief. Knowing this, you can then make up your own mind whether to try it.

Indigestion

Indigestion or heartburn is an unpleasant side-effect of pregnancy. As the uterus rises it puts pressure on the stomach, forcing it up against the diaphragm. Some people have a rather loose opening in the diaphragm where the oesophagus (food tube) enters the stomach. Pregnancy can cause pressure against this area and further laxity, allowing some of the food in the stomach to reflux into the oesophagus. Food in the stomach is mixed with a very strong acid, whereas the climate in the oesophagus is alkaline. Acid reflux of even a small quantity of food causes a burning, lump-in-the-throat sensation which is worse when the body is horizontal. Because of the effect of pregnancy hormones on involuntary muscle tissue, food may remain in the stomach for up to 48 hours, which further exacerbates the condition.

Propping yourself up with pillows in bed and avoiding stooping positions is advisable. You might need to take some sort of antacid preparation or a little milk after meals. Eating small meals and chewing everything well helps, as do stretching exercises over the back of a chair (see page 126).

Constipation and flatulence

During pregnancy hormones reduce the motility of the whole intestinal tract. In some women this leads to constipation. On the other hand, because of the added support to internal organs from the uterus, there are women whose insides behave better when they are pregnant. Diet is probably the most important factor to keep bowel motions comfortable and normal. If you add unprocessed bran or rolled oats to your diet, more water will be taken up in the food mass and there will be better stimulation of peristalsis (intestinal movements). There should also be less of a tendency towards flatulence. If wind is a problem, there are exercises which can help, such as stomach tightening, hip-hitching, and humping the back on all fours, known as the donkey exercise (see pages 126, 128). All these exercises have a mechanical effect on the abdomen, acting as a stimulus to the passage of food residue and gas.

Breathlessness and palpitations

The modern pregnant woman often goes to some trouble to maintain her fitness. She attends antenatal, fitness or yoga classes. She may participate in sport. Nevertheless changes to the body mean that few will go through the whole pregnancy without becoming breathless. The body adjusts to the extra demands for oxygen by increasing the lung capacity. In ordinary circumstances a pregnant woman can keep up with the need for extra oxygen (but if you run upstairs or climb a long slow hill, you will puff a bit!). The same type of adjustment affects the action of the heart. More blood has to be pumped around the body. Most women are unaware of these changes but some develop a sensitivity to a heartbeat that has become stronger and more rapid and once it is noticed, it may concern them. Neither breathlessness nor rapid heartbeat should worry you in pregnancy unless there is some known malfunctioning of the heart or lungs, in which case a specialist will be brought in for consultation by your doctor.

Stress incontinence

Stress incontinence is a distressing condition that is dealt with in detail on page 181. A mild form is common in pregnancy. If a sneeze or cough erupts suddenly, it is quite likely that you will not be able to hold your loaded pelvic floor muscles against the onslaught and will leak a little urine. Pelvic floor exercises are a necessity during pregnancy, not only to help prevent this situation but to make the area flexible for the stretching it will have to undergo during the birth. No one need be unduly worried about mild stress incontinence in pregnancy. A more serious form of stress incontinence involving loss of a considerable quantity of urine several times a day is another matter. If this happens you should check with a physiotherapist. You may be exercising the wrong muscle. (It is quite easy to check that you are using the correct muscle by tightening your pelvic floor while passing urine at the toilet. If you can slow or stop the stream, there is no doubt that the right muscle is working.)

Insomnia

In the first trimester the extra hormones in the system may make for excessive drowsiness. In the third trimester wakefulness may be the bane of your existence. Discomfort from the large uterus, cramp and other aches and pains can interrupt sleep, as can pressure on the bladder and irritation of its muscular wall.

If you use relaxation techniques conscientiously you should be able to sleep or go back to sleep once awakened. A semi-prone position with a pillow in the bed under your upper knee will prevent the weight of the top leg dragging on the uterus. The baby may wriggle a bit when you first adopt that position but will soon settle down. Unfortunately there is no cure for urinary frequency at this stage of pregnancy, but at least it gives a chance to reposition the pillow.

Fainting

A condition called supine hypotension, or the 'cut-off', affects some pregnant women when they are lying flat on their backs or reclining. The symptoms are cold clamminess, a sick sinking feeling, and finally fainting. The condition is caused by the baby lying on the large blood vessel which brings blood back to the heart from the lower part of the body. Many women are not affected by this because the blood quickly finds other channels to the heart. But in some the blood flow to the heart is slowed down, temporarily prejudicing the supply to the head. The simple remedy is to move the baby out of the way! The hands and knees position works best, but rolling over onto your side or lying semi-prone will also soon relieve the symptoms. Some women have low blood pressure during pregnancy. There is nothing abnormal about this; in fact it is quite a healthy state of affairs. However, it does make a woman more susceptible to fainting feelings. It *can* occur in labour, and if it does, a high sitting, kneeling or semi-prone position should be comfortable.

Problems needing special care

There may be other problems that beset you in pregnancy, marring an otherwise idyllic period. Don't hesitate to voice your worries, either in class or afterwards in the privacy of the physiotherapist's office. You are sure to find a sympathetic ear. A number of problems that occur in pregnancy need special care: they will be supervised by your doctor. They include high blood pressure, toxaemia, fluid retention, bleeding, placenta praevia, incompetent cervix, irritable uterus and excessive vomiting. In some cases strict rest is ordered and, if this happens to you, you may be hospitalised. If the problem is less serious and you are still anticipating a vaginal birth, you will be able to continue to go to antenatal classes. Sometimes the outcome

Exercises During Pregnancy

1. Capsule
Lie in a slightly propped position with your knees bent. Hold your 'bulge' with your hands and lift your head and shoulders. To maintain supportive stomach muscles, it is also a good idea to tighten your stomach at least 10 times a day (this can be done in any position).

2. Treadle
Do a lot of foot pedalling – feet up – feet down; and move your hips (hip-hitching), making one leg shorter than the other while keeping the knees straight. These movements will help to prevent or control varicose veins and leg cramps.

3. Stretcher
Stand and stretch your parallel arms over your head and move them to right and left. If you have pain on one side on your chest wall, stretch away from that side.

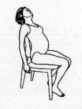

4. Reliever
If you have indigestion or heartburn, sit on a straight-backed chair and hang your shoulder blades over the back of the chair. This helps to stretch out the food tube to your stomach.

5. Donkey
If you have wind pains, position yourself on all fours and hump your back. Relax to your original position and repeat. Drawing in the stomach may help as well.

may be a caesarean birth, but in any case nothing but good can come of learning to relax and use breathing to maintain a state of calm in the face of the problem. However, more care must be taken and your physiotherapist will advise which exercises are suitable and which should be discontinued. In conditions such as placenta praevia or low 'marginal' placenta which might slip down below the fetus and which may have been associated with episodes of bleeding, you should probably not do exercises that increase abdominal pressure. The same might be said for women with an irritable uterus who are having frequent strong contractions but are not due for some time (early contractions can cause softening of the cervix or rupture of membranes).

High blood pressure

When the blood pressure is raised to a level that has warranted a warning from your doctor, do tell your physiotherapist. Apart from reviewing the exercise routine, special daily relaxation sessions can be suggested in an attempt to control blood pressure and prevent the situation from worsening. Relaxation means deep rest, not just sitting with the feet up reading or knitting. Two half-hour periods a day are not too much. In a few cases, I have known mothers-to-be claim they have kept out of hospital by strict daily relaxation and concentration on lowering the heart rate and blood pressure.

If the doctor finds protein (albumin) in the urine as well as high blood pressure, the patient may be put in hospital for bed rest. The physiotherapist can visit and supervise some easy bed exercises which will keep the circulation moving along and the lungs clear, and at the same time give you some reassurance about techniques for labour which may still be needed. Indeed, women sent to hospital days or weeks before the birth often manage well in labour, partly because they have become accustomed to the staff and the hospital's ways.

Fluid retention

Fluid retention can be an isolated condition or be associated with high blood pressure. If it is the only abnormal symptom, it is unlikely that you will find yourself in hospital. However, you may

Bed Exercises

These exercises can be done after abdominal or pelvic surgery or if hospitalised during pregnancy.

1. Pedalling
Press both feet down as far as you can, working the calf muscles. Pull your feet back to make an acute angle with the legs. Then move the feet alternately – one up, one down.

2. Stiffening
Press both knees back hard onto the bed. Relax and repeat the exercise or do one knee at a time.

3. Hip hitching
Edge one leg down so that the heel is below the other foot. Then edge the other one down. As one leg goes down pull up the other leg from the hip so that you keep sitting in the same place.

4. Stretch and pull
Grasping the bedhead or overhead bar pull the whole of your body weight slowly up the bed using your arm muscles, not your stomach muscles.

5. Breather
Take a slow breath, letting the air fill your lower chest and slightly expand the midriff. Let the air out, sighing softly.

These exercises should be done every hour on the hour (while you are awake!) They accelerate blood circulation which helps prevent clotting. Full expansion of the lungs assist in keeping the chest clear of mucus. When you are in bed for any length of time, your body is fairly dormant. These exercises keep important systems stimulated without putting pressure on the uterus. No. 5 will ease Braxton Hicks contractions.

be uncomfortable. Tight, puffy hands and swollen ankles can be a legitimate cause for complaint. Circulation exercises, as have been described for varicose veins and cramp (see page 120), can be done many times a day and should help. Hand and wrist movement, squeezing, bending and stretching are beneficial too but, as the real problem is that your overloaded kidneys are not excreting wastes fast enough, this may be only a partial solution.

Vomiting

Nausea and vomiting are usually managed simply by finding out what suits you, such as small meals fairly often, cutting out certain foods or relaxation training. Unremittant vomiting (hyperemesis) means being hospitalised so that adequate nutrition for both mother and baby can be ensured. (The English novelist Charlotte Brontë is thought to have died from untreated hyperemesis.)

Early contractions

Early contractions are usually only a nuisance, but they should be reported to your doctor because if they persist, they could open the cervix prematurely. Your doctor may examine you vaginally to determine if this is happening. If left untreated, a bit of membrane may be nipped in the opening and rupture, which can lead to premature labour. Ultrasound techniques are also helpful in diagnosing this eventuality. In some cases when the cervix is incompetent, a stitch (suture) is inserted until term, then removed when it is time for the cervix to open.

Total rest is often advised and possibly drugs to weaken and discourage contractions, as the aim is to keep the baby in the uterus while conditions are favourable there: the mother is normally the best incubator. The reason for premature labour is not entirely understood. Heredity is probably a factor, but tiredness and overwork could be predisposing causes and should be avoided as far as possible.

Pregnancy can so often be an intensely happy vigorous optimistic time. There is no need for you to fall victim to nagging complaints when so often they can be forestalled or at least investigated. And if there is a real problem and adjustments have to be made, you will find yourself responding cheerfully and constructively.

Early caesarean section

In a few cases pregnancy problems become so serious that the doctor decides to perform an early caesarean section rather than risk the baby's safety. If this happens to you, it might seem that your antenatal course has been wasted. This is not so, as your relaxation techniques will be useful for any stressful experience and, if a general anaesthetic is to be given, breathing exercises will need to be done for several days afterwards to keep your lungs clear. Besides this, the antenatal course is likely to have prepared you well for just such an eventuality, making it less of a shock and easier to accept. A caesarean leaves only a thin scar along the pubic hairline, often known as a 'smile' because of its shape. Most women recover quickly, especially if they are exercising 'little and often'. If the scar is sore or lumpy, ultrasound treatment can help.

Inductions

The hormone oxytocin is the key to the start of labour. This hormone stimulates the uterine muscles to work and start the labour process. The uterine muscles are crucial to the progress of labour. They are the powerhouse for labour, and are known as the Powers which pass the Passenger through the Passage—the 3Ps of the whole operation.

During the 1970s a great many inductions of labour were done by drip infusion, feeding a synthetic form of the hormone oxytocin in solution into the body via a vein. The amount of hormone added determines the strength of contractions.

This practice has been largely discontinued because it did not always work, particularly if the natural process was not ready to begin; if very strong contractions were produced with little time for recovery between each contraction, the baby might suffer distress (usually recorded in the fetal heart beat); and a quick labour was often harder for the mother to bear, as *she* had no time to recover between contractions.

The practice now is only to augment a labour with a drip induction if the labour is sluggish, and to tailor the amount of hormone added carefully to suit each individual labour. Prostaglandin gel applied vaginally is another gentle induction which is growing in popularity.

An induction is also used if you are days overdue, and the doctor thinks it inadvisable to let the situation drag on any longer. Occasionally a drip might be necessary for psychological reasons to bring on labour at a certain time or for physiological reasons if there are pregnancy problems.

Quite often the bag of waters (membranes) will be ruptured as well. This makes it easier for the cervix to open as the membranes can be swept free of the cervix as the waters are broken.

There is no real increase in pain as the induction is only supplying the power that the uterus, under natural conditions, has failed to do.

When the issue of induction is raised in antenatal classes, there is generally a unanimous vote against it. The subject may not come up with your doctor until the last week of pregnancy when she or he is reviewing your condition and the likelihood of problems for you or your baby if you go over your due date. The doctor may even give you a deadline date after which she/he will induce you. It is probably good policy to tell your doctor your feelings about an induction earlier in the pregnancy, although a decision can't be made until the time for labour approaches.

You might be able to activate the uterine muscles yourself: by having intercourse around about the due date. Intercourse brings on the right climate for oxytocin production, partly because it is inclined to be deeply relaxing. And if your body is ready to begin labour, presumably because the baby is well down and the cervix is soft, sex might set it off as there are prostaglandins in semen!

Due to the bulge, sex in pregnancy may have to take place from behind. You often have quite high libido (wish for sex) in the middle three months, but there will usually be less inclination in the last three months. Intercourse is not dangerous unless there is a risk of premature birth, so if you have been given a time for the induction (tomorrow or next week), you can experiment by doing your own relaxing inducement!

Home birth or hospital?

Three considerations should form the basis of a woman's choice of birth place: maximum safety for mother and child; the ability to have a reasonable say in how the labour will be conducted; and the mother's confidence in feeling secure, relaxed and cared for. When a mother-to-be crosses a hospital's portals her fight-flight hormones can put her temporarily out of labour. In fact the modern midwife may advise her to stay in familiar surroundings until labour is well established, provided it is safe to do this.

Historically women have mostly laboured and delivered at home, mainly because there was no other choice. But home birth was never the exclusive rule. An engraving in a fifteenth century treatise on midwifery entitled *The Garden of Roses for Pregnant Women and for Midwives* shows a woman sitting upright on a birth stool, surrounded by flowers. Possibly she was not at home, but in a sort of early birth centre.

An infusion of herbs in hot water might be placed underneath a labouring woman to 'draw' the child out. Midwives were often accused of being witches because of these herbal brews. However, providing they were thought to be white witches, they were tolerated because they were supposed to be able to transfer the mother's pain to a domestic animal!

Hospitals such as the Hôtel Dieu in Paris were built to provide medical care. They were largely run on charity and were frightfully overcrowded. Patients with infectious diseases, wounded soldiers and children were all treated together. Even when lying-in hospitals began to appear, the death toll from puerperal fever was fearful, partly because the medical men and their students made vaginal examinations without washing their hands. It would not have helped that they used cadavers to instruct their students in anatomy. This was before people understood the essential role of cleanliness in medical care and especially when dealing with that perfect climate for infection, the open womb. Under the circumstances to have a baby at home was probably much safer.

In the eighteenth and nineteenth centuries doctors, who were exclusively male, made house calls only when there was dire need. The woman was expected to be passive or prostrated, and to give as little trouble as possible. Language changed: the doctor 'delivered' the baby, or delivered the mother of a baby.

Fortunately women have always helped each other. Midwifery was a very early development in human history. Egyptian art shows many midwives helping at a delivery, and use of the birth stool was common in Egypt, Greece and Palestine, though difficult cases may have been delivered in bed. The birth stool was part of the marriage portion until quite recently in parts of Europe, or was owned and transported by the midwife.

Midwives in ancient Greece were either skilled, taking on medical and surgical intervention when necessary, or unskilled, looking after routine confinements. One midwife called Agnodice tried to improve her skills by attending medical lectures dressed as a male. The men were outraged and she was arrested, but women rose in protest and she was acquitted.

Early last century women were left to suffer pain in the first stage of labour only to be anaesthetised for the actual birth. Even if they were conscious during the birth, they were made to lie on their sides with one leg in the air, tied up or held by a midwife, or flat on their backs. Other procedures were mandatory and invaded personal privacy—such as enemas, shaving of all the pubic hair, or wearing gowns with no back to them.

Technological development has brought new 'interventions': epidurals, inductions, monitoring the fetal heart (which involves wearing a belt to strap the electrodes on, or clipping an electrode to the baby's scalp once the waters have broken—although some hospitals have telemetry, a remote controlled method of monitoring).

It is not entirely safe to give birth to a baby at home. Emergencies can arise very quickly and often cannot be foreseen.

Labour wards are changing to fit in with the expressed wish of many women: to give birth with a minimum of medical intervention. Birth centres have been set up to feel more like home, with the added safety of a hospital labour ward next door. The modern obstetrician is usually understanding as well as highly skilled. Part of labour can often be carried out at home, but the risk of maternal haemorrhage and the possible need for quick resuscitation of the baby make a medically supervised delivery the wisest option.

A shared experience: the male role

The biggest alteration in male behaviour in recent years has been an enormous increase in interest and involvement by men in the birth process. A passage out of Charles Dickens's *Martin Chuzzlewit* epitomises the old-style father-to-be: 'he went and stopped his ears in an empty dog kennel and never took his hands away nor came out until he was shown the baby'. We have to remember that birth then could be nothing short of horrific. The local midwife might be unskilled and ignorant; faced with a hopeless situation she might have to perform a bloodthirsty operation like crushing the skull of a fetus to get it out. No wonder husbands were squeamish!

Over past centuries males have either absented themselves from the birth process or were excluded by women. This seems to have been the case all over the world and as far back in human history as we can trace. In a study of fifty-eight primitive cultures, the anthropologist Ford found male partners were usually relegated to the background when labour started, although women giving birth might be ostracised instead by the men or by religious taboo. Sometimes women were deemed unclean for some weeks after the event. However, women were never left alone: they were tended by their own sex. In Samoa it was found that women who were barren were allowed to be midwives to compensate them for their loss. If a woman had a baby on her own by accident, she was gossiped about and branded as feckless, rather like the woman today who inadvertently gives birth in a toilet or a taxi and makes headlines in the local newspaper.

Ford found that about a third of the cultures surveyed practised the *couvade*, a custom in which the father vicariously shares his wife's discomforts, morning sickness, baby's kicks or labour pain. The *couvade* is thought to have survival value in locking the father, potentially a free agent, onto his child. In modern society it is fascinating to see fathers-to-be begin with a rather cavalier attitude after the initial euphoria of 'I'm going to be a father!' Then, at antenatal classes and films, it begins to dawn on them what a wonderful process they have started off. Practical help that men are taught to give for labour brings out the male protectiveness which will quickly extend to the child. They learn touch relaxation (see page 47), assisting with movement and positions. They learn about the changing patterns of labour, and how to guide their women when they are too tired to initiate the response themselves. Verbal encouragement for all labour stages is greatly appreciated.

It is always the hope of society and of the couple themselves that the exhilarating experience of shared childbirth and its emotional closeness will bind the two protagonists together forever. Unfortunately, in the modern world, there seem to be too many other separating influences. If general statistics are any guide, this new practice of sharing the delights of birth which has such potential for good, does not prevent future marriage break-ups. Paradoxically, a couple may be more likely to stay together if they have to cope with a tragedy. When there is a stillbirth, or the baby survives only a short time, the father usually rises magnificently to the challenge of building up morale. Some physiotherapists include in the class programme a section on acting out such a scene, the rationale being that if it happens it won't be such a shock. My feeling is that it always *is* a shock, and there is no need to add to people's fears. If anyone asks about perinatal death, which they often do, they should be answered honestly. But to dwell on the negative side of birth seems morbid.

The men who attend classes appear to take their partner's worries very seriously, often raising them when the woman has been more reticent. This shows how much positive good antenatal classes can do in producing a climate where man and woman can encourage each other. For this sort of interchange to happen, class sizes need to be kept small so that all the couples get to know each other. No one is going to ask questions or make comments about intimate subjects in a large group.

Taking on responsibility for another person is a sign of maturity. For men, just as much as for women, having a child is a commitment to take care of that child. Many men are anxious to make this commitment and are rewarded by being part of the joy of child development.

The female pelvis

Human labour which culminates in vaginal birth is a complicated exercise in mechanics. Without being dogmatic about why some women can give birth through the pelvis and some can't, it is interesting to investigate what is known about female and fetal physique, as their interaction decides whether a birth will be easy, difficult or impossible.

The female pelvis has evolved differently from that of the male so that it is capacious enough to allow a mature fetus to pass through it unharmed. Stone age artists seem to have observed this, judging by their votive figures depicting pregnant women. These figures have large breasts and wide hips, the ideal gynaecoid pelvis. Shaped like a basin, this type of pelvis is wide from side to side at the top or inlet, and long from front to back at the bottom or the outlet. The fetus has to corkscrew through, normally leading with the crown of the head, chin on chest, and rotating inwards to appear at the outlet with its face towards the mother's backbone. This is the best way to negotiate the pelvic basin, which is also curved forwards, as if the basin were tipped slightly on its side.

This rather complex arrangement for birth is due to two evolutionary factors: the development of an upright posture, and the large size of the human skull at birth (due to brain size). Anthropologists now think that the precursors of humans, the australopithecines, walked upright several million years ago. Many bones have been found with the typical upright pelvis which supports the weight of the trunk and allows easy bipedal walking. Skulls also show that the head was erect because the large hole for the spinal cord, the foramen magnum, is placed horizontally (not vertically as it is in animals on all fours). Precisely when or how the female pelvis became differentiated from the male is not known, although very ancient female pelves have been found which strongly resemble the male form.

The most suitable pelvis for birth has a wide, curved, Norman-style pubic arch, whereas the male pelvis is pointed or Gothic shaped.

Another unusual feature in the human female is that the vagina curves forward, following the pelvic curve. In other large mammals the vagina tends to be straight.

Not all female pelves are of the ideal, or gynaecoid, type. Some women have a male-like pelvis which is roughly heart-shaped with less usable space for the fetus in the posterior half. Other pelves are anthropoid (ape-like), being long from front to back at the inlet. A few are flattened and very narrow from front to back. Considering that human beings are wanderers about the globe, it is not surprising that there are many types of pelvis. The gynaecoid type is common among Europeans and Asians, though the latter are lighter boned. Africans have the anthropoid type, with a long oval from front to back. Some individual shapes make vaginal birth simply unworkable. Others cause long, painful labours which may succeed eventually with a certain amount of medical help. If obstructed labour occurs among primitive people it may result in rupture of the uterus, which is often fatal for both mother and baby. If vaginal birth is finally achieved it may result in irreparable damage to the cervix or vagina or nerve damage leading to bladder problems or partial paralysis. A primitive tribal or simple village life is no guarantee of a painless, trouble-free labour.

Because of the complex contours involved in the process of fitting the fetal head to the maternal pelvis, the issue is not whether the head will go through, but which way it will go through. If the head is turned the wrong way, or is not sufficiently flexed forward, there is a risk not only of a tight fit but of a wrong fit. Both tight fit and wrong fit are liable to produce greater pain and more delivery problems.

Good musculature is a factor in pushing a baby through the pelvic canal but it obviously cannot achieve the impossible if the bony proportions are mechanically problematical. The pelvic floor muscles form a gutter which can guide the fetal head into successful rotation. An Australian researcher who specialises in gynaecological anatomy has found that the Asian type of pelvis has a well-shaped pelvic floor with a large area of muscle attached to bone and a good depth and thickness to the muscle, on the whole more efficient than its European counterpart. The modern practice of working the pelvic floor muscles in pregnancy is beneficial for supporting pelvic organs and may also help rotate the fetal head into the most favourable birth position.

Effective pushing is achieved by good muscles, quick reflexes and mobile joints so that the upper trunk can fold around the uterus, increasing the uterine effort to widen the outlet to its utmost limit.

The fetus

In many mammals the position of the young within the uterus is immaterial and often there are multiple young. In the human womb there is usually only one fetus. By about eight months the baby has turned head-down. The head is the largest part of a human baby and the best portion of the anatomy to prise open the cervix. The only other candidate is the baby's bottom or breech (resulting in a breech birth). When a human fetus reaches full term, it is considerably heavier than the young of large primates. Its brain is three times as large and still growing, and the labour is usually longer. The gestation period in the human is not very different from the ape, perhaps because the pelvis could scarcely cope with much extra weight or a larger growth of head. Consequently the human new-born is not as well developed as other animal young and is very dependent on its mother or other adults for quite a long period.

A baby's brain grows until the age of about two, which is allowed for by the slow union of the cranial bones making up the skull. Some separation of skull bones can be seen at the front fontanelle, a soft, pulsating spot on top of a baby's head. Fetal cranial bones can to some extent mould to the mother's pelvic contours. Sometimes the moulding can be very obvious and a baby's head is egg-shaped at birth and often has additional lumps and bumps on it, depending on how the head has come through the pelvis. Moulding usually subsides quickly and the head resumes normal shape in a day or two.

It is possible that Neanderthal people (an ancient branch of ape-like beings who lived in Europe about 200,000 years ago) died out because their young had large and rather rigid skulls, making birth extremely difficult. Their human 'cousins' developed a head that is more versatile. The front part of the brain, considered the seat of intelligence, has enlarged to replace the receding forehead of earlier forms, giving the head a domed appearance. This is why the fetus needs to tuck the head in at birth, presenting a smaller circumference, the crown, to the birth outlet.

Breathing for labour

If you are expecting a baby, preparations for the big day will include learning labour techniques, such as relaxation and breathing, which can turn an ordeal into a labour of love. Women are no longer required to remain in bed for the duration of labour. You can sit, stand, walk, kneel, rock, lie down (though not flat on your back) or curl up in a ball. Upright positions are good to start with. They help 'drive' the baby downwards. But the bed is there, and you should never feel that it is wrong to lie on it if you are tiring.

Painless births can occur under hypnosis, but results depend on your response to the hypnotherapist. Usually there is no memory of events afterwards, which is a pity because many women like to recall the high points of birth. Relaxation and breathing techniques (see pages 44–49) will help you remain awake and aware.

Women beginning antenatal classes often say, 'I want to learn the breathing', as though it were a magic formula, the open sesame of the cervical portal. Any breathing pattern *not* based on relaxation is more or less doomed to failure and some antenatal educators would go so far as to say that, if relaxation is properly learned, breathing can be left to the whim of the moment, or rather the demands of the particular contraction. This can work for some women in some labours. However, trained breathing can still follow the dictates of labour, tuning in to contraction after contraction. You will learn to be aware of movements of your diaphragm and ribs and become adept at flowing from one level of breathing to the next. You may even know where you are in labour by the breathing level you instinctively seek, whereas without training instincts can be misleading. Any new physical skill needs practice, whether it be sport or giving birth, and it is no help to the novice to be thrown in at the deep end.

Breathing can be used with different emphasis at different rates and depths. The subconscious nervous system is a past master at changing rate and depth to suit any activity or lack of activity.

Diaphragm breathing

The diaphragm is a dome-shaped muscle acting as a partition between the abdomen and the chest. It is involved in every breath we take, providing it is not paralysed. Emphasis on using your diaphragm brings on deep breathing. It becomes convex like the dome of a mosque when you breathe out, and flattens downwards when you breathe in. By late pregnancy the diaphragm will press on the top of the uterus (the fundus) if a reasonably deep breath is taken. If the cervix has softened and labour is under way, this pressure is useful, gently pressing the fetus's head against the cervix. Pressure of the presenting part of the fetus against the cervix releases more of the stimulating hormones which tell the uterus to contract more firmly (a feedback mechanism). By aiding relaxation diaphragmatic breathing helps to add momentum to the labour.

If the diaphragm is used correctly the upper abdomen (the midriff area) will rise and fall, but not the chest. Some women will be comfortable when they breathe slowly, even to the extent of only four to six breaths per minute. It is very difficult to feel nervous for long while doing deep slow breathing. Of course, some people's nervousness moves with them in every situation like a second skin but, if you combine deep breathing with the technique of word repetition, eventually the rhythm will take over and bestow its beneficial effect. Repetition can be monotonous, but the rewards are worth the trouble and, if carried out conscientiously, each practice session will make it easier to achieve a deeper state of calm (see page 47).

During early labour, when the contractions are niggly but not really painful, diaphragm breathing is comfortable and practical. There is no need to continue it in the rest periods between contractions. That is a time to forget about breathing and let nature take over the rate and depth of your breathing.

Rib (mid-chest) breathing

When you concentrate on fully expanding the diaphragm, there is a tendency to 'go to the limit' in breathing in, followed by a gentle release and a definite pause before the next breath. As the uterus becomes firm to hard and rock-like in a contraction, diaphragm breathing may feel uncomfortable. When this happens the easy solution is to abandon it and move to the mid-chest, a slightly higher level of breathing with a different emphasis.

The body doesn't seem to require a full breath in this area, yet mid-chest, or rib breathing, is equally relaxing. Each person develops a rate and depth to suit the level of the contraction, which can be quite variable. In contrast to your earlier piston-like diaphragm breathing, mid-chest breathing involves a flaring, lateral movement of the ribs, so that the lower ribs act like a bucket handle, moving up and out in an arc. You can achieve deep breathing if desired, or shallow breathing.

When practising the mid-chest level of breathing, it is important to recognise that the depth of the breath is a personal choice, so is the rest or pause between breaths. The deeper the breath, the longer the rest period. In other words, depth affects rate.

If labour is progressing fast, you might use mid-chest breathing for only a short time, if at all. This is not an excuse to leave it out of your practice programme. The mid-chest level of breathing is probably the closest to physiological at-rest breathing. Breathing at this level therefore feels natural, and is not hard to learn.

Upper chest breathing

The relaxed uterus is shaped like an upside-down pear but it becomes harder and rounder when it is contracting in strong labour. Women who have not been trained tend to pant when the contractions become really painful because they instinctively feel that the tight uterus needs room to contract without having to submit to too much pressure from respiratory movements.

To prevent chaotic fast breathing it is an advantage to learn to use the upper chest. Upper chest breathing expands the top five or six ribs upwards, reducing interference with the now very tight uterus. You can vary the depth and rate of this breathing to suit your needs.

Upper chest breathing technique is not as easy to learn as diaphragm or mid-chest breathing. You should start with a short up-and-down movement of the upper ribs, taking and releasing a few shallow breaths on the words 'in-out'. Elastic recoil on the 'out' breath allows the chest to subside back to a neutral position. This breathing is easier to learn using the mouth. Later, nose breathing can be substituted to prevent dryness of the lips, although the urgency of the contractions often encourages mouth breathing in spite of the drying effect. There should be a slight pause after each breath so that the breathing is not 'in-out-in-out' but 'in-out-rest-in-out-rest'. The rest period is very short, but if it is not there, nature will have no time to normalise the blood gases which may alter to the point of discomfort. People who stress the 'out' breath too much will be inclined to hyper-ventilate. Physiotherapists sometimes suggest that the breath be 'sighed' out, which is a relatively slow action.

Some women are naturally good at distinguishing between levels of breathing. Others fail to see much difference. There is no need to be too purist or perfectionist about it. The diaphragm is pro-grammed to work in every breath, so that when you are using the upper chest a beat can also be detected at midriff level. Those who can't distinguish area change will generally be able to understand rate change, depth change and the general principles of 'lighter', 'higher' and 'shallower' as the contraction increases in intensity. In any case, rhythm is probably far more important than which area of the chest moves.

Lung activity follows chest activity so that there is likely to be a greater oxygen exchange when deeper breathing is used. However, upper chest breathing for labour is not harmful, provided it doesn't cause hyperventilation. Trained breathing in labour is an on-off process, carried out only during a contraction, which will occupy at most a minute to a minute and a half. After that there is a rest period when breathing rhythm returns to normal. Labour is not something that is likely to happen more than a few times in a lifetime; but upper chest breathing will help you tolerate any pelvic or abdominal pain.

Hyperventilation

Hyperventilation occurs when the carbon dioxide in the blood falls below a critical level. It is also known as carbon dioxide wash-out. Normally the dissolved carbon dioxide gas in the blood keeps a balance between acidity and alkalinity. When this balance, known as the pH, goes up there is a shortage of carbon dioxide, the blood becomes more alkaline and this state is registered in the brain. Symptoms of over-breathing then make themselves felt: everyone knows the sensation of giddiness that comes from blowing up too many balloons. In labour, giddiness is usually the first symptom, followed by pins and needles or numbness in the face or hands. There can also be faintness or nausea. These unpleasant symptoms act as a warning from the brain that all is not well with the blood gases. The remedy, as in the case of blowing up balloons, is simple: rest for a while and nature will redress the balance. If hyperventilation develops during a contraction, there is a quick way of raising the carbon dioxide level—by breathing into cupped hands. The carbon dioxide lack is made up by temporarily breathing back your own breathed-out air. But this quick cure has only a short-term effect; it doesn't attack the cause. You can avoid hyperventilation by obeying the body's dictates on pauses between breaths.

No matter which level of breathing is used, the components are: a breath in, a breath out and an appropriate pause before the next breath. When breathing is deep and slow, the pause is quite long. When breathing is shallow and rapid, the pause can be very short. In normal activities such as walking, running and speaking, nature looks after breathing by automatically adjusting to the activity. If more difficult activities are attempted, for example swimming or singing, breathing may have to be trained. The same can be said for labour. Labour may well be a difficult activity where no real experience can be gained before the actual event. This is why it lends itself to hyperventilation. Training in breathing rhythms appropriate to the level used will lessen the possibility of hyperventilation, which often happens when you're trying too hard.

If you are having strong, painful contractions, your body may wish to react with shallow breathing which is, of necessity, fairly fast. In this case look to your rhythm of breathing, count (or hear it counted for you by your partner) 'and one, and two, and three', and take each breath *when* it is needed and not *before* it is needed.

Transition

The changeover period between first and second stage, or the passage of the presenting part through the cervix, is considered a turning point in labour. Technically speaking, transition is when there is one centimetre of cervix still to open at the front, but the baby's head (or breech) has actually entered the vagina at the back. This often causes a desire to push, because of that pressure on the vagina. The pushing urge is strongest at the peak of contractions when the uterus is pressing the head down most firmly, and it can feel exactly like an urge to go to the toilet to empty the bowel. But it is really pressure from the baby, the 'I'm here!' signal. Labour ward staff may tell you not to push because there is a 'rim' of cervix at the front rather like a crescent moon which is preventing the baby from full access to the vagina.

A satisfactory breathing technique to deal with this situation is one which will divert the pushing urges temporarily until the cervix is fully open and at the same time keep you in control of the process. Transition is often quite short—twenty minutes or so, although it can take an hour or more. You will be so pleased to have reached this encouraging point in your labour that you won't mind putting up with a few extra discomforts.

Physiotherapists generally teach 'panting and blowing' for use at transition and many midwives are conversant with this excellent pattern of breathing which so exactly fits the situation. It is satisfying both physically and psychologically, having a rhythm and sequence that usually prevents hyperventilation and can be used at any speed. You can begin slowly, 'in-out-in-out-in-blow', and accelerate like a steam train gathering speed and slow as the end of the contraction is reached. The right rest period between sequences tends to be inserted automatically, depending on the overall speed, and this is the secret of preventing hyperventilation. It must be remembered that the actual sequence is 'in-out-in-out-in-blow', not 'in-in-blow'.

A transition examination may reveal a rim of cervix in front which is quite thick, or thin and pliable and easy for the midwife to push back out of the way. If the latter is the case, you will be ready to push. Sometimes the midwife, knowing that the cervix is very nearly open, may be able to allow pushing when the push urge asserts itself, although there is some evidence that the head rotates more easily if it is allowed to descend to the pelvic floor without pushing. The midwife may actually be able to see the baby's head in the vagina or her gloved fingers encounter the head. It may be a little uncomfortable as the midwife tries to determine which way the head is lying, so that she knows where the face is and how flexed the head is on the neck.

If you are in transition, yet have no urge to push, don't be discouraged. An epidural (see page 53) might have numbed the sensation of pushing and delayed rotation of the fetal head; or the fetal head might not be pressing firmly enough on the back wall of the vagina to produce the urge signal. No push urge at this time suggests that the head has not begun to rotate or has not descended into the vagina where the pelvic floor muscles form a gutter which helps to rotate the baby.

Sitting upright allows gravity to act on the baby to bring it through the cervix. Relaxing the pelvic floor is very important. You may also wish to change to transition breathing (panting and blowing). It can be psychologically encouraging to use this breathing, which is suggestive of progress. Alternatively you can use the oxygen mask (see page 54).

A full bladder can impede progress at transition. If it remains distended while the baby is being pushed past, the bladder might be bruised. Emptying the bladder at this late stage of labour is not easy because the position of the baby's head tends to close off the urethra. However, a soft catheter, a thin flexible plastic tube, can be pushed painlessly up into the bladder to siphon off the urine. The whole operation takes only a minute. There is no real discomfort.

A quick crossing from transition to second stage without problems is desirable and not uncommon, particularly for women having a second or subsequent child. To your joy, the midwife pronounces the cervix open and you may begin pushing. However, the baby sometimes moves very fast down the vagina and may pop out, tearing tissue in the process. In this case you may be asked to employ delaying tactics, such as panting, which will usually forestall a strong pushing urge, if only for a short time.

The best kind of panting for this purpose is a repetitive 'in-blow-in-blow-in-blow', taking very shallow breaths and blowing out in a short, sharp action. The cheeks can be used to blow like those cherubs that blow the winds on old maps. If this is done fairly fast, it will prevent tearing and allow a smoother birth, which is of benefit to the baby as well as the mother.

In the short term 'blowing-panting' should not cause hyperventilation, as it is seldom needed for more than a few contractions. What is more, the contractions themselves have become shorter (30–40 seconds) and the rest periods between contractions have lengthened. During late first stage it was the other way around. The contractions could last up to a minute and a half and the rest period be cut to a minute or less. When the cervix is fully opened there is often a lull in contractions and then the timing balance changes. (Many text books say that all strong contractions, both first and second stage, last 60–90 seconds but their authors cannot have spent many hours in a labour ward timing contractions!)

Some women have great difficulty preventing pushing at this time. The push urge can be an overwhelming bodily sensation, very compelling and immediate. Even if you have practised the anti-pushing panting, there is a tendency to say, 'I've just got to push!' Speech at this vital moment is not advised! The only way to stay in control of the situation is to continue non-stop panting until the contraction (which is really very short) is over. You will not only be pleased with yourself, you will win the praise of those around you! Control is in the breathing. It is not a holding back with the muscles of the pelvic floor. The pelvic floor or perineum, the skin and muscle behind the vagina, must be allowed to stretch, and these short blows give it time for that stretching.

Second stage—birth

Imagine a circle at cervix level large enough to allow passage for the baby's head. The cervix is open when it is no longer palpable, having become one with the wall of the uterus. In a pushing contraction, the upper two-thirds of the uterus contracts while the lower third and the vagina stretch. The mechanics of pushing involve the presenting part (usually the head) navigating a curve in the bone structure of the pelvis known as the curve of Carus. While this is happening the vulval opening stretches, the coccyx moves back and the vagina itself is stretched to capacity. The vagina is concertina-like, full of folds which can open, usually painlessly, as the baby is pushed from the uterus to the outside world.

If you look at the bony pelvic outlet in antenatal classes, you can see the pubic arch, the bones you sit on and the sacrum and coccyx (tailbone) forming a bony ring and you will be reassured that there really is room! Still, there is an enormous stretch of the soft tissues. A 'panic stretch reaction' or 'Chinese burn' sensation may be experienced if the baby comes out so quickly that there is no time for natural numbing to occur. Given time, the doctor or midwife will numb the vulval area with local analgesic and there will be no feeling of stretching. Whatever happens, try to keep the pelvic floor relaxed. This is not as difficult as it sounds. It is much easier to relax the pelvic floor than to contract it while actually pushing.

A good position for pushing is comfortable upright sitting with knees as wide apart as they will go, feet planted firmly and hands under your upper thighs so that you can use your arms in the pushing effort. Or you might prefer to squat, kneel upright, or rest on all fours (though this last position does not have the same good gravity effect and the baby will come out behind you, so you will not *see* the birth). Squatting and upright kneeling are mechanically excellent but in these positions it is more difficult for a doctor or a midwife to intervene if the need arises. Your arm and neck muscles help you push, fixing your ribs so that the main muscle, the diaphragm, has a firm base to work from. Knees held apart helps with the leverage, particularly as the head or breech begins to 'crown', that is, appear at the vaginal opening.

In second stage the push urge lasts for the whole contraction. As it starts to build up you should take a quick deep breath through the mouth for bearing down. Then hold your breath while you push. Each hold lasts up to ten seconds. If you prefer, you can hiss out 'sh-sh-sh' as you push.

Women who have no push urge in second stage need help from a midwife, who places her hand on the abdomen and gives the signal to push when the uterus contracts. Epidurals are the main reason for lack of push urge. The epidural does not prevent pushing; it merely means there is no sensation of pushing if the epidural is still operating.

Don't hold your breath for too long because this might temporarily reduce the baby's oxygen supply. On the other hand, you must be able to make an impression on the baby's movement down the birth canal. An obstetrician may be more inclined to use forceps if the mother doesn't make progress with her pushing. It is very tempting to help a baby out when the head recedes and the baby loses as much *between* contractions as it has gained *during* contractions. There is a happy medium, which you will find for yourself, between long breath holding and short inefficient pushes.

Delivery

It is very satisfying if you can push the head out to about ear level yourself. You then pant ('in-blow-in-blow') while the neck is born; the head 'restitutes', that is, turns back to where it was before it rotated (being now free of the pelvis), and the body is born. Sometimes the doctor will ask for a small push for the shoulders, but often that is not necessary. Panting for delivery is usually only for a few seconds, unless the umbilical cord is around the neck. This is not an unusual or alarming situation, but it does help if you can pant briefly instead of pushing while the doctor untangles it. Use 'in-blow-in-blow'.

Episiotomy

An episiotomy is a small cut made to the perineum to ensure more room, to prevent tearing and overstretching of the vagina and to let a baby out quickly. The practice is very old, having been documented in Indian literature from 1500 BC. Many deliveries need this incision which is later stitched.

Ask your doctor about episiotomy and the answer will often be that, between you, you will try to avoid one. Some women like to prepare for the stretch of the vulva by stretching the opening with their thumbs before labour. A little KY® gel will help to lubricate the area. The bridge of tissue that separates the vulva from the anus should be stretched downwards.

Forceps

The Romans undoubtedly used forceps for freeing the fetus as there are friezes showing a crude instrument of this type. But a rather fearsome device called the crochet, a kind of hook, became more popular. Forceps that fitted the fetal head and did not damage the mother unduly were invented by the Chamberlen family in England in 1588 but kept secret and used only by successive Chamberlens for four generations. Princess Charlotte, daughter of the notorious Prince Regent and heir to the throne of England, lost her life after a twenty-four-hour second stage. Her son died too, although he was reputed to be strong and healthy. The obstetrician would not use forceps. Realising his mistake afterwards, he shot himself out of remorse.

Today forceps might be used to aid delivery if you can't push the baby right out by yourself or if your baby's heartbeat indicates that he or she is suffering a lack of oxygen. Another reason for using forceps is to turn the baby's head into the right position so that you can push it out. A lift-out is a *low* forceps delivery, whereas turning usually requires a forceps rotation or *mid*-forceps delivery. Differently shaped forceps are used for these two types of delivery due to the different situations. High forceps, which drag the baby down from cervix level, are no longer used. A baby can sometimes be brought down from cervix level with a vacuum extractor, a kind of suction device that fits on the baby's head. However, it may be decided that a caesarean is the safer course if the baby is hard to reach.

Breech and twin labours

In breech or twin labours, the cervix still has to dilate. There will still be some sort of transition or cross-over period. For a breech birth there is often quite a bit of pushing to do, particularly if it is a first baby. It is a great help if you push well until the breech appears. Then the doctor can help extract the arms and legs. He turns the body so that the baby is face-down and forceps are used to protect the head coming afterwards. Sometimes the doctor will ask for a brief period of panting while the head descends into the pelvis. If you have a breech position for your first baby, a caesarean might be considered. In any case the obstetrician will be sure to order an ultrasound scan so that he can look in detail at the baby's position, its head size and the capacity of your pelvis.

Twin births are often quite easy. There are two small babies in the womb instead of one large one and the first twin opens the cervix. It is interesting that the second twin has no moulding of the head as the 'door' has been pushed open by the first twin. The babies may be in almost any position: both heads down and anterior, both posterior; one breech, one head down; both breech, and various other combinations. A scan will be done to sort it all out. Most twins are born vaginally, although triplets and quads are usually not because the babies are likely to be small and immature. A caesarean could be the only way of saving them.

Caesarean section

There are, of course, reasons for having a caesarean section other than for breech or multiple births. The main ones are:

- disproportion, where the baby is too big for the mother or in an awkward position
- an emergency situation for the mother, such as eclampsia (fits) due to sudden high blood pressure
- an emergency situation for the baby, such as erratic heartbeat due to lack of oxygen (fetal distress)
- cord prolapse, where the cord comes down the vagina before the baby
- placenta praevia, where the placenta comes first, before the baby, thereby endangering the baby's blood supply
- separation of the placenta from the uterine wall before the baby is born
- the baby is very small (including multiple births)
- the mother has a medical condition incompatible with vaginal birth (for example, vaginal herpes).

A caesarean birth may be elective (decided on and carried out before labour starts) or it may become a necessity during the course of labour. If the caesarean has to be performed as an emergency, a general anaesthetic is often administered, but if it is elective or if there is no special hurry when the situation has arisen during labour, an epidural can be given.

Preparation for this kind of birth can be supplied by the physiotherapist. In fact many of the techniques taught in classes will still
be useful if a caesarean is the option chosen late in pregnancy or
during labour. If the caesarean is an elective one, you may well be a
little nervous. Relaxation and slow breathing will help you to keep
calm. These techniques are useful as a tranquillising injection is seldom given because extra analgesic drugs might harm the baby.

Most caesareans take place before the transition period. However, there are a few women who actually begin to push, then, due
to a tight outlet or malpositioning, find it impossible to deliver the
baby vaginally. Having a caesarean after starting to push is fairly rare,
which is fortunate as it must be disappointing to do all that work
and then miss the final act!

The newborn

The average newborn is a tough little creature but he or she must be
kept warm after leaving the tropical waters of the uterus. It was
understood very early in the history of human birth that cold had a
drastic effect on the newborn. Unwanted babies were exposed and
left to die of cold. Swaddling was used by the ancient Egyptians and
continued until relatively recently. Australian Aboriginal babies
were once smeared with ash and goanna fat. Both practices were to
retain warmth, though swaddling was also thought to straighten the
limbs after being flexed in the uterus. Incubators with an envelope
of hot water under or round the bedding were designed more than
a hundred years ago.

Premature babies are more susceptible to cold than full-term
babies because they have little or no 'brown' fat, fat that can be simply
converted into energy. Today they may be wrapped in cellophane to
conserve as much heat as possible. The lungs in the premature infant
respond less readily because they are less expansile. A slippery substance (surfactant) is secreted into the lung fluid during the final
weeks of pregnancy and this helps the lungs to overcome surface tension and therefore to expand. Women who are likely to give birth to a
premature baby may be given an injection of a drug which stimulates
surfactant production and helps to produce the right conditions for
breathing in the baby's lungs. Premature babies under 30 weeks may
need to be placed on a ventilator to help them breathe normally.

Breathing

There is an exquisite timing in physical mechanisms which contributes to causing the first breath, and this usually ends in a cry. The chest wall is squeezed, compressing the lungs. Then the chest is released as the body is born. The ribs expand, a vacuum is created and air rushes in. Before birth there is fluid in the lungs, some of which is expelled by compression and elastic recoil and some of which is gradually absorbed. At the same time the baby is experiencing a lowering of oxygen and a rise of carbon dioxide; the blood becomes more acid and this stimulates the respiratory centre in the brain. External stimulation tends to trigger breathing: noise, light, initial heat loss and sucking out of mucus from the breathing passages.

In the fifteenth century an Italian, Bagellardo, noted that babies could be stimulated to breathe by having their faces blown on. The kiss of life is older than we might imagine. Babylonians swung asphyxiated newborns in a specially constructed swing, while Scythians dropped them into icy cold water as a test of endurance! In some cultures alcoholic stimulants were administered.

It is realised now that if a baby is very slow to take the first breath, the brain may suffer an oxygen lack and brain cells may die. Every effort must be made to make sure this does not happen. A tube can be passed into the baby's trachea through which oxygen is administered at the right pressure. All labour wards have this type of resuscitation gear and a heating element to keep the baby warm. Although breathing into or blowing onto the baby might have the effect of triggering respiration, this is not certain. If the baby doesn't breathe, oxygen is needed.

After the first gasp, most babies give a spontaneous cry. However, if the baby has been intubated because breathing has not started, the tube will prevent crying. The mother will be reassured that her baby *is* breathing, though she can hear no noise. The majority of newborns breathe spontaneously and this is followed by a lusty yell as the air is expelled.

Cutting the cord

The cord is clamped and then cut. As an added precaution the baby is given an injection of vitamin K (konakion) to aid clotting. Modern practice is to lift the newborn straight up to the mother even before the cord is cut. The mother supplies warmth from her body and hands for a few minutes before baby has to be wrapped. Some people believe that it is a good idea to wait until the cord stops pulsating before cutting it. This actually happens quite quickly because cold affects the cord. If a mother is Rh negative, the cord is cut quickly to limit the potential effect of jaundice-producing antibodies (see page 154). Otherwise it probably doesn't matter just when the cord is cut.

Apgar score

The nursing staff are trained to note five points about the baby within a minute of birth. This is called the Apgar score. It is repeated again five minutes after birth. Two points are given for each of the following five categories: heart rate; respiration; muscle tone (whether baby is normally active or flabby); reflex irritability, such as a cry or a grimace; and colour. Babies who score less than seven need to be watched and lower scores will be accompanied by obvious signs of needing resuscitation, but most babies score seven or over and rise to ten in a short time.

Cot position

Newborns used to be placed in the cot with the head slanting down, mimicking the position in the uterus. This is now considered undesirable. Moulding of the skull usually occurs during labour and is accompanied by some swelling of brain tissue. Newborn babies are now slanted the other way to relieve the pressure inside the head. Their heads are generally cowled for extra warmth for the first few hours. Some babies have a soft swelling lying over one of the skull bones. This is known as a haematoma, a collection of blood which has been trapped under the covering membrane of the bone, and is due to pressure build-up during the birth process. It looks ominous but it is not dangerous and will disappear in a day or two.

Observation

It has been suggested that labour is an ordeal for the baby. Contractions certainly do affect the fetus's heart rate, which is an outward sign of shortage of oxygen. However, normal monitor tracings show that the baby quickly recovers as long as the initial handling is gentle. The baby usually sleeps for a while, then there is often a wakeful period. It is a good idea for baby to be observed by trained staff at this time (usually in the nursery) so that any small problems can be treated. Some babies are 'mucusy', or they grunt, indicating that they are still a little short of oxygen.

Baby then may sleep for another two hours or so. After this the nappy is often wet, showing that the kidneys and bladder systems are functioning. Boiled water is given to check the swallowing reflex and to make sure there is not a 'blind gut', a food tube that does not reach the stomach in one piece but ends in a blind sac. The anus must be checked too, to see if it is open; and rectal temperature is taken. The face is washed free of mucus, vernix and blood (which may have come from a graze or cut received by the mother) and later on the baby is bathed. (Bathing used to be carried out immediately but now it is postponed, allowing the baby time to rest after birth.)

Patent ductus

Blood circulation in the unborn is different from circulation after birth because the baby in *utero* is not breathing. The fetus picks up oxygen not from the lungs but from the placenta via the umbilical cord. A short tube called a ductus, which has allowed blood to pass from the aorta to the pulmonary artery during intra-uterine life, must close off at birth. Otherwise the lung circulation will be compromised by diverting into the general circulation with consequent deficit of oxygen. The tube normally seals automatically but a few babies are left with a 'patent ductus' which causes inefficient blood circulation. (Badly affected babies were known in the past as 'blue babies'.) Nowadays they are operated on to correct the defect and this is being done much earlier than previously, usually in the first year. Paediatric surgeons are highly skilled at working on tiny organs and there is obvious benefit to the child to have the operation as soon as practicable, to restore normal circulation and therefore normal growth.

Overdue birth

Overdue babies progressively lose the greasy protective covering that they wear in the uterus, known as vernix. When born their skin looks dry, red and cracked. Skin cells flake off and may be ingested into the lungs. Also, the placenta becomes less efficient as it ages. It is then less able to purify the amniotic fluid of a greenish-black motion known as meconium that is passed from the bowel. It is quite normal for the baby to pass meconium in the uterus but it is not normal for meconium to remain in the fluid so that the baby is living in a dirty pond. Meconium is an irritating substance, particularly if it finds its way into the lungs. It is very sticky and sometimes stains the skin and nails of overdue babies. A newborn that has aspirated foreign matter such as meconium may contract pneumonia so the obstetrician keeps a watch on overdue pregnancies and might advise an induction of labour for the baby's sake.

Jaundice

Jaundice is quite common in newborn babies. Developing about the third day, it is due to immaturity of function of an enzyme in the liver. The baby becomes slightly yellowish. So-called physiological jaundice will usually disappear by the end of two weeks; but putting the newborn under an ultra-violet light has been found to speed recovery.

Another form of jaundice due to blood incompatibility is more serious. This is caused by a difference of blood grouping between mother and baby, making the baby's blood cells 'foreign' to its mother. She develops antibodies against these foreign cells which can then migrate back to the baby via the placenta and destroy some of the baby's red blood cells. It is now possible to prevent the mother from making these antibodies in many cases, but jaundice does still occur as a result of some blood incompatibilities. The severity of the jaundice can be measured by the amount of bile pigment (bilirubin) in the blood. If this becomes too high for safety, the baby can be given a transfusion in which his or her blood is exchanged for blood without the damaging factor.

Congenital problems

Congenital defects are those that have developed during pregnancy and are present at birth. They may involve some growth abnormality; for instance, pressure within the uterus sometimes causes foot deformities called talipes.

Modern results in correction of talipes are very good if the correction process is begun immediately following birth, when the tissues are very soft and malleable. Congenital dislocation of the hip is another condition which is reasonably easy to correct. Untreated, it leads to an ugly lurching walk. Babies are routinely examined at birth for 'clicky hips', a looseness of the hip joints which allows the head of the femur to ride up on the pelvis and partly come out of its socket. Placing the baby on its stomach helps to correct this. If there is a true congenital dislocation the baby will probably be put into a frog plaster with the legs bent up and rotated out like a frog's hind legs. When a good socket has formed, the plaster can be removed. Wry neck (torticollis) is another orthopaedic problem which usually corrects easily. It is caused by a short knotty muscle on one side of the neck pulling the head out of alignment, possibly caused by the fetus's position in the uterus (but other developmental factors may have been involved). Stretching the muscle as the baby grows corrects the condition, while ensuring that both sides of the face receive adequate blood circulation.

There are many other minor defects that can occur and most of them are simple to correct. However, as some are serious, all babies are thoroughly investigated at birth. A blood test called the Guthrie test is done by pricking the baby's heel to test for an enzyme deficiency which affects one child in several thousands. Some defects are obvious at birth, such as cleft palate or missing fingers or toes, whereas others can be discovered only by exhaustive tests.

Babies whose mothers are on toxic drugs such as cocaine run a great risk of suffering withdrawal symptoms (because they also are high on the drug). This can cause feeding difficulties, painful diarrhoea and incessant crying, which can last for months. A urine test in pregnancy identifies mothers who are at risk.

Movement tests

As well as bones and joints, the baby's movements and behaviour are observed as evidence of the brain's control of nerves and muscles. Through recognised tests paediatric specialists—doctors and physiotherapists—can diagnose neurological problems at birth instead of waiting till a baby fails to walk or talk, and treatment can begin earlier.

A good many of a new baby's actions are performed by reflex action. There is a very complex relationship between reflex action involving little actual thought and purposeful movement, and innovative action initiated by the higher centres of the brain. The learning process consists of laying down patterns in the brain. The brain chooses the behaviour most likely to be profitable to the individual; and much of this learned behaviour, particularly if it is repetitive, becomes reflex. As we have seen, some reflexes are innate, some are learned. A baby functions mainly at a reflex level but is wonderfully ready to store up memories and learn to cross reference them. The brain is growing, laying down nerve pathways, and a normal baby learns fast. Babies are born programmed with the ability to perform rudimentary movements that will enable them to acquire skills later on. Tests show how well a newborn can make grasping movements, crawling movements and walking movements. Many other tests involve eyes and ears, balance, alertness and co-ordination.

Neonatal physiotherapy

Working in neonatal nurseries is a fairly new area for physiotherapists. Babies who are chesty can be freed of mucus by vibrations and gentle percussion of the ribs, perhaps many times a day. Healthy infants are good at dealing with mucus whereas sick babies not only tend to make more but are too weak to clear their own airways. To catch pneumonia would be disastrous for a sick baby.

Orthopaedic problems are often treated by a physiotherapist as it is likely that tight tissues will need to be stretched, limbs positioned and exercised, and bandages or splints made. Parents can be shown home treatment which is just as important as treatment initiated in hospital. The physiotherapist will also work closely with the paediatrician if the baby has not passed all the neurological tests. Although there are variations in how early babies roll and crawl, talk and walk, it is possible to see by the tests which babies are likely to have learning difficulties and activity problems. The sooner the treatment is begun the better the result.

With good diagnosis and early practical management many of the orthopaedic and neurological disabilities that made life difficult for a child in the past are now totally compatible with a full and useful life.

Breast-feeding

Breast-feeding from birth is extremely valuable, the rich creamy colostrum that is secreted for two or three days before the milk being especially nourishing and potective. In the past, babies were quite often denied colostrum as it was thought harmful in some way and an older baby was brought in to suck it off. (It might seem extraordinary to us that people could watch domestic animals suckling from the moment of birth and not apply it to themselves. But perhaps it is not so odd when we remember that until the nineteenth century humans did not regard themselves as animals.) Often breast milk was not considered enough sustenance. In the book of *Isaiah*, 'butter and honey shall he eat' refers to the newborn, and other erstwhile authorities suggest sops of bread, baked apple and roast pork! Opium drops were sometimes given on a sponge to stop a baby crying, and if the mother was well off she could farm the

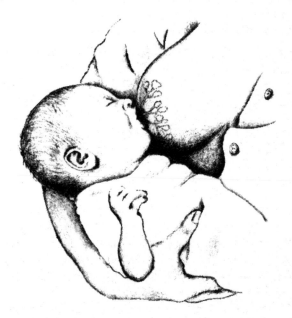

The baby takes the nipple and areola into the mouth

baby out to a wet nurse. There was a condition called overlaying, which referred to the suffocation of a baby enveloped in pendulous breast tissue by a comatose surrogate mother!

Breast-feeding has been scientifically proved to be superior to all other substitutes. Breast milk contains trace elements such as iron, zinc, copper, selenium, aluminium and titanium in comparable levels in women all over the world, whereas cow's milk has variable trace elements, fewer vitamins and is less digestible. Cow's milk gives less protection against disease and allergic reactions. It has been established now that if a baby is breast-fed adequately, no supplementary foodstuffs are necessary for six months.

Baby massage: bonding

Mothers instinctively caress and fondle their babies and this expression of love is almost as important to the child as food. Babies are quite discriminating and they differ in the kind of touching they prefer. Baby massage is a way to increase the sensory input to the brain. It should be pleasurable to the baby, the effect soothing. Many mothers will develop little exercises and games as well. Jittery babies often become quieter and more manageable after massage and babies with neuromuscular problems can increase their learning skills by the greater sensory stimulation it offers. There is no mystique about massage technique; in fact many mothers begin it by enfolding their child soon after birth and maintaining that closeness from then on.

Ward staff notice a mother who does not enfold her baby, who tentatively touches only with fingers, never using the whole hand. There may be reticence in accepting the baby, a psychological reluctance to bond. Although there is no need to worry if a relationship between mother and child takes a few days to develop, a lack of enfolding by the time they go home may point to future problems in the relationship. There is much to be said for teaching baby massage to mothers identified in this way. Once they begin to handle the baby with confidence, bonding follows. Instead of love inspiring handling, handling can inspire love; and firm but loving handling is every child's birthright.

The mother

No sooner is the challenge of labour over than another rapidly takes its place: the newly born personality wastes no time in making demands and letting mother know its likes and dislikes in a very forthright way. Perhaps the post-natal mother already has an idea of the character traits of her child from the way it behaved *in utero*. An active baby with long waking periods may continue to be lively and wakeful. Rather than trying to change what is innate, mothers would be better advised to learn about their baby so that mutual adjustment can take place. Babies are very adaptable, but mother is the adult and should set the pace.

The following two scenarios represent extreme post-natal situations, but are not too far from reality.

Scenario 1

The new mother has been to baby-care classes and has practised handling a neighbour's newborn—just holding and nappy change. She has read up on breast-feeding and knows she must make sure that her baby is really drinking, not just nibbling and making her sore. She also knows that squeezing drops of milk out and rubbing her nipple on baby's lips will make him open his mouth as he smells the rich colostrum. This mother asks the nursing staff *not* to give her baby complementary feeds so that baby always arrives hungry.

A female relative visits while she is feeding and it happens to be a time when baby is restless. The relative says she can't understand why women insist on breast-feeding when bottles are so handy and anyone can give them. The new mother feels angry and upset; it is day three, her breasts are tight and she is a little frazzled. She goes home on the fifth day, still breast-feeding. Baby doesn't settle that night, but each time he wakes she changes him, gives him a short top-up and firmly puts him down, telling him it is dark and everyone is supposed to be asleep (she understands that it was always dark in the uterus and baby needs to learn to associate darkness with sleep). For the next few days life is very up and down, but little by little baby learns how this household runs and begins to fit in with it. Fitting in is made easy for baby because both parents unanimously make it clear that they expect it.

Scenario 2

The new mother has never handled such a tiny baby before. She holds her new daughter like fragile china. Baby has a thin, piercing cry. She jiggles her head to try to find the nipple, misses and gets more and more agitated. With help, the new mother manages to attach baby tenuously to the nipple, which gets sorer by the minute. Next feed, baby seems completely uninterested and is not crying but half asleep, having filled up in the nursery. By day three the new mother has breasts like footballs. Staff suggest a nipple shield as baby finds it impossible to latch on and mother's nipples are cracked and bleeding. She feels inadequate, cries almost as often as baby does and is devastated when mother-in-law says she could have predicted this. She (mother-in-law) had *exactly* the same experience with baby's father. *He* wouldn't feed. She was told her milk was no good, too thin or something. She assures her daughter-in-law that she'd be better off giving up now. Doctor and staff are non-committal about it, leaving the new mother to make up her own mind. The last straw is when her husband sides with his mother! The new mother leaves hospital on the seventh day but finds bottle feeding doesn't stop baby crying for a large part of the night. In the daytime baby sleeps (sometimes), but after her bottle she regurgitates and clothes and bedclothes are beginning to smell. Baby's behaviour changes as the months pass, but not really for the better. She demands attention of one kind or another and the harassed parents do their very best to comply with what she seems to want, although sometimes this is difficult to determine.

The first two or three days, while the breasts are secreting colostrum and are not tight, afford a good opportunity for mother-baby co-operation in sucking expertise. The baby must be taken off the nipple gently (a finger in the mouth breaks the suction) if she or he is not taking the whole of the areola into the mouth. This prevents nipples from becoming really sore. Some babies have tremendous suction power, which can create soreness even when the feeding technique is correct. Also during this period the new mother can learn to relax (using skills taught in antenatal classes) which will encourage a let-down, making it easy for the baby to get milk. The uterus might contract as the baby feeds. This is because oxytocin, the hormone that causes the let-down reflex, also stimulates the uterus. After-pains are actually achy contractions which are seldom a worry to new mothers. After second and subsequent births they tend to be stronger and pain-killers might be needed. Presumably oxytocin is in greater supply the second or third time around. Experienced mothers do tend to have a better let-down reflex.

Three post-natal problem conditions, known as the three Bs, appear within days of or immediately following birth; they are sore breasts, a sore bottom and a sore back. When the new mother (or mother of two, three or more children) returns home, she is likely to be not only busy but subject to overtiredness, and any additional physical problem could be the last straw, so treatment in hospital is best.

Sore breasts

Post-natal breast problems follow four progressive stages:

- engorgement
- a blocked milk duct
- infection and inflammation (mastitis)
- a breast abscess.

New mothers may be disturbed by the feeling in the breasts when the milk is coming in. At that time breast nerves have heightened sensation. They are tingly, tender, distended. Many women find this sensation exquisitely pleasurable, but the few who are likely to be repelled by it react better if they are warned.

An engorged breast is congested and feels heavy, warm and painful. If the breasts become distended or the baby doesn't feed well on one breast, a blocked duct can result. The baby's mouth germs flow into the milk ducts during feeding. This does not matter so long as the ducts stay open, but a blocked duct gives germs a chance to multiply in the warm environment. A blocked duct feels lumpy and sometimes sore. It usually appears in one quadrant only but it may affect the whole breast.

Mastitis is an infection which often causes soreness and sometimes red streaks radiating from the infected area. Tender glands in the armpit can make it painful to raise the arm and there is often a generalised fluey feeling. Neglected mastitis can lead to an abscess of encapsulated pus, which might need to be surgically drained.

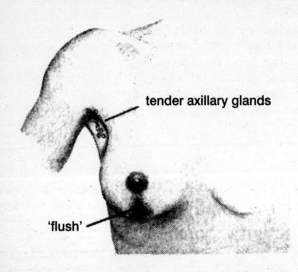

tender axillary glands

'flush'

Engorgement and blocked ducts can be successfully treated with ultrasound or IFT by a physiotherapist. Mastitis needs the same treatment; however, if you are running a temperature, antibiotics will be prescribed. Physiotherapy treatment should not cease until the breast has returned to normal. Drugs will neutralise the infection, but it is the treatment (and the baby) which normalises the ducts.

Sore bottom

A sore 'bottom' is usually the result of cutting or tearing while giving birth. Torn nerve endings can cause the pelvic floor muscle to lose tone (firmness) in the long term. Damage to the perineal area might take the form of significant bruising, a haematoma under the skin or a slow seepage of blood into the tissues. A very large episiotomy might have been necessary and many stitches inserted.

Problems such as these are bound to make the whole area tender. If not treated, discomfort can continue for two or three weeks. Time will bring healing, but meanwhile you will want to resume normal activities which include feeding a new baby. Sometimes sitting is painful, so the baby must be fed lying down, and this doesn't suit all babies.

Ultrasound helps a perineal problem of any significant magnitude. It reduces the swelling by improving circulation and stimulating cell activity. Soreness quickly disappears and bruising diminishes. The immediate increase in comfort makes the treatment worthwhile. Surgery is sometimes indicated in cases where the underlying problem, particularly bleeding into the tissues, is still apparent. Ultrasound will aid healing after surgery.

Sore back

It is not unusual for post-natal women to complain of aches in the lumbar spine and sacroiliac region when they bend over to change nappies and bath their babies. Obviously the change-table and bath should be at the right height to avoid this problem, but some women are extremely sensitive to the slightest amount of forward bend in the first post-natal week. For the last months of pregnancy the enlarged uterus has essentially acted as a splint for the spine, and it would seem that the sudden change in centre of gravity, with no extra weight in front, could be the reason for painful twinges in the back. On examination, muscle spasm and tenderness can often be found along the lower spine, radiating out to the hip area on one or both sides. A simple remedy is to lie on your stomach and let your back muscles totally relax. Postnatal backache is seldom a serious worry unless there is some long-standing problem, but as any interference to the initial bonding time for mother and baby is undesirable, the condition deserves attention. Ultrasound is a simple treatment which seldom fails to relieve this condition.

Sometimes back pain is so low that it might be classified as a sore 'bottom'. But this is coccyx pain, not damaged perineal tissue. As the fetal head passes through the pelvic outlet the coccyx bends backwards. In a tight fit, this bone might be briefly pushed out of joint or even fracture. It generally returns to its usual position, but overstretching of the sacrococcygeal joint can make the whole area extremely painful. Any attempt to move the coccyx, which occurs automatically as you sit, and move from sitting to standing can be excruciatingly painful. Daily treatment with ultrasound will help, and sitting on a hollow foam ring so that the coccyx is spared pressure. If this condition is not treated, it could be weeks, or even months, before you can sit comfortably. When you leave the hospital, ultrasound treatments might need to continue. The only alternative to physiotherapy is to remove the coccyx, and few women want such surgery at any time, let alone soon after giving birth. Most women are willing to try the more conservative method to relieve their pain.

The first six weeks

For six weeks after the birth of the baby, your body will be gradually returning to its pre-pregnant state. During this period the uterus bleeds, ridding itself of its pregnancy products. The placenta has come away at birth but the lining of the uterus must also be shed. You should use pads, not tampons, unless you go swimming. The shed uterine lining is a nutritious substance which is an ideal medium for germs to grow in, particularly if this fluid is dammed up for any length of time by a tampon. If this happens you could get toxic shock, a rare condition caused by an accumulation of infectious organisms that multiply rapidly and, in some cases, lead to a kind of rapid blood poisoning. A sea sponge may be less irritating than a tampon but it must be rinsed out frequently or changed.

Post-natal women tend to disregard exercises, being more interested in their new child than themselves. Fearing total collapse of their partner's shape, some men encourage all sorts of fitness routines but women should be warned against excessive exercising too soon after birth.

Though extremely rare, a condition called air embolus can occur while the uterine arteries are not firmly sealed. It involves the obstruction of a blood vessel by an air bubble. The cause is thought to be turning upside down—standing on the head or shoulders, or bicycling with legs over the head. These positions could draw air into the uterus. When the body is righted again, an air bubble can be sucked into a uterine blood vessel by the sudden lowering of the diaphragm and can pass into the circulation, blocking a main blood vessel which supplies oxygen to the lungs, the heart or the brain.

There is no need to worry, however, provided you stick to the recommended exercises for six weeks. Women who swim in the

Home Exercises

(until baby is 6 weeks old)

1. a) Pull your tummy in.
  b) Pull your waist in; make it small like an hourglass.
  c) Pull your pelvic floor up.
(Do these exercises whenever you think of them, many times a day.)

2. Lying with your knees bent, place both hands on your stomach and press inwards. Raise your head. (This narrows the 'gap' between the rectus muscles.)

3. a) Lying on your stomach with your hands under your forehead, raise your head, hands and arms (torso off bed from the waist up).
  b) Raise your legs, holding them straight with heels together. (This strengthens the lower back.)

4. Press and pull. Stand with your palms pressed together, elbows out. Then grip interlaced fingers and pull. (This prevents saggy breasts and round shoulders.)

5. Walking. Walk on tiptoes, knees straight like a tin soldier or marionette. (This will help correct any postural mistakes.)

Breast engorgement remedy
A simple, homely salve for sore breasts: insert a cabbage leaf inside the cup of your bra. The leaves are thought to contain a soothing substance which takes the heat out of tight, swollen breasts.

post-natal period should not duck-dive and fitness fanatics should ride stationary bicycles (the right way up). After six weeks the bleeding has usually dwindled or stopped altogether. Then handstands and headstands can be resumed, with nothing more harmful than a potentially embarrassing 'plop' when you right yourself, expelling the uterine air.

During the first post-natal week, exercise classes held in hospital ensure that all post-natal women progress at their own pace. The class will include those who have had a difficult forceps delivery or a caesarean section. The only difference for these women is that they might have to progress more slowly. Ideally a physiotherapist is

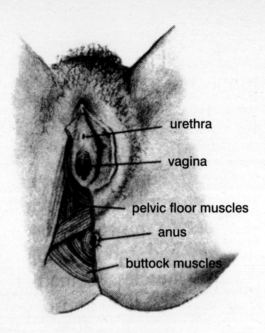

The pelvic floor

available every day and women are encouraged to continue the exercises when they go home. Post-natal exercises are quite demanding, not because they take a long time to perform, but because overstretched muscles need to be worked many times a day to regenerate. There are two sets of muscles which have been excessively stretched: the abdominal muscles and the pelvic floor muscles (if there has been a vaginal birth). Additionally, the muscles of the thighs and buttocks need toning up because when you are heavily pregnant at eight months or so you do not maintain the activity level normal for your age. You seldom dash upstairs or run for a bus!

Abdominal exercises

There are three layers of muscles in the abdomen and each must be given its own special emphasis to assist in firming up all over and seaming together in the centre. At first a definite valley can be felt between the two straight (rectus) muscles down the front. When you lie on your back and raise your head, your fingers will find a trench running up and down from the navel. This may come as a bit of a shock, but resistance exercises help to broaden the muscles out and fill in the gap. Just after the birth the midriff area can be grasped in folds of 'extra skin'. This too will respond to tightening, done many times a day, and crossover resistance exercises.

Crossover exercises follow the direction of pull of the oblique muscles, internal and external. These form a cross and add strength like a natural corset with fibres running in opposite directions. Crossover resistance exercises have been found to be the strongest and most useful of all isotonic exercises for the abdominal muscles. Isometric or static exercises are also important.  The physiotherapist may suggest up to fifty stomach and waist tightenings per day, in a 'little and often' routine.

Pelvic floor exercises

Pelvic floor muscles also respond well to high-repetition exercises. However, because the pelvic floor has been stretched to capacity during birth, it will tire easily, so the exercises should be done with caution. Some patients are told to work the pelvic floor by slowing or stopping the stream of urine at the toilet. This is a reasonable practice if used as a test, but if it is done habitually, it could cause problems for later life. A post-natal mother of one or two days might find she simply can't have any effect on the stream at all. The best way to work the pelvic floor is to remember what it felt like before the baby was born and try to reproduce the same action at any time in any position, not necessarily at the toilet. No more than five repetitions should be done at one time in the first week. Sometimes the pelvic floor is so weak and stretched it will tolerate only one repetition, after which the nerves won't conduct for several seconds. You will find out how soon your pelvic floor tires and gradually increase the

Pelvic Floor Exercises

1. Relativity
Sit on a chair with your knees apart. Sit back and pull the back passage in and up off the chair seat. Hold for two to four seconds then relax. Sit forward, elbows on knees. Pull the front passage in and forwards towards the pubic bone. Feel it slide forwards on the chair seat.

2. Tailwag
On all fours, contract the pelvic floor muscles on one side and then the other.

3. Elevator
While standing try to pull the pelvic floor up in stages, like a lift stopping at all floors (about four floors is quite good). As proficiency increases try to let the PF down stopping at all floors!

4. Feet up
Lie on an inclined plane and move your feet up and down and in a circle. Pull in the pelvic floor and relax it in rhythm with your feet.

No. 4 will help you to get rid of excess fluid.

number of contractions you can do at one time. Women who have had a caesarean section still need to exercise the pelvic floor because the hormones active in pregnancy generally cause some lack of muscle tone. Quite a number of post-natal women have haemorrhoids which developed during late pregnancy or when the anus was stretched during the birth. Pelvic floor exercises will help establish better blood flow in the area until the condition disappears. Ultrasound can be very helpful, too.

Swelling or vein problems

Circulation exercises are vital for residual swelling or vein problems. An aching leg might develop when periods return. Exercises that work the feet, knees and hips, interspersed with rest times with the foot or feet up on a stool, should be done often during each day. Plenty of brisk walking and keeping the sore leg up as much as possible prevents further damage to veins.

Posture

Postural exercises are important because your body's centre of gravity has moved backwards during pregnancy owing to the added weight in the front. In the first days after the birth some women retain the pregnant posture, leaning back and almost looking as though they were still pregnant.

Post-natal mothers have to carry their baby, nurse their baby, bath and change their baby—all positions where the shoulders are rounded. To prevent neck and high thoracic (chest) pain and aches between the shoulder blades, exercises for the shoulder girdle and scapular (wing) muscles are given. Birds have enormously strong scapular muscles for flying. The corresponding set of muscles in humans is necessary to retain an upright posture. These muscles also help prevent sagging breasts.

During this six-week period your pelvic bones are tightening up (their ligaments softened a little during pregnancy so that the pelvis could stretch). It is best not to lift heavy objects, especially in a bending over position. Careless lifting can cause back strain.

After six weeks

Do not attend aerobics classes until after six weeks. Even low-impact aerobics are hard on the pelvic floor. There is risk of doing unsuitable abdominal exercises, straining your back and the chance of forgetting you should not turn upside down.

At a time between six weeks and three months after the birth, you might feel ready to try harder exercises such as aerobics. However, it is quite likely that you'll feel a bit sluggish due to lack of sleep and a lot of sitting while feeding. If you don't feel fit enough for aerobics or sport, or if you are overweight, you can go to a physiotherapist's remedial exercise class and work up gradually.

You should probably not start jogging until after the first six weeks as the impact tends to strain the stretched pelvic floor. And it is wise to postpone very active sport until your body has had a chance to return to normal. There are exceptions to this and if you must play in a match before the six weeks are up, ask your doctor or your physiotherapist. Some people do seem to zip back into shape very quickly.

So enjoy your post-natal interlude (if you can!), let everyone wait on you, and don't worry if you have no time for serious exercising. A few muscle contractions and stomach and posture exercises are quite acceptable for that special time, and will prevent you from seizing up altogether. And if you are breast-feeding five or six times a day you will be producing the hormone prolactin which switches off ovulation, so you have a natural contraceptive. However, just to be on the safe side, your doctor might prescribe a mini-pill.

Constipation muesli

2 cups of rolled oats

2 cups of Allbran

2 cups of natural bran

½ cup of sunflower kernels

½ cup of crushed nuts

½ cup of sultanas (optional)

Have a bowl of this, with milk or fruit juice,
last thing at night.

5

GYNAECOLOGICAL AND BLADDER PROBLEMS

All muscle strengthening for any gynaecological problem involves exercising the pelvic floor muscles, a small group of vital muscles that guard the entrance to the genital and excretory organs. The female pelvic floor is much more at risk than the male, as men have other safeguards for supporting their organs. If you have been sent to a physiotherapist to learn pelvic floor exercises, the effectiveness of your muscles as a support and closure device will first be evaluated. The physiotherapist will ask you to describe your symptoms and probably examine you vaginally, in the way a midwife does. (Some women go to their first session armed with tracksuits, but these aren't necessary unless you are also attending a remedial fitness class.)

Physiotherapists can help with a range of gynaecological and bladder conditions including weak pelvic floor muscles, prolapse, vaginal air intake, episiotomy scarring causing sexual difficulties, and pelvic pain and tenderness. They can also counsel patients before and after an operation. Exercises and electrical treatment are the standard conservative methods for this bracket of disabilities.

Weak pelvic floor

The pelvic floor is a complex muscular platform which contains the pelvic organs. A normal pelvic floor does not sag. It forms a plane and its axis is a straight line between the coccyx and the pubic bone. A neglected pelvic floor sags like a worn out trampoline. In order to understand your condition and the state of this strategic muscle, the physiotherapist will examine you by inserting two gloved fingers gently into the vagina to feel which part of the muscular platform is not working efficiently. When you are asked to contract your muscles, pulling inwards, the strength of the pelvic floor can be felt and any weak areas or overall weakness can be discovered and brought to your attention. Sometimes one side of the muscular ring is weaker than the other, possibly due to damage caused while giving birth. Often the muscle layer at the entrance to the vagina is weak and thin, resembling a rubber band. Muscular tissue should extend all the way up the vagina so that, in the normal state, the constricting pressure is spread out. Occasionally no muscular contraction can be felt at all. This might sound like a hopeless situation, but muscles can be retrained. Any muscle has the ability to improve its tone if its nerve supply is intact. If a woman has symptoms in spite of having a good pelvic floor, another explanation for the symptoms must be sought and treated.

Exercising the pelvic floor will improve the blood supply to the muscles and the response of nerves in the area, making for more rapid repair of any birth damage (see page 00). Start by pulling in the anus as you do in controlling the passing of wind, and once this action is registered in your mind, try for a forward pull bringing in the sling action around the vagina. The pelvic floor works as a unit. As you learn to use it you may be able to identify separate parts of that unit, but at the beginning, keep it simple. The exercise can be done in any position and should be practised many times a day. No one will know you are doing it unless you assume strange facial expressions!

In the old days it was thought that women who habitually rode horses could become 'muscle bound' which could lead to difficult births. It is now known that exercising the pelvic floor makes it more resilient; much more stretchy and pliable. Although a good time to become conscious of your pelvic floor is when you are having or have just had a baby, it is never too late to begin. You will always reap rewards; sexually, supportively and in controlling body outlets.

Uterine prolapse and low cervix

When a pelvic organ drops or falls from its usual position, the condition is called a prolapse. Giving birth is the main cause of prolapse. The soft tissues in the base of the female pelvis have to stretch to capacity when the baby is pushed through. Post-natal exercises help to tighten up a weak, gaping vaginal area, but few women realise just how much work they have to do! Correct pelvic angulation also helps to contain the pelvic organs which should rest on the pubic bone rather than dropping through the 'hole' of a weak pelvic floor. The best position for the non-pregnant uterus is kinked forward over the bladder. Any other position makes it more likely to prolapse.

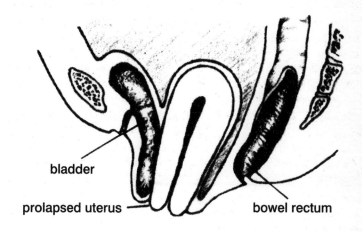

bladder

prolapsed uterus

bowel rectum

A gynaecologist might refer you to a physiotherapist if you have the beginnings of a uterine prolapse, a low cervix. If you also have a weak pelvic floor and a wide vaginal opening, you have all the indications for trouble in the future, but the condition can often be rectified by early treatment.

Symptoms of uterine prolapse could include:

- discomfort in the vagina (a full feeling)
- a sensation of pressure (a pushing feeling)
- a dragging, drawn-down sensation.

The physiotherapist will feel your cervix during the vaginal examination. If the cervix is easy to reach, it is described as 'low' and may be classed as a first degree prolapse. In second degree prolapse the cervix is close to the entrance to the vagina. If this is the case an operation is likely to be suggested. If the uterus is completely prolapsed, a condition known as procidentia, the vagina turns inside out and appears at the vulval entrance. Fortunately this condition is rare. It requires surgery and cannot be cured by physiotherapy.

When you have any of the symptoms described above, you may wake up feeling fine. This is because you have been horizontal for some hours. By lunch time or late afternoon you are very uncomfortable and it is a good time to do what we call 'posturing' for a period of ten minutes or longer, allowing the prolapsed tissue to move back upwards. You can also exercise your pelvic floor in this position. If there is no other bodily condition which prevents it, it is a good idea to raise the bottom of your bed, a brick under each leg. The sloping position allows you to do some posturing while you are asleep and is often very effective in helping to reduce the prolapse.

Vaginal (partial) prolapse

Vaginal prolapse is usually less serious than uterine prolapse. There are three main types:

- cystocele (prolapse of part of the bladder)
- urethrocele (prolapse of the urethra)
- rectocele (prolapse of the rectal wall).

Any of these partial prolapses can occur on its own or in addition to each other or a uterine prolapse. A urethrocele and a cystocele are often combined (cystourethrocele) and can cause bladder weakness, and a rectocele can make it difficult to empty the rectum completely. These conditions are usually not dangerous, but they make you feel uncomfortable and vulnerable. They are not uncommon in women who have had several children but can occur after the first child. Pressure from the baby's head might stretch the ligaments that support the bladder, and as the vagina shares its back wall with the rectum, stretching can cause the formation of a sort of pocket just inside the anus. Faecal matter can become trapped in this pocket and is sometimes difficult to expel. Rather than straining, which is usually useless and may be damaging, you can press firmly on the bridge of tissue between the vaginal opening and the anus. This action dislodges any matter that has been caught in the pocket. Surgery is seldom suggested for a rectocele, unless a repair for some other form of prolapse is being done. The situation improves markedly if you strengthen the relevant part of the pelvic floor.

Posturing for Prolapse

1. Sit on a padded chair. Draw the muscles around the back passage up off the chair.

2. Sit forward on a chair with your knees wide apart. Draw in the back passage, put your fingers on your pubic bone and try to pull the muscles forward towards your fingers.

3. Lie on your back, with your knees bent. Do a sit up while pulling your pelvic floor in. Relax the pelvic floor as you lie down again.

4. Bottoms up
Kneel and rest your elbows on the floor. Keep your buttocks high and your back low. Do some pelvic floor pull-ins. Stay in this position for ten minutes.

5. Bridging
Lying with your knees bent, lift your buttocks as high as possible. Stay in this position for ten minutes.

Vaginal air intake

If the vagina is very open, there is a tendency for air and water to enter it in certain postures. Water can enter the vagina during a bath or a swim but as soon as you stand up it flows out again. Air, however, can remain longer in the vagina and its exit is not easily controlled. It may make an embarrassing noise as it plops out. The vaginal walls might even make a flappy clicky noise as you walk like billiard balls meeting! The condition is usually cured by rigorous exercising of the pelvic floor. Exercising tightens the muscles which to some extent determine the size of the vagina; a wide vagina—one that will admit three fingers—is normal soon after giving birth, but a five finger vagina gives very little support and lends itself to air and water intake problems.

Sexual problems

There are two vaginal conditions which may interfere with sexual satisfaction: a vagina that is too loose and a vagina that is too tight. The looseness is natural soon after childbirth, but the vagina should not remain like this. Weak, stretched vaginal walls have no resilience. The result is very little satisfaction for both partners. The tightness, accompanied by soreness, is usually caused by scarring either after episiotomy or after surgery. Scar tissue will not 'give'. Obstetricians and general surgeons are aware of these difficulties and will always try to leave you with a mobile vagina. However, if there is a problem, electrical treatment given by a physiotherapist can help resolve the scar tissue and regenerate the required flexibility.

Pelvic pain

Women are very subject to vague pains in the pelvis and low abdomen. Pain may be due to periods, ovulation, endometriosis, ovarian cysts, or even some more remote source. And conversely, pain deriving from pelvic organs often involves the back and because of this an orthopaedic condition can be difficult to distinguish from a gynaecological one. If there is any suspicion that a disease process is present, the gynaecologist will investigate by making a small incision in the navel and inserting a laparoscope, an instrument with an eye-piece attached which is used to examine the organs of the abdomen and pelvis. If the laparoscope shows no disease, the cause could be a spinal problem or some pelvic functional disorder. Either of these might be referred to a physiotherapist. Quite often pelvic pain is very difficult to track down and cure. The list below gives some of the answers physiotherapists have for a few common types of pelvic pain.

Proctalgia fujax (spasm of the pelvic floor)

This minor condition has a very complex name! It means 'fleeting pain in the rectum' and it may be fleeting but anyone that has it knows all about it! Spasm of the pelvic floor occurs in men and women, but more often in women. A short, sharp episode of pain caused by cramp in the surrounding muscles is felt in or near the rectum, often on one side though it may spread to the other. The spasm can be confused with pain in the colon and lead to inappropriate exploratory investigations. The pain is often accompanied by a feeling of fullness in the bowel and is severe and temporarily incapacitating. Electrical treatment soothes over-active nerves and has proved very beneficial, causing the painful episodes to abate after two or three treatments and often disappear altogether.

Endometriosis

Endometriosis was once dismissed as a figment of female imagination. It is now realised that it has a very real cause and is responsible for much pain and misery, even cases of suicide.

Endometriosis is a condition in which some of the membrane that lines the uterus migrates to the wrong place, such as the ovaries, the bowel or the uterine ligaments, instead of passing down the vagina during menstruation. The membranous lining is subject to hormonal influences, so it swells during the menstrual cycle even if it is in foreign territory. This means that monthly bleeding is occurring in abnormal places which can cause quite severe pain. Endometriosis abates during pregnancy and in the menopause because there are no periods, but it can leave painful adhesions.

Women describe various types of pelvic pain and any of these might be due to chronic endometriosis. Pain is often bad before and during menstruation. It may hurt to use the bowels or to pass urine and it is often painful to have intercourse or a pelvic examination. There might also be diarrhoea or constipation, bleeding from the bowel, spotting from the uterus or swollen abdomen. Symptoms are mentally and physically debilitating and often result in lack of sleep. In the long term endometriosis can cause infertility.

There are drugs that can be used to suppress ovary function and hence swelling of endometrial tissue, but they often have side-effects and are never prescribed unless there is a reliable diagnosis, usually reached by doing a laparoscopy. The option of physiotherapy, using a harmless interferential current, should not be discounted as it aids blood circulation, tissue healing and resolution of adhesions. Acupuncture may also help with pain and it is worth trying vitamin supplements, a low fat high-fibre diet, and evening primrose oil. Any of these may give some much needed relief.

Low abdominal bloating

Women sometimes complain of low abdominal pain and bloating; some even say they feel as though they were four months pregnant or have a football inside! There is no swelling in the morning but by afternoon or evening the abdomen is prominent, uncomfortable and very tender to any pressure. When not associated with endometriosis, the cause of this curious condition is obscure. It might be related to fluid retention or postural drag on ligaments supporting the reproductive organs or gas in the bowel. It is often impossible to hold the abdominal muscles in because the condition is just too painful. Going to bed usually relieves the pain in time, but it can recur day after day. Interferential therapy (IFT) is very helpful in treating this condition.

Physiotherapy for gynaecological conditions

Physiotherapists use various types of machines to help women with the conditions mentioned above and also bladder problems (see pages 180–186). Some of the machines stimulate muscles with an electrical current or an electromagnetic impulse and tone up the tissues generally, while a biofeedback machine gives you information about how much muscle power you can achieve.

The current devised to treat structures within the pelvis must be able to penetrate skin, bone and muscle to the right depth, and it must be of the right type and strength to stimulate the electrolytes (substances which conduct electricity) operating in body tissues. Two electrodes (covered with damp gauze which is discarded after treatment) direct the current to the right place. One electrode is placed under the buttocks and one on the pubic area. Sometimes four electrodes are used.

The current stimulates internal muscle tissue, promotes cell activity and blood flow and tends to activate normal nerve responses. No harmful effect has ever been documented. The treatment is not uncomfortable, apart from the fact that the area, including the pubic hair, must be very wet to facilitate conduction through the skin. Although water combined with electricity is considered dangerous, this treatment is safe because the currents are small and they are designed to match the type of current that works naturally within the human body. Electrically charged particles (ions) move from one part of a cell to another. Stimulation of this process has a cumulative effect, promoting healing and activating crucial mechanisms.

Pre- and post-operative physiotherapy

Gynaecological surgery is commonplace. For some women it is utterly necessary, in fact life-saving. For others its purpose is to relieve pain and discomfort or remove a potentially malignant growth. Hysterectomy (removal of the uterus, with retention of the ovaries if possible) is necessary if the uterus or the ovaries are diseased. For cases of prolapse where there is no disease in the organs, a hysterectomy is not necessary. An operation that repairs or stitches up the prolapsed tissue is performed instead.

Any operation carries less risk if the patient is well, both before and after surgery. Physiotherapists can help prevent problems by advising patients a few days before surgery on how to prepare for a quick recovery. After surgery, physiotherapists supervise breathing exercises and encourage productive coughing to help dislodge lung secretions sometimes caused by the anaesthetic, especially in smokers. Leg exercises before and after surgery are also encouraged, to aid circulation and prevent blood clots. Pelvic floor exercises taught before surgery will be gradually introduced post-surgically as soreness allows. After any pelvic surgery a catheter is inserted into the bladder where it stays for a day or two. When it is taken out, the bladder often goes on strike and is difficult to empty. The physiotherapist will have prepared you for this, so that you can ease your discomfort by full relaxation of the pelvic floor muscles and a gentle diaphragm pressure from above.

After the operation and once healing is complete, it is extremely important to continue with pelvic floor and abdominal exercises. Progressive strength contractions repeated at intervals throughout the day will achieve a good result. If you were proficient at pelvic floor contractions before the operation you will know what effect you are aiming at after surgery. A firm pelvic floor will help to make the surgery successful in the long term, particularly if it was a repair operation for a prolapse.

Surgeons are so skilful these days that few women are left with uncomfortable or unsightly scars. Nevertheless women who have had several operations may have sore lumpy scars because there is less undamaged skin to use in the sewing up process. Physiotherapists use ultrasound to soften the internal and external scarring and ease the movement of one layer of tissue over another. The sound waves have a mechanical shaking effect which resolves the hard areas by stimulation of circulation and cell activity.

After surgery, stomach and pelvic floor exercises will enhance muscular support for the newly positioned organs. They should also prevent the need for any further repair operations.

Bladder conditions

As many as one in three women will have problems at some time in their lives with urine incontinence. Incontinence is not a disease but a malfunctioning of the bladder and its outlet tube, the urethra. The condition ranges from the occasional loss of a few drops of urine, to a fairly constant dribble or a gush after going to the toilet, to a very embarrassing sudden flood. Many cases of minor or even sometimes serious incontinence can be remedied with exercises, simple electrical treatment or surgery, so there is no need to put up with damp pants or soggy pads. Women of all ages suffer all kinds of discomfort for years, embarrassed about admitting that they 'wet themselves' and have to wear a pad to play sport. Their quality of life is being thoroughly undermined and yet this type of problem is often pushed aside as being low on the list of health objectives.

Guided self-help is readily available. Urologists, writing about bladder incompetency, now include as possible solutions not only chemotherapy and surgery but physiotherapy. On balance the younger age group have a better chance of success than the middle-aged to elderly, but the treatment is conservative and inexpensive and any age can expect some improvement. The only excuse for not restoring the strength of the pelvic floor is if there has been nerve damage as in some back injuries, stroke, paraplegia or multiple sclerosis (MS). If nerves are damaged, messages to muscles are interrupted, but often people with these disabilities can be assisted by various prescribed medications and voiding techniques.

Some women are born with anatomical deficiencies, such as a short urethra or a lack of angulation of the urethra to the bladder. Men seldom have bladder incompetency until old age. Not only is the male urethra longer, but it is also looped up and supported by the prostate gland. If this gland is surgically removed, as it often is late in life (when it may grow to block the urethra), continence can be compromised to some extent. Women are biologically prone to bladder incompetence in the upright posture because the pelvic organs rest on a relatively unprotected area. Many older women have trouble containing urine when they first get out of bed in the morning—it's a mad dash for the toilet—hopefully an en *suite*!

The bladder is a hollow muscular bag which fills to a certain level and then alerts the central nervous system that it is ready to empty. It then voids (in a suitable place) via the urethra, a muscular tube connecting the base of the bladder to the outlet. The average female urethra is about three centimetres long and can elongate during labour when the bladder is pushed upwards. The middle third of the urethral tube is surrounded by muscle tissue to form a sphincter, a closure device like a tap. During childbirth the urethra, which lies close to the vagina, can become stretched and cease to work efficiently. If the urethral tube is not angulated to the bladder and not supported well enough from below by the pelvic floor muscles, the sphincter is liable to open under pressure. This is called stress incontinence.

Stress incontinence

Stress incontinence occurs when sudden pressure is exerted from above, as in coughing, sneezing, lifting, shouting, laughing, jumping and running. A urethra that is 'in place' can control the escape of a small amount of urine by milking it back into the bladder. If the bladder mechanism is competent, urine can be contained by the higher pressure in the tube until the person is ready to void. But if the urethra is saggy and unsupported, the urine simply flows down the tube when pressure is applied from above.

There is some controversy about what exactly alters the position of the urethra. It may be slackening of ligaments in pregnancy, fetal head pressure in labour or a bit of both. It is certainly advisable not to push before the cervix is fully open, and to use gravity (upright positions) as an aid to the expulsive force during birth.

When voiding takes place normally, the pelvic floor relaxes and causes a fall in urethral resistance. The muscle in the wall of the bladder then squeezes the bag to expel urine. Two types of muscle fibres maintain continence, namely the pelvic floor muscles which are voluntary (consciously controlled) and the small fibres at the bladder neck which are involuntary (subconsciously controlled). This means that urine control is partly willed and partly reflex. The voluntary muscles have fast twitch fibres that respond very quickly when needed (in coughing and sneezing you need sudden support from below). Slow twitch fibres do the holding over long periods— for instance, overnight, while you are asleep. Short elastic ligaments keep the urethra suspended at the right angle. Several ligaments maintain the height of the pelvic organs, but the ligaments hitching the urethra to the pubic bone are the most important ones for continence. In cases of intractable stress incontinence the surgeon loops the neck of the bladder up to the pubic bone so that the necessary angle of the tube to the bladder is restored.

But many cases of stress incontinence have been cured by physiotherapy. As the muscles gain strength, they are trained to respond in a way that is appropriate to the activity. For instance, a woman who is incontinent while playing sport will need to learn to 'switch off' while she is running and jumping. Like any other muscle, the pelvic floor muscles are affected by general fatigue. This is why so many women need to go to the toilet during an aerobics class. And a large number wear pads just in case!

Frequency and urgency

You are 'frequent' if you pass urine more than seven times a day or twice or more at night. It is a habit-forming condition which not only wastes time but also trains the bladder to hold smaller and smaller volumes of urine.

You are 'urgent' if your bladder insists on you going to the toilet— right now! An urgency feeling can be very awkward when you cannot find a toilet. It is also inclined to assert itself when you put your house key in the door having made a panic dash for home. Urgency is a combination of an incompetent closure mechanism and over-activity of the bladder muscle which contracts inappropriately. Urgency leads to urge incontinence.

The two conditions, frequency and urgency, are often associated. A person who experiences urgency thinks that by emptying the bladder more frequently the urgency will go away. This creates a habit of frequent visits to the toilet and is obviously not a good idea.

Incomplete emptying

The bladder should be emptied completely every time you go to the toilet. It is possible to be in such a rush to get on with the next thing that you cut off the slowing stream before the bladder is emptied. While it is good to be able to do this in dire emergencies, it shouldn't become a habit.

Another form of incomplete emptying is when a pouch of bladder traps escaping urine, usually because the bladder has a bulge in it, a cystocele. For some women this trapped urine can only be voided by standing up or wriggling backwards and forwards on the toilet seat or straining.

Overflow incontinence

If a considerable quantity of urine stays in the bladder all the time, the bladder neck becomes stretched and is more likely to leak. Older people are more susceptible than young ones to this problem and if the sensory nerves do not give the brain good information of the state of the bladder the person is unaware of the level of filling. Diabetics can sometimes be affected by overflow incontinence because of a tendency to thirst which makes them constantly fill the bladder. Added to this there may be some sensory loss. A voiding schedule can be helpful, making going to the toilet a routine every so many hours.

Tests and surgery

If surgery is contemplated for a bladder problem, some urological tests will need to be carried out to see what part of the system is malfunctioning. Using an instrument called a cystoscope, a urologist can look inside the bladder. Another simple test is to measure the capacity of the bladder and its reaction to changing pressure. Urologists can also diagnose a problem by injecting dye into the bladder and taking an X-ray video of the action of urinating. This is called a voiding X-ray.

Before you seek advice from your doctor, ask yourself a few questions:

- Do you lose small amounts of urine under pressure? (If so, you have stress incontinence.)
- Do you pass urine more than seven times a day? (If so you have frequency.)
- Do you suddenly have to go to the toilet rather than lose control altogether? (If so, you have urgency.)
- Do you need to revisit the toilet within ten minutes or do you lose a few drips after voiding? (If so, your bladder might not be emptying properly.)
- Are you aware of when your bladder is full or do you have sudden unaccountable leaks? (If so you could have overflow incontinence.)

All these problems can be sorted out and your doctor will be able to refer you to the relevant specialists.

Toilet training

Conditions such as urinary frequency have been blamed on toilet training. This is an ill-advised theory, likely to confuse parents and deny children a learning experience. Toilet-training is a process of teaching a child to train a reflex. Newborn babies have excellent micturition (urine passing) reflexes but no reflexes for continence. As they grow older, children are taught when and where to give 'permission' for urinating. Most children learn amazingly quickly. No doubt they are glad to be dry! Soon the reflex works so well that the child is 'safe'. Many animals teach their young to have this sort of control and we know how long the cat can hold on if it gets shut in the house! As the child grows, so does the bladder. A child under the age of two will need to empty the bladder much more often than a six-year-old.

My own observation is that there is an ideal time for training a child (which varies a bit from child to child) just as there is for learning to talk. Pre-school children learn languages much faster than anyone else. If you miss the bus on toilet training it probably sets the scene for bladder problems later in life.

There are people in the medical and allied professions who advise parents not to make their children go to the toilet before going to bed or going out. This is overreaction. It causes inconvenience and may result in wet beds. As a general rule it is good to encourage holding on, but certainly not if you are trying to teach a toddler to stay dry overnight! Toilet before bed is a good rule. Children usually teach themselves to hang on. Most schoolchildren are excellent hangers-on!

Bed wetting

Nocturnal enuresis is the medical name for repeated episodes of bed wetting. This condition usually has a psychological basis but it could also be associated with a weak pelvic floor. Children and adults can suffer from it, and the condition deserves attention because it causes much misery. Often the attempts made to correct this distressing problem have met with little success and the child, adult, or parents of the child are desperate.

Children of three and over can be shown how to flow-stop, switching off urination as they void on the toilet. This is the most graphic way to prove to a child that she (or he) has a mechanism for control. They should be encouraged to hold on longer in the day and have their volume measured, trying to increase the amount they can produce at one void. Proficiency will carry over to night time. This practice is also useful for adults getting up many times in the night to the toilet. The aim is to increase the interval between voids, even by five minutes, until the normal volume of urine can be stored. An adult bladder should hold 400 millilitres in the daytime between voids and about 600 millilitres at night. A child's bladder will hold up to 300 millilitres.

There is a misconception that it is dangerous for the bladder to be overstretched. This only happens in extreme cases, usually where there is nerve damage. In fact there is no need to worry about the child who hardly ever 'goes' unless she or he is drinking too little. Breast-feeding mothers pass very little urine. During lactation mothers should drink plenty as it will help the urinary system as well as the milk secreting system.

Bladder infections

Sometimes urinary urgency is caused by a bladder infection. If an infection is suspected, a mid-stream specimen of urine will be sent to a pathology laboratory. If the bladder is inflamed and hypersensitive it temporarily alters its behaviour. The acid urine scalds the sensitive tissue and is very painful to pass in spite of the fact that the bladder is trying to get rid of it. You may find yourself in the toilet every ten minutes!

A woman's urinary system is more open than a man's, and therefore more vulnerable to infection. You may have recurrent infections, and they may be linked to some activity or some food. Intercourse can trigger off urinary sensitivity. Another problem is that the infections sometimes become resistant to antibiotics.

Recurrent urinary infections can be treated with IFT which helps to normalise mucous membrane and to make the inflammation subside. The electrical impulses increase cell permeability which means waste products can be washed out of cells more efficiently. It is also a good idea to drink a glass of cranberry juice each day. Recent studies have shown that this reduces the ability of bacteria to adhere to the tissue that lines the bladder and urethra.

Faecal incontinence

Incontinence of the bowel, such as diarrhoea, might be caused by an intestinal problem or weak muscles after an operation. If the muscles around the anus are strong, they can help contain the faeces until a toilet is reached.

A certain type of bowel incontinence in women is due to a collection of faeces in a rectocele, a pouch or pocket in the rectum which discharges faeces bit by bit. A woman with a rectocele might have to visit the toilet many times a day. This is aggravating and distressing and is not uncommon in older women. Having a strong pelvic floor will tend to make the emptying process more efficient.

Constipation can cause faecal incontinence because the compressed bowel contents irritate the bowel lining and cause diarrhoea. A high-fibre diet helps to ensure a more even consistency, eliminating the need for straining which is potentially harmful. A bowel that is almost constantly full can actually cause incontinence of urine by altering the position of the urinary sphincter.

Faecal incontinence can be treated by strengthening the ring of muscle around the anus and the lifting muscle which supports the rectum. Barring radical nerve damage, most people can be cured of this condition. The earlier the symptoms are recognised and treated, the better the results.

Incontinence aids

Many kinds of aids such as absorbent pads and pants, sheets and drainage apparatus are available for people with incontinence. Medical supply firms stock these articles and it should be possible to choose the padding or appliance that suits your particular needs. However, before resorting to mopping up devices, first consider what you may be able to do yourself to rectify the situation.

Conservative treatment of incontinence

The symptoms of incontinence range from mild disturbances to serious conditions that spoil the quality of life. A physiotherapist is one of a team of medical people who can devise treatment that will help restore your control of continence and in many cases regain a normal lifestyle. The treatment aims are:

- to strengthen the pelvic floor
- to retrain the continence reflex
- to teach the bladder to hold a reasonable quantity of urine
- to improve the resilience of all tissues in the region of the problem.

All women with any kind of bladder problem are given exercises as compulsory homework. For a long-standing neglected problem much hard work will be needed over several months. You might have to resign yourself to a slow, gradual improvement. There will be plateau periods when you think you are never going to get better, but perseverance will usually pay off. The next plateau is reached and eventually improvement is sustained at an acceptable level.

6
MIDDLE LIFE

Middle life can be considered as the period of a person's life between the ages of thirty-five and fifty. It has traditionally been seen as a time of deterioration; middle age has meant loss of muscle tone, varicose veins, wrinkles and fixed attitudes.

In spite of the fact that this stigma is largely a thing of the past, there is a danger at this time of life of becoming complacent, to the detriment of one's own physical or mental well-being.

Women in middle life represent a range of lifestyles. Some will have children in their teens or even older; others will have much younger children, even babies, having put off having a family until they were well into their thirties or even forties. If you have a young family and you are also working, you are vitally dependent on remaining in good health.

So what are the factors that might undermine your health, either now or in the future?

Weight

Extra weight compounds other problems. It is worth paying some attention to it before it snowballs. Fat distribution does depend on body type, but if you are overweight you are sure to be taking in more energy than you are using up. Aerobic exercise helps to burn extra kilojoules, but it must be accompanied with a reduction in food; you will need to forego that extra slice of cake. If you are the main family cook, you are in an ideal position to taste without being reprimanded. When you make out your list of daily food and drink intake (see Sample Replacement Diet, page 72), do you include the little tasting snacks?

Women often want to know how to take off weight from a particular area. This is difficult to do because the body is programmed to deposit extra fat according to individual physique. However, you can tone up the muscles underlying the bulgy area and hopefully convert fatty tissue into muscle. You should exercise the whole body to get the best results. Advice is always available from physical education instructors and physiotherapists. Try to avoid the temptation of putting off a weight-reducing programme. It won't get any easier.

Lose weight gradually. Even taking one habitual item out of your daily diet will eventually make a difference. Crash diets usually don't work. You almost always put the weight back on again. What you need to do is re-programme your mind so that it becomes accustomed to the lower body weight and begins to like the new diet better than the old one.

The following tenets put out by the Commonwealth Department of Health will help:

1. Avoid eating too much fat.
2. Avoid eating too much sugar.
3. Eat wholegrain bread and cereals, fruit and vegetables daily.
4. Limit alcohol consumption.
5. Use less salt.

Avoiding fatty foods means not eating food such as pastries, rich cakes and desserts, ice-cream, rich sauces, gravies and fried foods. You can replace them with lean meat, fish, poultry, eggs, nuts and dairy products in moderation. You can learn to drink tea and coffee without sugar and substitute bread, and fresh vegetables and fruit, for foods with added sugar such as processed cereals and canned fruit. Use brown rice, wholegrain bread and cereals; and try rye, maize and soya bean products. One or two standard alcoholic drinks a day are considered a healthy limit. But you can drink low-alcohol beer or wine diluted with soda or mineral water. Chemical and bodyweight differences mean that women are generally more susceptible to alcohol than men. On the whole, women intuitively recognise this and drink less. Excessive alcohol consumption by males is one reason for the fact that, on average, men do not live as long as women.

High blood pressure and cholesterol

Some women will have had raised blood pressure during pregnancy. One reason for this may be an underlying tendency exacerbated by the pregnancy and recurring later in life.

It has been discovered that Australian Aborigines living on traditional food that they have gathered and hunted have very low blood pressure. One group was found to have a blood pressure of about 110/60 at fifty years of age, whereas a European might have a reading of 140/85 at a similar age. Inheritance might play a part, although Aborigines on European diets quickly acquire the equivalent blood pressure.

The Innuit have low blood pressure, despite their high-fat diet of fish, whales and other sea mammals. Recently it has been found that fish oil contains a cholesterol, the 'good' kind, which lowers the chance of collecting fatty deposits in arteries (atherosclerosis). Animal fats usually contain 'bad' cholesterol and our affluent Western diet is often high in this kind of fat. High salt intake is another factor; it can cause fluid retention and can also predispose towards hardening of the arteries. High blood pressure can cause slow damage to the heart, kidneys, brain or the retina of the eye.

Cholesterol has been painted so black that you might be forgiven for thinking of it as a wholly bad substance. In fact it is needed by every cell in the body, being a building material of particular value to growing children. However, the arteries of some adults are physiologically vulnerable to over-supply of cholesterol. Dense fatty bulges build up and cause bottlenecks in arteries. These can raise blood pressure or slow the bloodstream or both. Dieting helps to divert cholesterol to other parts of the body, hence people with high cholesterol are advised to lose weight.

Coronary disease occurs when the heart muscle is starved of blood. There are usually cholesterol-fed 'plaques' in the coronary arteries. It is apparently a new disease. Apoplexy was well known in history, and has nothing to do with the heart. It is a blockage of a brain artery, what we now call CVA (cerebrovascular accident or stroke). The increase in coronary disease can be partly attributed to the fact that people are living longer. But men are at risk much earlier than women. Women are thought to be protected to some extent by oestrogen until the menopause.

Gallstones

Fatty foodstuffs are digested by bile, a substance stored in the gall bladder. Bile is sometimes blocked from entering the digestive tract by gallstones. The medical model of a woman with gallstones is one who is fair, fat and forty—a little glib perhaps but there is no doubt that a fatty diet increases the possibility of gallstone formation. If a stone large enough to block the bile duct forms in the gall bladder, the pain is excruciating.

An ultrasound scan can locate the offending stone and then surgery might be recommended to remove it. The operation is called cholecystectomy. Another treatment for gallstones is to use a special type of ultrasound to break the stone up, unblocking the duct.

After any anaesthetic, there is a tendency for breathing to be shallow and for secretions to collect in the lungs. If a bronchiole (small breathing tube) becomes blocked, the lung tissue behind the blockage tends to become plugged so that air can't get into it. This is called atelectasis and it can lead to pneumonia. Added to this is the fact that after gall bladder surgery deep breathing is very painful.

Chest physiotherapy helps to keep the lungs clear. Usually you are asked to perform various breathing movements while the physiotherapist uses vibration of the chest wall to shake the mucus clear so that it can be coughed up. This treatment is an essential precaution; it can be life-saving.

Cancer

Cancer is an insidious disease and some of its originating factors are probably beyond our control. However, we can control our diet, and our exposure to sun and we can stop smoking or minimise our exposure to second-hand smoking. Smoking is implicated not only in lung cancer but also in cancer of the mouth and oesophagus. Diet is implicated in colon cancer and, to some extent, breast cancer. A connection has been found between excessive sugar consumption, behaviour of insulin and breast lumps. Glucose is used in many manufactured foods, such as confectionery, and is twice as harmful as sugar. Insulin production is triggered by a rise in blood sugar (glucose) which in turn promotes storage in the form of glycogen. The body looks for an organ of storage, and the female breast is the ideal candidate.

Another female anomaly is that liver adenoma, a benign tumour, can be a side-effect of taking oral contraceptives. The risk is very low, about 1 in 80,000, and research is mainly based on pills used in the past which had higher levels of hormones than the pills in use today. Excessive alcohol consumption can cause liver cancer. The Japanese, who eat a lot of salted fish, are prone to stomach cancer. Betel nut and tobacco chewing can cause oral cancer but so can smoking and heavy alcohol consumption.

Cancers of the cervix and uterus are usually not fatal, provided they are diagnosed early. This is the reason for regular Pap smears. Sometimes a colposcopy is ordered. A colposcope is an instrument like a spyglass used to view the cervix. The examination may corroborate the results of the Pap smear or there may be some erosion of tissue needing laser treatment. Suspicion of cancer could involve a cone biopsy, taking tissue from the affected part to be examined by a pathologist.

There are measures you can take to help you avoid cancer. They are:

1. Eat plenty of fibre (this could prevent colon cancer).
2. Limit sugar (this may help prevent breast cancer).
3. Limit alcohol (this could prevent liver cancer).
4. Do not smoke (this could prevent lung or oral cancer).
5. Do not expose your skin to strong sun (this could avoid skin cancer).
6. Eat five portions of fruit and vegetables a day and vary the types you eat. Include brassicas such as Brussels sprouts, broccoli and watercress, and red foods such as tomatoes, all of which have anti-cancer properties.

Breast lumps

Lumps in the breast are taken as a sinister sign, but often they are benign (not cancerous). Check yourself regularly and seek medical advice at once if you discover one. Sometimes a lumpectomy (removal of the lump) needs to be surgically performed. Occasionally a mastectomy (removal of a breast) is necessary; this can involve removal of the glands in the armpit as well. After a total mastectomy the arm affected will be stiff and sore. Physiotherapists gently stretch tight tissue and restore normal movement. This has to be done immediately after surgery, otherwise a 'frozen shoulder' can develop.

It is important for any woman losing a breast to become adjusted to this assault on her womanhood. Careful choice of a padded bra with assistance from a trained corsetry adviser will help overcome one of the hurdles. Fortunately radical mastectomy is not performed nearly as often as it was thirty or so years ago; good screening methods (mammography) now detect signs before they become serious.

Drugs

Many people start taking medicinal drugs, often prescribed, at middle age. The drugs might be necessary, indeed life-saving, but sometimes the reasons are rather dubious. It is worth asking yourself and your doctor whether the desired result could be obtained in a simpler way, a way that has no side-effects. It has been said that, for a drug to have an effect, there must be the possibility of a side-effect.

Let us take first the anti-inflammatory drugs which are prescribed for rheumatic problems. They usually have the property of reducing inflammation and also having a pain-killing component. The most widely used is ibuprofen (e.g. Brufen®, Nurofen®) but there are many more. Known as non-steroid anti-inflammatory drugs (NSAIDs), a name which makes them seem innocuous, these drugs can cause digestive upsets, though if they are taken with meals this is less likely. A rare effect is suppression of bone marrow which normally produces red and white blood cells. If this function is defective, the body's immune system can be sabotaged. Before you make a decision to take a non-steroid anti-inflammatory drug, have you tried the natural methods offered by physiotherapy? Your doctor might suggest you do both.

Painkillers such as aspirin can be helpful in many situations but the body grows accustomed to them; it ignores the effect and produces pain in increasing magnitude to alert the brain to the problem. Narcotic painkillers which contain codeine are habit-forming. Barbiturates can also cause dependency. In the end painkillers may defeat their own purpose.

Tranquillisers such as Diazepam® and Temazepam® are sedatives. Driving a car after taking one of these could be dangerous.

The tricyclic drugs for depression (Tryptanol® is one) also reduce alertness and should be used strictly as prescribed. Sleeping pills can also exacerbate incontinence. A recent finding is that taking long-term sleeping pills increases the likelihood of fracturing the femur.

Caffeine, alcohol and tobacco are all drugs. Tobacco can cause abnormal amounts of vitamin C to be lost, resulting in fragile capillaries which means you bruise easily. If you look at the legs of ageing smokers you will notice that parts of the legs are purple; this is caused by small broken blood vessels. Caffeine prevents the absorption of calcium, whereas camomile tea is rich in calcium. Try herb teas!

Diuretics and beta-blocker drugs are used to reduce high blood pressure and prevent coronary heart disease. Diuretics help the body rid itself of fluid, and beta-blockers lower blood pressure and stabilise the action of the heart. Factors taken into account when prescribing the most suitable drugs are age and severity of symptoms. And yet by adjusting your diet and lifestyle you can probably lower your own blood pressure and relaxation can cure insomnia. The modern doctor will often suggest the more natural methods of control before resorting to drugs.

Rheumatism

There are many types of rheumatism. You may be the victim of an auto-immune disease—the body working against itself, causing swelling and stiffness. Or, more simply, rheumatism is a localised, periarthritic condition with inflammation around a joint (*peri*, around; *arthros*, joint). Other conditions involve nerve pressure. The pinched nerve is often a spinal root, a part of a nerve which will mesh with others to form a whole nerve such as the sciatic. However, the nerve itself can be trapped, and this can happen to the ulnar nerve as it crosses the elbow joint. Another cause of nerve pressure is when a nerve has to cross a bony arch such as the first rib. Pressure on the first thoracic nerve by this means can cause pain or tingling or numbness or temperature change in the arm and hand. Women appear to be quite susceptible to some rheumatic conditions such as RSI and calcium deposits forming in structures around joints such as the shoulder. One theory suggests that this may be due to alterations in collagen, which is a body protein in skin, bone, cartilage and connective tissue. Collagen may be sensitive to change in female hormones.

There are many rheumatic conditions, causing anything from neuralgia in the face to pain in the big toe. Physiotherapists can diagnose where the pain is coming from, analyse the symptoms and treat you until you can move freely, sleep at night, and feel your old self again.

Diabetes

If you are constantly thirsty and passing a large quantity of sweet-smelling urine, it is possible that you have diabetes. Diabetes mellitus is defined as a series of disorders or a syndrome in which the body is unable to properly regulate the processing, or metabolism, of carbohydrates, fats and proteins. It is caused by an absolute or partial deficiency of the important hormone insulin, which is produced and released by specialised cells (known as beta cells) located in the pancreas. The function of insulin is to regulate the levels of glucose (the body's energy source) in the blood in order to ensure that enough is made available at all times to all the various tissues and organs, so that vital life-processes can continue.

There are two main forms of the syndrome: Type 1 which is insulin dependant, and Type 2 which is non-insulin dependent. On a worldwide basis, Type 2 diabetes accounts for over 85 percent of cases, although incidence varies between different ethnic groups. In the UK, more than 1.4 million people are known to have diabetes and about 80 percent of this is Type 2.

There is a long, asymptomatic period in Type 1 diabetes (called the prodromal period) during which the beta cells are progressively being destroyed. The peak age for symptoms to appear and for diagnosis to be made is 11 to 13 years. However, this is not always the case, and mature and even elderly people are occasionally diagnosed. Diabetes is sometimes inherited but genetic factors at present identified do not account for all the incidence of Type 1 diabetes. It is believed that environmental factors such as viruses may be involved.

Type 2 diabetes is the more common form and it too has a long asymptomatic period lasting many years. Usually people are not diagnosed until they are over the age of 40. In contrast to Type 1 diabetes, in Type 2 disease people have a relative, rather than an absolute, loss of insulin. However, the disorder is a progressive one and in many cases the situation, both with regard to insulin secretion and the effectiveness of its action, may worsen with time. Type 2 diabetes is now reaching epidemic proportions and medical experts agree that the rising tide of obesity among people in Western countries is closely linked with this.

Many people are newly diagnosed with diabetes each day in the UK. Although some will have gone to their doctor feeling unwell or with symptoms that have indicated diabetes, for many others the diagnosis comes as a complete surprise. This is because it is quite common for diabetes to be detected during a routine health check or during a period of hospitalisation for some other problem. Quite often, initial suspicion of diabetes is raised when sugar is found to be present in a urine sample. However, further testing of blood samples is needed for the diagnosis to be confirmed. It is estimated that 50 percent of those with the commonest form of diabetes—as many as one million people—are at present undiagnosed and unaware that they have the syndrome. It is probable that many of these people either have no symptoms or that symptoms have developed so slowly and insidiously that they have not recognised that anything is amiss.

Women with diabetes need to be extra careful during pregnancy as there can be an increased risk of heart defects in babies. Although rare, recent research has found defects to be five times more common, occurring in 3.6 percent of babies. Gestational diabetes mellitus (GDM) is a type of diabetes that arises during pregnancy, usually during the second or third trimester. As the baby's major organs are quite well developed at this stage, the risk to the baby is lower than for women with Type 1 or Type 2 diabetes. In some women, GDM occurs because the body is unable to produce enough insulin to meet the extra needs of pregnancy. In other women, GDM may be found during the first trimester of pregnancy, which means the condition probably existed before the pregnancy. In many cases blood glucose levels can be controlled by diet but some women may have to take insulin injections.

Diabetic clinics teach people about diabetic diet and weight control—which is, to some extent, the key to controlling diabetes. Your condition will be constantly tested and thus stabilised by adjustment of diet and perhaps administration of some form of insulin. After this you will be taught to test yourself.

Unfit diabetics need a course of exercise, and sometimes bladder stress causes mild incontinence (either feeling 'urgent' or inadvertently losing drops of urine) which can be relieved by toning up the pelvic floor muscle. A physiotherapist can treat you if you have this condition and help to restore your bladder control (see page 180).

Disability

People who have been involved in serious accidents and have suffered nerve or spinal damage learn physiotheraphy techniques, first in the hospital and then at a rehabilitation centre. Others who have muscle-weakening diseases such as multiple sclerosis (MS) need physiotherapy to help make use of remaining muscular abilities. MS sufferers can benefit enormously from modified fitness classes given by a professional who knows how far to push their weakening muscles. It has been found that weekly fitness classes can lengthen the remission periods for MS patients.

Depression

Every woman experiences varying degrees of depression at some stage in her life. The condition ranges from low feelings to the true medical condition of depression, of which many sufferers are women. This illness, once described as a 'heavy heart' due to the burdensome feeling of weight in the chest, causes a seizing up of all motivation—a kind of inertia. Low self-esteem, poor sleep patterns, inability to concentrate, reluctance to converse and a wish to be left alone are all possible by-products. Depression can masquerade as pain, exhaustion, anxiety and bizarre bodily symptoms, even paralysis. If a physiotherapist examines a patient with pain all over her body that forms no known pattern, she or he suspects an underlying psychological cause which could have its roots in a depressed state of mind.

If the depressed person can overcome the inertia and exercise, it seems to help. A sense of achievement can help raise self-esteem, and the process of exercising can switch off the body chemicals dominant in the depressed mood. As depressed women are known to resort to tranquillisers, many of them addictive, it is very important that professional advice be sought. With so much new information on how body chemicals act on the brain, we can soon expect a reliable cure, possibly involving such a simple expedient as change of diet. One researcher found that going without breakfast could initiate an attack of depression in susceptible people. If you are depressed, try to overcome your inertia and explore one of the many avenues available for help.

7

MENOPAUSAL CONFIDENCE

The word menopause refers to the last menstrual period as menarche refers to the first. The term climacteric is used to describe the whole period when there are menopausal symptoms, which can span several years. Menopause is apparently unique to human females. Development of the brain and of cultural evolution are probably responsible. Ninety percent of women in developed countries can expect to experience menopause.

A healthy way to view the menopause is that you will be liberated from the nuisance value of monthly periods. You will not lose your femininity and, although naturally you are gradually ageing, you need not suddenly become unattractive at the menopause. Women are at the peak of their careers at menopausal age and are able to continue a well-adjusted, productive life for many more years.

Since menarche the uterus has been continuously preparing to receive a fertilised ovum. Females have a quota of eggs when they are born, which are shed each month in reproductive years (though many eggs fail to reach maturity). Often the menopause is a welcome rest from the body's intense monthly preparation for fertilisation.

Sometimes women can experience an artificial menopause. The removal of ovaries will bring on menopausal symptoms, even in a woman of thirty. If a hysterectomy is necessary in a young woman gynaecologists always try to leave the ovaries, or at least one or a part of one, because menopausal effects can then be postponed until the normal time. If, however, the ovaries must be removed, the oestrogen hormone can be replaced chemically to delay menopausal symptoms such as premature ageing.

Menopausal symptoms include irregular periods, hot flushes and sweating, palpitations, giddiness, tiredness, a crawling sensation on the skin, dry flaky skin, noises in the ears, lack of concentration, and a tight, 'thick' head or a headache. Some symptoms are particularly alarming—palpitations might be thought to presage a heart attack; a recurring splitting headache could mean all kinds of sinister things. It is best to investigate the cause of such symptoms and, if they are found to be normal conditions, to accept them pragmatically. Over-reaction tends to prolong and strengthen the symptoms.

Periods

Periods usually become irregular and gradually dry up. Sometimes they are excessively long, copious and painful; or they might be brief and frequent. These hormonal imbalances can be upsetting and may be considered serious enough to be referred to a gynaecologist. A hysterectomy is sometimes advised, but oestrogen therapy has been very helpful in making these serious menopausal symptoms more bearable.

Oestrogen, HRT and alternative therapies

Oestrogen secretion does not cease altogether at the menopause. When the ovaries stop producing oestrogen the adrenal glands take over, providing a rather weak form of oestrogen. Women who carry quite a bit of fat are better at converting adrenal hormones into oestrogen, an ironic and rather heartening twist of fate for the overweight menopausal woman!

Many women reaching menopause are unsure whether they should take hormone replacement therapy (HRT), a synthetic product, to help combat some of the symptoms. There are different forms of HRT, including oestrogen-only HRT, combined (oestrogen and progestogen) HRT and tibolone (Livial®) which is a different type of HRT.

Oestrogen-only products are available as tablets, implants, patches, vaginal rings, gels and a nasal spray. In combined HRT-products, the oestrogen and progestogen may be taken in the same tablet or patch or they may be taken separately. The progestogen may be taken every day (continuous combined HRT) or for 12–14 days of each monthly treatment cycle (sequential combined HRT). Doctors will evaluate a woman's suitability for such treatment, if she believes she needs it, and recommend it if necessary

In 2002, a large clinical trial investigating combined *HRT* was halted after results found the drug increased the risk of breast cancer, strokes, heart attacks and blood clots. However, the Committee on Safety of Medicines (CSM) advises that for many women the benefits of short-term use of HRT outweigh the risks. For longer-term use women should be aware of the increased risk of breast cancer, particularly with the combined form of HRT. Women who are taking any form of HRT should see their doctor at least once a year to have their treatment reappraised.

The recent backlash against HRT has resulted in many women seeking alternative therapies such as dietary changes, and vitamin supplements and herbs. Scientists have also now begun to study the benefits of a group of plant hormones known as phytoestrogens which occur naturally in certain foods such as soya.

Hot flushes

Hot flushes are the result of vasomotor instability. The body's temperature control is not working as well as it has in the past. People who once noticed the cold will be peeling off cardigans and sweaters.

At least 70 percent of women of menopausal age will experience hot flushes, or a sudden rise in temperature, a reddening of the face and neck and then sweating. The flushes appear to be worse at night, sometimes in bed, and they are sometimes heralded by a feeling of anxiety. Flushes are thought to be linked with a lowering of oestrogen. HRT seems to help overcome this symptom but it has also been found that taking vitamins C and E helps to reduce hot flushes.

Osteoporosis

Oestrogen depletion at the menopause is cited as the main cause for women's bones becoming brittle in old age. There is a rarefaction of bone cells, particularly in the long bones. Some women are more prone to osteoporosis than others, and those who are will be more likely to break bones. Certain fractures such as broken hips, wrists and upper arms are much more likely to occur in older women than in older men. Spinal compression fractures can also happen quite easily in susceptible people. African women appear to be largely immune. Asian and Caucasian women are at risk, but only about half will sustain fractures in old age, and even fewer if the problem is diagnosed and treated. If you are thin, white and a smoker, you are a likely candidate for osteoporosis. But overweight people are also susceptible.

Two dietary supplements can help prevent the problem. They are calcium (found in dairy products) and vitamin D (found in fish oils and milk products and processed by sunlight). These should be integrated into your diet, and your doctor may advise calcium supplements. Eating foods that contain plant oestrogens (phytoestrogens), for example soy foods, can also help prevent osteoporosis, as can HRT. A reasonably active lifestyle is beneficial—it keeps the muscles working which stimulates bone cell regeneration.

Genital changes

The genital tissues—vulva, vagina and urethra—lose their elasticity and fatty deposits during the menopausal years. The vagina becomes paler and its acidity level drops, encouraging the multiplication of bacteria. If the vagina becomes inflamed by bacteria it may look red and angry, feel itchy and burning, and exude discharge. At the menopause the vagina may narrow and lose its folds, and the tissues become smoother and thinner.

The narrowing can be an advantage because the genital structures are apt to prolapse at this time of life. Good muscles will help you to keep your genito-urinary tissues healthy and will support and contain the organs. It is never too late to start an exercising programme.

Another change is that the vagina can become quite dry. Women who have this condition can find intercourse painful. HRT will alleviate this problem and some women find that an oestrogen cream, applied directly to the mucous membrane of the vagina by applicator is very effective in restoring a jaded sex life. But, although hormone replacement therapy improves the texture of the lining of the pelvic organs and their outlet tubes, only exercises can regenerate muscles. It is vital to maintain the muscles in the pelvic floor adequately.

Urinary symptoms

The urethral closure mechanism, a muscular cuff called the sphincter, cannot control the pressure from the bladder as efficiently after the menopause. The sphincter normally receives a good blood supply which furnishes the turgidity required to keep the tissues firm, but this supply deteriorates with age. Muscles tend to diminish in bulk and tone. Collagen in ligaments (the elastic component) is reduced. Ageing kidneys may pass a higher volume of urine, particularly at night. It is not unusual for an older woman to be up once or twice at night (or even six times!). There may be a lack of sensation and slower nerve responses. Neither is helped by the administration of sleeping pills.

Incontinence can be treated. A physiotherapist with an interest in gynaecology and urology can teach a woman to exercise the muscles which support the vagina and the urethra. After doing these exercises women report greater control, less nocturia (getting up at night) and fewer voiding difficulties. An added benefit is greater tolerance for exercise. Older women can have a tendency to dribble urine when moving from a lying position to a standing position, particularly when getting up in the morning. This disability often responds quickly to a sphincter control learning programme.

Medication can be prescribed to help the body get rid of excess fluid. Many menopausal women are put on diuretics to control fluid retention. Such drugs should be avoided, if possible. They are inclined to make incontinence problems more difficult to deal with. Doctors can also prescribe an antispasmodic drug which is helpful in preventing bladder instability (dribbling). But there is everything to be gained if older women with any form of incontinence, including frequency, urgency or voiding difficulties, learn to control their pelvic floor muscles. Incontinence in old age should not be regarded as an inevitability if treated correctly. Many people can remain continent all their lives.

Anxiety

If menopausal signs give rise to anxiety, secondary stress symptoms such as insomnia, depression, sustained headache or backache might appear. The more you are weighed down by the awareness of being menopausal, the more likely you are to develop psychological signs which you attribute to the menopause. Perhaps you become forgetful, feel touchy or easily put out. Then other people react to and aggravate your condition; thus a vicious circle is created. 'It's her time of life' dismisses uncharacteristic behaviour.

Perhaps the menopause is depressing because it is related to the ageing process. But, like any other obstacle in life, undue pessimism is immediately counterproductive.

Anxiety and depression can be alleviated with relaxation techniques which slow down breathing and heart rate and bring calm. If you remain calm, in control and refuse to overreact, your body's little aberrations will not distress you. Relaxation does not come promptly to everyone and many people are surprised at the unexpected results they achieve by learning the knack of quickly releasing tension (see page 44). In fact, minor irritating menopausal symptoms can virtually disappear.

Smoking, caffeine ingestion

The habits of a lifetime are hard to break. If bad habits have not been broken earlier there should be added incentive at the menopause. The incentive is to remain relatively youthful and in good health; to be able to manage one's own life for many years to come and not be a burden to someone else.

Smoking causes cancer, artery damage, bronchitis and emphysema. In bronchitis, the lungs produce mucus that clogs the bronchial tubes, leading to chronic cough and debility. Emphysema (which can also be caused by long-term asthma in non-smokers) involves stretching of the air sacs which lose their elasticity and coalesce so that the person loses the capacity for transference of oxygen from the lungs to the tissues.

Arteriosclerosis (hardening of the arteries) is a more insidious part of the ageing process which, to some extent, can be warded off by healthy habits. Its common sequel, deterioration of the mental powers, seriously undermines the quality of life.

Excessive ingestion of caffeine stresses the adrenal glands which produce oestrogen. Oestrogen production diminishes at the menopause, and drinking copious cups of coffee and tea (tea also contains caffeine) further prejudices its production. Oestrogen is responsible for soft feminine contours and fatty tissue under the skin, and it is worth taking measures to maintain its production.

8

GRACEFUL AGEING

Ageing is a corollary of living. Fortunately, and rather oddly, most of us accept it without wanting to go backwards. What we do not accept, and should not, is becoming decrepit. We should fight deterioration in every way we know. Physiologically, ageing changes our bodies. It starts at birth, but appears to accelerate from the menopause. The heart decreases its output, blood pressure is more likely to rise and hardened patches in the arteries may cut down vital oxygen supplies to organs, the brain and the heart itself. But muscles can deteriorate at any age and their degeneration can still be checked to a certain extent in old age. A healthy muscle is a muscle that does work, and healthy muscles promote healthy bones and joints.

Sight and hearing

The senses are not as acute as they were. As the eye structure changes with age the eyes' focus becomes less flexible. It may be more difficult to read telephone numbers or thread a needle. You might actually benefit from long-sightedness if you were previously short-sighted. Eye muscles work all the time but they also need to relax. When practising general relaxation, remember your eyes!

Hearing also changes with age. Deafness or an inability to separate sounds, especially in large gatherings with much background noise, can occur.

Some people are offended when told they are going deaf and do not realise that they can improve the quality of life into advanced old age by acting on the information. It can be difficult to learn to use bifocal or varifocal spectacles or hearing aids at this age. But this is a great pity, as modern technology has so much to offer.

Memory and efficiency

Short-term memory is known to deteriorate as we get older. But memory should be exercised like any other part of the body. If you don't use it, you lose it! It may be necessary to write things down, have a pen attached to the telephone, or a diary by your bed or on your desk. Advancing age is quite often used as an excuse for laziness; and this won't do!

The brain needs to be exercised in the same way as the muscles and joints do. Longer life expectancy, increasing numbers of elderly and some grim economic facts have made it vital for us to remain mentally alert. A course or a hobby can help stimulate interest and activate the thinking processes. Note-taking helps the learning process and recreational writing, for letters and diaries, can be very satisfying.

Balance impairment

With age, the myelinated nerves, which tell the brain what conditions the body is experiencing, gradually lose their outer covering or sheath and don't transmit messages as accurately. This means that activities that were easy in youth are more difficult and dangerous as we get older. Accidents can be prevented if you engage in activities that accurately reflect your capabilities. Performing quick movements in safe circumstances, for instance exercising to music on a carpeted floor, will improve cardiovascular fitness and can postpone loss of balance. Some instructors use rebounders (miniature trampolines) to help the muscles absorb any shock. Naturally you must be reasonably fit to undertake such exercise. See a doctor first to check your cardiovascular fitness.

Spinal mobility

The normal spine can withstand a reasonable amount of torsional strain. As we grow older, it is not as easy to go quite to the end of the range when twisting the spine. The same can be said for bending and stretching. Stretching the muscles and ligaments to their limit is uncomfortable and it can be painful. Elderly people turn the whole body, rather than the head or head and shoulders. Some find it hard to reverse the car. A certain amount of torsional strain on the spine is healthy; without it the pivotal joints at the back of each vertebra will deteriorate. Mobilising activities involving spinal rotary movements are vital in slowing down the ageing process.

X-rays of the spines of people over the age of forty often show signs of wear: narrowing of the intervertebral discs and the formation of extra bone on the edges of the vertebral bones called lipping. Sometimes these signs appear long before the age of forty. When told of this deterioration, some people believe they must limit their movements to preserve their spine but this is not so. Only occasionally does spinal movement need to be limited; in such cases several vertebrae might be fused together through surgery; or the part of the spine affected might be encased in a collar or a corset. Physiotherapy is invaluable in either case. The best treatment for slightly deteriorated vertebrae is an increase in movement. Although a *hyper*mobile spine can cause problems such as instability, most people are *hypo*mobile as they age and a normally mobile spine is usually free of pain, and if one part of the body can't move, it is necessary to compensate by good mobility in other areas.

Circulatory fitness

The cardiovascular organs—the heart, the arteries and the veins—age along with other structures of the body. Oestrogen may protect women from cardiovascular problems during their reproductive years, but after the age of fifty just as many women as men experience coronary thrombosis, strokes and high blood pressure. Doctors can prescribe oestrogen, and other medication is available to stabilise blood pressure, to steady heart rhythm or to increase the force of contraction of the heart. Additionally, you can ensure circulatory health by adopting a nutritional, non-fattening diet with a minimum of processed items containing little or no food value, and a routine of daily exercises or activity.

By increasing your exercise tolerance, that is your ability to exercise to a point that is mildly testing, your cardiovascular fitness will be improved. The heart is a muscle, and all muscles are improved by exercise. If you have a heart or circulatory disease, or have had heart surgery, a cardiac physiotherapist, who has special knowledge of circulatory problems, can devise a suitable exercise programme and recommend the right balance between exercise and rest by carefully checking the effects of exercise and taking pulse and blood pressure.

Stroke

Minor strokes are not uncommon. Known as a CVA (cerebrovascular accident), they involve a clot lodging in an artery, preventing blood from getting to a part of the brain and thereby starving it of oxygen. This situation is often temporary. The clot clears, the blood flows adequately again and the tissue regenerates to some extent. But the person could be left with movement disorders which ought to be treated as soon as possible while the regeneration is taking place, to maximise the return of function. Stroke patients may exhibit loss of speech and loss of muscular power with overactivity (spasticity) of some muscle groups. Sometimes there is incontinence or a balance problem; and there is nearly always lack of co-ordination. Physiotherapy is a vital part of the team approach to rehabilitate stroke patients, who can often expect many years of fairly active life without a repetition of the accident.

For serious strokes, physiotherapy and speech therapy are often given on a daily basis, in either hospital or day-care centres. Through rehabilitation, patients learn to walk again, use the affected hand and arm, eat and talk.

Continence

Our homes for the aged are cluttered with people who are incontinent, urinally, faecally or both. Many of them are women because, as you will have gathered by now, women are anatomically prone to leakage! Many of these unfortunates are only there *because* of their incontinence. The family has found it impossible to manage. Rather than expecting families to be superhuman in their caring, physiotherapists and other health professionals are making enormous efforts to provide help.

Task forces are working to heighten awareness of this huge problem. Physiotherapists are concerned mainly with the preventive aspects so that the next generation of elderly will be continent. Nurse continence advisers assess individuals in homes and hospitals, teaching staff how to cope and improving the comfort and self-esteem of people who have lost hope. A great deal can be done by regular visits to the toilet, even for the elderly who are mentally impaired. By working for continence not only will money and effort be saved (laundry bills for homes are staggering), but dignity and sanity will replace degradation and despair.

A healthful routine

Routine is essential in making things happen on a daily basis. You can think of routine as automating the body, making it work *for* you.

In retirement we need self-discipline to invent a suitable routine and stick to it. When we were in the work force, routine was imposed on us. Often it was irksome. In some cases longed-for release from a working routine brings with it a *laissez faire* attitude in retirement.

The routine should consist of at least two daily exercise periods. Morning exercise could be housework, gardening or both. The afternoon exercise period needs to be more recreational—a walk, movement to music, or a session on an exercise bike. At least once a week outside social activity, such as golf, tennis, bowls or croquet, is desirable, though not mandatory for those who are more comfortable with their own company. Make sure you have plenty of mental activity; for example, learn a new skill that you have always wanted to try. It is never too late!

One of the weekly activities that should rate high is an exercise class. Many community centres have them at low cost. They are healthy, and they are fun!

Remedial fitness

Fitness classes for older women ideally should be taken by physiotherapists, who understand postural adjustment, muscle fatigue, joint strain and the importance of limiting exercise so that the heart rate keeps within the right range for the person's age. Disabilities must be taken into account, but exercise should be energetic enough to increase the heart rate and respiratory effort. Aerobic fitness can be worked up gradually, thereby increasing blood supply to muscles, organs and bones without a corresponding increase in heart rate. Balance and co-ordination can also be improved by progressing from easy movements to harder movements, from slow to faster and from simple to complex. To achieve tangible results and improve capillary blood supply, low-impact aerobic exercises should be carried out for a minimum of twenty minutes, two or three times a week.

Some people associate ageing with loss of independence, deterioration of self-image and withdrawal from enjoyable activities. Society does tend to dictate what activities are suitable for different age groups, but that should not deter an older person who feels energetic from enjoying life. If you fit the archaic picture of an ageing woman who is overweight with flabby muscles, have varicose veins discolouring the skin, a dowager's hump and a slow ponderous gait, a brisk daily walk will soon invigorate your spirit and improve your appearance. Exercise enhances circulation, increases calcium absorption, decreases the chances of obesity and promotes your sex drive!

Relaxation

The value of relaxation has been extolled as a gateway to a heightened consciousness. Mastery of relaxation can make us feel light, floating, even high, as if we are on drugs. Use it as a way out when circumstances become intolerable, in danger of overwhelming you. It will help you find peace. No matter how bad the situation is, physically or mentally or both, if you can relax, you can escape. Instinctive control of our bodyworks is a primitive facility lost in the race for civilisation. It can be relearnt with great benefit by early contact with the tenets of physiotherapy. If the contact comes late, in mature age, it is still not too late.

Emotional stability

Freed from hormonal dominance, women should find their later years to be a time of stability and quiet contentment. However, they may well bring disappointment, disillusion and grief. Even in times of extreme mental torment, attention to the body's needs can divert the mind. Constructive physical work is extraordinarily therapeutic. Our minds can be switched off by our bodies if only we will allow the body to take over. It is all a matter of switching on the right chemicals!

Pain is too often a companion of old age but there are many ways of overcoming it. A Canadian researcher has analysed the language used to describe pain and devised a test to quantify it. The test consists of eighty-three words, grouped according to intensity and ranked by patients. For instance 'pinching' pain is mild compared with 'crushing' pain; 'vicious' pain and 'killing' pain imply mental suffering; 'lacerating' pain is quite different from 'gruelling' pain. Physiotherapists use this type of approach, listening carefully to how a person describes their pain. The description is usually very accurate. It may be a question of learning to live with it. If so, you will need instruction at a pain clinic.

Assistance

Medical assistance of all types becomes more necessary as life advances. It is important to be knowledgeable about the options available and to ask questions such as the following:

- Am I being blinded by science? Bamboozled by impressive-sounding jargon?
- Is this procedure/test/X-ray/manipulation/treatment really necessary? What are the advantages of this treatment? What will happen if I don't have it?
- Is this procedure vital *now*? Or is there a simpler option to try first?

The physiotherapist must be able to offer real service, to compete with the many options which range from highly sophisticated medicine to unproven quackery. The individual's needs must be met at a cost that is within reach of the average pocket. When assessing the assistance and treatment you are receiving, you should expect your physiotherapist to:

- consider your welfare while you are in session
- spend adequate time with you
- treat you in a private area

- explain the treatment to you
- evaluate your progress and keep you informed of the number of visits you will need.

The word physiotherapy means body healing. The profession achieves an improvement rate of about 80 percent overall. This may not mean complete cure in every case; but it does mean less pain, more freedom of movement, and more strength and resilience.

If a situation seems bad, despair can't right it. Despair is always an inappropriate response because the unseen future may hold a solution. Whenever a new discovery is made it has a habit of revealing something bigger, smaller or more fantastic than anyone could ever imagine.

> And though thy soul sail leagues and leagues beyond—Still, leagues beyond those leagues, there is more sea.
>
> —Dante Gabriel Rossetti, *The House of Life*.

GLOSSARY

acne vulgaris a chronic inflammatory disease of the sebaceous glands and hair follicles of the skin. Cysts and nodules may develop and scarring is common.

adenoma a type of tumour.

AIDS acquired immune deficiency syndrome.

amenorrhoea absence of menstruation.

amniotic fluid fluid surrounding baby in the uterus.

anaemia reduction in red blood cells or haemoglobin in blood.

anorexia nervosa chronic loss of appetite for food.

Apgar score system of scoring an infant's condition at birth.

areola pigmented area around nipple.

arteriosclerosis loss of elasticity of artery walls.

asthma breathlessness caused by spasm of the bronchial tubes due to swelling of the mucous membrane.

atherosclerosis localised accumulations of fatty deposits in artery walls.

bio-feedback training to gain control of the involuntary or voluntary nervous system.

brachial plexus network of nerves supplying the arm.

Braxton Hicks contractions intermittent painless contractions.

bursa padlike sac which acts to prevent friction in and around joints.

cardiovascular pertaining to the heart and blood vessels.

cervix the neck of the uterus.

chlamydia micro-organisms that cause genital inflammation and conjunctivitis.

cholecystectomy removal of gall bladder.

cholesterol a sterol, or oil, widely distributed in animal tissues.

cirrhosis a chronic degenerative disease of the liver.

climacteric cessation of a woman's reproductive period.

coccyx small bones at the base of the spine.

collagen a fibrous insoluble body protein.

colostrum secretion from breast before onset of true lactation.

crabs crab louse which can infest pubic hair.

cystocele a bladder hernia.

diuretic agent which increases the secretion of urine.

dysmenorrhoea painful or difficult menstruation.

embolus mass of undissolved matter, such as fat, a blood clot or an air bubble, in a blood vessel which can cause blockage.

emphysema distended or ruptured air sacs in lungs.

endometriosis condition occurring when patches of uterine lining are found outside the uterus.

endorphin morphine-like substances found in nervous system.

enuresis involuntary urination.

epidural injection injection of local analgesic into space outside dura (hard layer surrounding spinal cord.)

episiotomy incision of perineum during second stage of labour.

Escherichia coli the colon bacillus, its normal habitat—the intestine.

faradism interrupted current to stimulate muscles and nerves.

ferning palm leaf pattern which cervical mucus assumes usually at mid-cycle in menstruating women. The mucus has a beaded pattern at other times and during pregnancy.

fight-flight reflex autonomic nervous system response to sudden stress.

galvanism a direct current which is used to relieve chronic pain.

glucose a type of sugar, also known as dextrose, important in body metabolism.

gonorrhoea catarrhal contagious infection of genital mucous membrane.

GUM genito-urinary medicine.

gynaecoid pelvis feminine type of pelvis.

haematoma a swelling which contains blood.

haemoglobin the iron containing pigment of red blood cells.

haemorrhoids a mass of dilated, tortuous veins in the anorectal area.

hepatitis inflammation of the liver of virus or toxic origin.

herpes (genital) vesicular eruption on the genitalia.

histamine a metabolic by-product which can cause discomfort and pain.

HIV human immunodeficiency virus damages a body's defence system so that it cannot fight certain infections, leading to AIDS.

hormone chemical activator stimulating increased functional activity.

HPV human papilloma virus, one of the most common sexually transmitted infections.

HRT hormone replacement therapy.

hyperemesis excessive vomiting.

hyperextension movement beyond the normal range.

hypermobile excessive mobility of joints leading to instability.

hyperventilation carbon dioxide depletion resulting in fall of blood pressure, vasoconstriction and anxiety.

hypomobile lack of flexibility of joints.

hypothalamus an area of the brain which controls metabolic activities, temperature control and hormones.

incontinence inability to retain urine or faeces.

induction (of labour) to cause labour to proceed.

insufflation (of tubes) to blow carbon dioxide into tubes to test patency.

insulin a blood sugar regulating hormone.

interferential therapy (IFT) medium frequency currents which 'interfere' with each other to produce a physiological low frequency current within the body.

ischaemia local and temporary anaemia due to obstruction to circulation.

konakion vitamin K injection to prevent newborn bleeding from cord.

kyphosis humpback or upper spinal curvature.

laparoscope instrument used for exploring abdomino-pelvic cavity.

lordosis exaggerated convexity of spine at waist level.

mastectomy removal of breast.

mastitis inflammation of the breast when lactating.

meconium first faeces of newborn infant.

menarche onset of menstruation.

menopause permanent cessation of menstrual activity.

migraine paroxysmal attacks of headache, frequently one-sided with disordered vision and gastric disturbances.

mononucleosis glandular fever.

muscular contraction
  Isometric—tension is developed but no mechanical work performed.
  Isotonic—tension is maintained while the length of the muscle is decreased during the performance of work or exercise.

myelinated nerve nerve with a fatty covering or sheath.

oestrogen the female sex hormone.

osteoporosis softening of bone.

oxytocin a hormone which stimulates the uterus to contract.

parasympathetic system autonomic nervous system responsible for the smooth running of body systems.

patent ductus opening between aorta and pulmonary artery.

periarthritis inflammation of area round joint.

perineometer apparatus for measuring pressure in vagina when the pelvic floor muscles are contracting.

perineum the external region between the vulva and the anus.

periosteum fibrous substance that covers bones and nourishes them.

peritoneum serous membrane reflected over viscera and lining abdominal cavity.

PID pelvic inflammatory disease.

placenta praevia placenta implanted low in the uterus, possibly below the baby.

procidentia a complete uterine prolapse.

proctalgia fujax rectal pain.

progesterone a hormone which has an effect on the lining tissue of the uterus.

progestin a hormone which has an effect on the lining tissue of the uterus.

prolapse a falling or dropping down of an organ or internal part.

prostaglandins group of fatty acids which cause the uterus to contract.

pulsed electromagnetic energy (PEME) a treatment achieved by creating an electromagnetic field within the body to alter physical or chemical processes.

rectocele a pouchlike protrusion of the rectal wall into the vagina.

relaxin hormone responsible for softening of ligaments, cervix and so on in pregnancy.

sacrococcygeal joint the joint between the coccyx and the sacrum.

sacroiliac joint joint of hip bones with sacrum.

salpingitis inflammation of the Fallopian tubes.

Scheuermann's disease a developmental condition in which several vertebrae grow asymmetrically.

scoliosis lateral curvature of the spine.

short wave a high-frequency current including the patient in an electrostatic or electromagnetic field producing deep warmth.

sphincter circular muscle constricting an orifice or tube, such as the anus or urethra.

STD sexually transmitted disease.

STI sexually transmitted infection.

surfactant an agent which lowers surface tension in lungs.

sympathetic system autonomic nervous system activated by stress.

syphilis an infectious chronic venereal disease.

thrombosis, coronary clot in an artery supplying the heart muscle.

thrush fungal infection of the mouth, throat, intestines or vagina.

toxaemia distribution of poisonous substances throughout the body.

transcutaneus electrical nerve stimulation (TENS) an electrical device with analgesic properties.

trichomoniasis inflammation of vagina by protozoan agent.

trimester three month period during pregnancy.

trochanter bony ridge at the top of the thighbone (femur).

ultrasound a treatment that uses acoustic vibrations for diagnostic or therapeutic use.

ultraviolet electromagnetic rays with antibiotic effects.

urethrocele a pouchlike protrusion of the urethral wall into the vagina.

vaginismus spasm of muscles surrounding vagina.

vaginitis inflammation of the vaginal tissues.

vas deferens excretory duct of the testes.

venereal warts moist reddish elevations on genitals or the anus.

vernix a waxy secretion covering the fetus.

visceroptosis downward displacement of visceral organs.

vulva the exterior opening of the vagina.

WHERE TO FIND HELP AND SUPPORT

Association for Post-Natal Illness
145 Dawes Road
Fulham
London SW6 7EB
Helpline: 020 7386 0868
www.apni.org

AVERT
(AVERTing HIV and AIDS)
4 Brighton Road
Horsham
West Sussex RH13 5BA
Tel: 01403 210202
www.avert.org

British Association for Counselling
and Psychotherapy (BACP)
BACP House
35–37 Albert Street
Rugby CV21 2SG
Tel: 0870 443 5252
www.counselling.co.uk

British Complementary Medicine
Association (BCMA)
P.O. Box 5122
Bournemouth BH8 0WG
Tel: 0845 345 5977
www.bcma.co.uk

British Infertility Counselling
Association (BICA)
69 Division Street
Sheffield S1 4GE
Tel: 0114 263 1448
Fax: 01663 765285
www.bica.net

British Pregnancy Advisory Service
(BPAS)
Austy Manor
Wootton Wawen
Solihull
West Midlands B95 6BX
Tel: 01564 793225
Fax: 01564 794935
Helpline: 08457 304030

Brook
(Sexual health advice for young
people up to age 25)
421 Highgate Studios
53–79 Highgate Road
London NW5 1TL
Tel: 020 7284 6040
Fax: 020 7284 6050
Helpline: 0800 0185 023

CHILD
(The National Infertility Support
  Network)
Charter House
43 St Leonard's Road
Bexhill On Sea
East Sussex TN40 1JA
Tel: 01424 732361
www.child.org.uk

Continence Foundation
307 Hatton Square
16 Baldwins Gardens
London ECIN 7RJ
Helpline: 0845 345 0165
www.continence-foundation.
  org.uk

Diabetes UK Central Office
10 Parkway
London NW1 7AA
Tel: 020 7424 1000
Fax: 020 7424 1001
www.diabetes.org.uk

Eating Disorders Association
103 Prince of Wales Road
Norwich NR1 1DW
Helpline: 0845 634 1414
www.edauk.com

Electronic Infertility Network (EIN)
Woodlawn House
Carrickfergus
Co. Antrim
Northern Ireland BT38 8PX
Tel: 07885138101
www.ein.org

Fertility UK
Tel: 020 7371 1341
www.fertilityuk.org

fpa (formerly Family Planning
  Association)
2–12 Pentonville Road
London N1 9FP
Helpline: 0845 310 1334
Tel: 020 7837 5432
Fax: 020 7837 3042
www.fpa.org.uk

Human Fertilisation and
  Embryology Authority
Paxton House
30 Artillery Lane
London E1 7LS
Tel: 020 7377 5077
Fax: 020 7377 1871
www.hfea.gov.uk

Mental Health Foundation
83 Victoria Street
London SW1H 0HW
Tel: 020 7802 0300
Fax: 020 7802 0301
www.mhf.org.uk

Mind (National Association for
  Mental Health)
15–19 Broadway
London E15 4BQ
Tel: 020 8519 2122
Fax: 020 8522 1725
Infoline: 0845 766 0163
www.mind.org.uk

Miscarriage Association
Helpline: 01924 200799
Scottish helpline: 0131 334 8883
www.miscarriageassociation.org.uk

National Centre for Eating
  Disorders
54 New Road
Esher
Surrey KT10 9NU
Tel: 01372 469493
www.eating-disorders.org.uk

National Childbirth Trust
Alexandra House
Oldham Terrace
Acton
London W3 6NH
Tel: 0870 7703236
Enquiry line: 0870 444 8707
Membership line: 08709 908040
Breastfeeding line: 0870 444 8708
Fax: 0870 770 3237
www.nctpregnancyandbabycare.
    com/nct-online

National Drugs Helpline
Tel: 0800 776600
www.ndh.org.uk/facts.html
www.drugs.gov.uk

National Endometriosis Society
Tel: 0808 808 2227
www.endo.org.uk

NHS Direct
Helpline: 0845 4647
www.nhsdirect.nhs.uk

Organisation of Chartered
    Physiotherapists in Private
    Practice (OCPPP)
PhysioFirst
Cedar House
The Bell Plantation
Watling Street
Towcester
Northants NN12 6GX
Tel: 01327 354441
Fax: 01327 354476
www.physiofirst.org.uk

Overeaters Anonymous
PO Box 19
Stretford
Manchester M32 9EB
Tel: 07000 784985
www.overeaters.org.uk

Playing safely (Advice on
    contraception and STDs)
www.playingsafely.co.uk

Rape and Sexual Abuse
    Counselling
Tel: 01962 848018
Women's helpline: 01962 848024
Monday 11.30 am to 1.30 pm
Thursday 7 pm to 9.30 pm
http://rasac.org.uk

Rape and Sexual Abuse
    Support Centre
Helpline: 020 8683 3300

Rape Crisis Federation
Unit 7 Provident Works
Newdigate Street
Nottingham NG7 4FD
Tel: 0115 900 3560
Fax: 0115 900 3562
www.rapecrisis.co.uk

SANE
1st Floor Cityside House
40 Adler Street
London E1 1EE
Tel: 020 7375 1002
Fax: 020 7375 2162
Helpline: 0845 767 8000
www.sane.org.uk

Sexual Health Line
(24-hour, 7 days-a-week advice
    about STIs, clinics and support
    services)
Helpline: 0800 567 123

Sexwise
(7 days-a-week, from 7 am to 12
    midnight, advice for under-18s
    on sex, relationships and
    contraception)
Helpline: 0800 28 29 30

Stillbirth and Neonatal Death
  Society (SANDS)
28 Portland Place
London W1B 1LY
Helpline: 020 7436 5881
Fax: 020 7436 3715
www.uk-sands.org

Threshold-Initiative for
  Women and Mental Health
14 St. George's Place
Brighton BN1 4GB
Counselling: 01273/622886
Helpline: 0845 3000911
www.thresholdwomen.org.uk

Verity (The Polycystic Ovaries Self
  Help Group)
52–54 Featherstone Street
London EC1Y 8RT
www.verity-pcos.org.uk

BIBLIOGRAPHY

Abt A. F., Garrison M. D. 1965, *History of Paediatrics*, W. B. Saunders, Philadelphia.

Anyon W. R. 1978, *Adolescent Medicine in Primary Care*, John Wiley & Sons, New York.

Balfour H. H., Heussner R. C. 1984, *Herpes Diseases and Your Health*, University of Minnesota, Minneapolis.

Bates R. G., Helm L. W. 1986, 'Epidural analgesia during labour: why does this increase the forceps delivery rate?' *The Association of Chartered Physiotherapists in Obstetrics and Gynaecology Journal* 58:3.

Bensen H., Klipper M. Z. 1976, *The Relaxation Response*, Collins, London.

Blum R. W. 1982, *Adolescent Health Care*, Academic Press, New York.

Booth D., Chennells M., Jones D., Price A. 1980, 'Assessment of abdominal muscle exercises in pregnant, non-pregnant and post-partum subjects using electromyography' *The Australian Journal of Physiotherapy* 26:5:177.

Boston Women's Health Book Collective 1985, *The New Our Bodies, Ourselves*, Harmondsworth Press, Penguin Books Australia.

Bowsher D., Frampton V., Wells P. E. 1988, *Pain Management and Control in Physiotherapy*, Heinemann Medical Books, London.

Briggs N. D. 1981, 'Engagement of the fetal head in the negro primigravida' *British Journal of Obstetrics and Gynaecology* 88:1086

Bullock J. E., Bullock M. I., Jull G. A. 1987, 'The relationship of low back pain to postural changes during pregnancy' *The Australian Journal of Physiotherapy* 33:1:10.

Bundsen P., Peterson L., Selstram V. 1981, 'Pain relief in labour by transcutaneous nerve stimulation' *Acta Obstet Gynecol Scandinavia* 60:459

Chase A. 1983, *The Truth About STD*, Quill, New York.

Chiarelli P. E. 1989, *Women's Waterworks*, Century Magazines, N. S. W.

Coates T. J., Peterson A. C., Perry C. 1982, *Promoting Adolescent Health: a Dialogue on Research and Practice*, Academic Health, New York.

Collins M. 1987, *Women's Health Through Life Stages*, Australian Physiotherapy Association (NSW Branch), Sydney.

Comfort A. 1986, *The Joy of Sex*, Mitchell Beazley, London.

Corsaro M., Korzeniowsky C. 1980, *STD—A Commonsense Guide*, St. Martin's Press, New York.

Cotteril J. A. 1980 'Acne vulgaris and its management' *Physiotherapy* 66:1:41.

Coyne T. M., Peck C. 1980, 'Pain and Depression as a Function of Effectiveness of Perceived Control' in Peck C., Wallace M. (eds.) *Problems in Pain*, Pergamon Press, Sydney.

Davies R. 1989, 'An evaluation of transcutaneous nerve stimulation for the relief of pain in labour' *The Association of Chartered Physiotherapists in Obstetrics and Gynaecology Journal* 65:2

Dobzhansky T., Ayala F. J., Stebbins G. L., Valentine G. W. 1977, *Evolution*, W. H. Freeman & Co, San Francisco.

Flynn A. M., Kelly J., Holmes G., Lynch P. F. F. 1978, 'Ambulation in labour' *British Medical Journal* 11:591.

Forbes G. B. 1981, 'Pregnancy in the teenager: biologic aspects' *Birth Defects: Original Article Series* 17:3:85.

Ford C. S. 1946, *A Comparative Study of Human Reproduction*, Yale University Publications in Anthropology, New Haven.

Gold P. W., Chrousos G. P. 1986, 'Abnormal hypothalamic-pituitaryadrenal function in anorexia nervosa: patho-physiologic mechanisms in underweight and weight corrected patients' *New England Journal of Medicine* 314:21:1335.

Greenhill J. P. 1971, *Office Gynaecology*, Year Book Medical Publishers Inc., Chicago.

Hall D. C., Kaufmann D. A. 1988, 'Effects of aerobic and strength conditioning on pregnancy outcomes' *The Association of Chartered Physiotherapists in Obstetrics and Gynaecology Journal* 63:21.

Houck J. C., Kimball C., Chang C. 1980, 'Placental beta-endorphinelike peptides' *Science* 207:78.

Howe C. L. 1982, 'Physiologic and psychosocial assessment in labour' *Nursing Clinics of North America* 17:1:49.

Kapandji I. A. 1974, *The Physiology of Joints*, Churchill Livingstone, Edinburgh.

Katona C. L. E. 1981, 'Approaches to antenatal exercises' *Social Science and Medicine* 15A:25.

Keay A. J., Morgan D. M., Stephen J. J. 1982, *Craig's Care of the Newly Born Infant*, Churchill Livingstone, Edinburgh.

Kistner R. W. 1985, *Gynecology: Principles and Practice*, Year Book Medical Publishers Inc., Chicago.

Kohl S. G. 1953, 'Transverse Narrowing of the Pelvis as a Cause of Dystocia', in Mayo L. W. (ed.) *Prematurity, Congenital Malformations and Birth Injury*, Association for the Aid of Crippled Children, New York.

Lacroix M. J., Clarke M. A., Carson-Bock K. L. et al. 1983, 'Biofeedback and relaxation in the treatment of migraine headache: comparative effectiveness and physiological correlates' *Journal of Neurology, Neurosurgery and Psychiatry* 46:525.

Lambley P. 1983, *How to Survive Anorexia*, Frederick Muller Limited, London.

Lawrence H. 1988, 'Sources of Pain in Labour', in McKenna J. (ed) *International Perspectives in Physical Therapy* (3), Churchill Livingstone, Edinburgh.

MacIntyre S. 1977, 'Childbirth: the myth of the golden age' *World Medicine* June 15:17.

McKeown T. 1988, *The Origins of Human Disease*, Basil Blackwell Inc., Oxford.

Martin R. 1989, 'Hormones and the menopause' *The Association of Chartered Physiotherapists in Obstetrics and Gynaecology Journal* 64:6.

Mattock E. 1986, 'The menopause' *The Association of Chartered Physiotherapists in Obstetrics and Gynaecology Journal* 58:13.

Melzack R. 1975, 'The McGill pain questionnaire: major properties and scoring methods' *Pain* 1:277.

Melzack R., Taenzer P., Feldman P., Kinch R. A. 1981, 'Labour is still painful after prepared childbirth training' *Canadian Medical Association Journal* 125:357.

Millard R. J. 1987, *Bladder Control*, Williams and Wilkins, Sydney.

Mitchell L. 1963, *Physiological Relaxation by Voluntary Control*, Recorded Sound Limited, U.K.

Moir D. D. 1982, *Pain Relief in Labour*, Churchill Livingstone, Edinburgh.

Moore M. L. 1978, *Realities of Childbearing*, W. B. Saunders, Philadelphia.

Morris D. 1978, *The Naked Ape*, Jonathan Cape, London.

National Conference on AIDS 1985, 'Meeting the challenge' *Australian Government Publishing Service*.

Nicosia J. E., Abcarian H. A. 1984, 'Levator syndrome—a treatment that works' *Paper given to the American Society of Colon and Rectal Surgeons*, New Orleans.

Nikolova L. 1987, *Treatment with Interferential Current*, Churchill Livingstone, Edinburgh.

Noble E. 1978, *Essential Exercises for the Childbearing Year*, John Murray, London.

Odent M. 1984, *Birth Reborn*, Souvenir Press, London.

Oxnard C. 1975, *Unique Diversity in Human Evolution*, University of Chicago Press, Chicago.

Oxorn H., Foote W. R. 1980, *Human Labour and Birth*, Appleton-Century-Crofts, New York.

Page E. W., Villee C. A., Villee D. B. 1981, *Human Reproduction*, W. B. Saunders, Philadelphia.

Ricketts O. S., Delpack K. D. 1980, 'The role of the physiotherapist in an addiction unit' *Physiotherapy* 66:12:409.

Russell J. G. P. 1982, 'The rationale of primitive delivery positions' **British Journal of Obstetrics and Gynaecology** 89:712.

Shearin R. B., Wientzin R. L. 1983, **Clinical Adolescent Medicine**, G. K. Hall, Boston.

Stace W. T. 1960, **The Teachings of the Mystics**, Mentor, New York.

Stanton S. L. 1984, **Clinical Gynecologic Urology**, C. V. Mobsby, St Louis.

Tanner J. 1988, **Beating Back Pain**, Lothian, Melbourne.

Twomey L. T., Taylor J. R. 1984, 'Old age and physical capacity: use it or lose it' **Australian Physiotherapy Journal**, 30:1:115.

Utian W. H. 1978, **The Menopause Manual**, MTP Press, Lancaster.

Wadsworth H., Chanmugam A. P. P. 1983, **Electrophysical Agents in Physiotherapy**, Science Press, NSW.

Williams M., Booth D. 1985, **Antenatal Education**, Churchill Livingstone, Edinburgh.

Wood N. F., Dery G. K., Most A. 1982, 'Recollections of the menarche, current menstrual attitudes and premenstrual symptoms' **Psychosomatic Medicine** 44(3):285.

Ziai M., Clarke M. A., Merritt T. A. 1984, **Assessment of the Newborn**, Little Brown, Boston.